ISBN 978-1-332-18000-4
PIBN 10294573

The Poultryman's Handbook

A CONVENIENT REFERENCE BOOK

For All Persons Interested in the

Production of Eggs and Poultry for Market
and the Breeding of Standard-Bred
Poultry for Exhibition

BY

International Correspondence Schools

SCRANTON, PA.

2nd Edition, 38th Thousand, 8th Impression

SCRANTON, PA.

INTERNATIONAL TEXTBOOK COMPANY

1920

Press of
International Textbook Company
Scranton, Pa.

76519

PREFACE

This handbook is intended as a book of reference for poultrymen generally. The publishers have not attempted to produce a condensed cyclopedia covering the broad field of poultry husbandry, but they have aimed to present to the public a handy reference book convenient to carry in the pocket—a pocketbook in reality—and containing such information as is most often needed by poultrymen who handle fowls commercially in large numbers, by persons who keep a few fowls in the back yard, and by breeders who aim to produce poultry of the best quality for exhibition. Although the treatment of some subjects is of necessity brief, it has been the aim so to distribute the space available that it would cover the more important subjects as fully as possible.

The more important poultry foods are briefly described and discussed, and sample rations are given for the feeding of fowls, chicks, turkeys, guinea fowls, pheasants, ducks, geese, pigeons, etc. Much useful information in regard to incubation and brooding is given. Eggs and market poultry, the various methods of breeding, and the enemies and diseases of poultry are discussed,

iii

and the insecticides and remedies for poultry are given. The various methods of poultry judging are explained and samples of the various score cards shown.

The glossary of technical terms is a feature that will be appreciated by poultry fanciers, as it is one of the most complete that has ever been compiled. The book closes with several pages of miscellaneous information, which will be found of general interest.

This handbook was prepared under the personal supervision of Thomas F. McGrew, Principal of the School of Poultry Husbandry, assisted by A. F. Stokes and H. D. Boone.

INTERNATIONAL CORRESPONDENCE SCHOOLS
SCRANTON, PA.

June, 1919

INDEX

The Poultryman's Handbook

POULTRY RAISING

Poultry and poultry products add to the wealth of the country each year more than wheat, cotton, or gold. Poultry can be kept successfully in almost every part of the world and is the most profitable kind of live-stock that can be kept. A few fowls can be kept by the intensive system in very confined quarters, and enough to provide poultry and eggs for a small family can be raised profitably in a corner of a small town lot; more can be kept on a little additional space.

An attractive feature of poultry raising is that fowls may be kept for pleasure as well as profit. A fancier may use the best of all the fowls he raises for exhibition, sell a few of equal or almost equal quality to others for the same purpose, sell eggs from pens of mated fowls for hatching, and the culls of the flock will be the best of market poultry. At the same time the flock will furnish a large part of the egg and meat diet for a small family.

Poultry farming can be followed by almost any one who has a small piece of ground and a few dollars to begin with. The business should be begun in a small way and built up gradually. Thousands of men and women are becoming independent each year from a beginning with a little piece of ground on which they raise poultry and vegetables. On a small town lot 50 ft.×100 ft. almost enough vegetables may be raised to

provide for a family for a year, and at the same time a small enclosure for poultry may be built on a corner of the lot.

It will be an advantage in raising vegetables and poultry on a small piece of ground, to practice migratory yarding. This consists in moving the house and yard or simply in moving the fence to enclose a different spot of ground. In this way space occupied by the poultry one year will be highly fertilized for the growing of vegetables the next year, and the fowls will be benefited in health and vigor from having new, sweet earth to travel over and scratch in.

VALUE OF POULTRY AND POULTRY PRODUCTS

The U. S. census of 1910 places the value of poultry and poultry products at $663,858,452. This amount is the value of these products from farms, and does not include poultry and eggs raised in towns and villages and on small farms by persons who made no returns.

The census separates poultry into two classes, the mature fowls kept for egg production and the young ones raised each year. The figures for the value of each class as well as for the total value of poultry and eggs are as follows:

Total value of mature fowls.....................$154,663,220
Total value of young fowls raised in 1 year... 202,506,272
Total value of all eggs produced in 1 year..... 306,688,960

Total value of both poultry and eggs.........$663,858,452

The following table, taken from the U. S. Census, shows the number, total value, and average value of fowls and eggs as reported for 1910. The table also gives the number of farms reporting and per cent. of all farms reporting.

NUMBER OF FOWLS AND VALUE OF POULTRY AND EGGS IN THE UNITED STATES IN 1910

	Number	Value	Average Value	Farms Reporting	Per Cent. of All Farms Reporting
All fowls ..	295,880,190	$154,663 220	$ .52	5,585,032	87.8
Chickens ..	280,345,133	140,205,607	.50	5,578,525	87.7
Turkeys...	3,688.708	6,605,818	1.79	871,123	13.7
Ducks.....	2,906,525	1,567,164	.54	503,704	7.9
Geese.....	4,431,980	3,194,507	.72	662,324	10.4
Eggs......	19,095,736,452	306,688,960	.016	5,634,780	88.5

In 1910 there were also reported 1,765,000 guinea fowls, valued at $613,000; 2,731,000 pigeons, valued at $762,000; and 6,458 peafowls, valued at $18,300.

The total value of all poultry and eggs in the United States in 1910 is estimated to have been more than $750,000,000, and for the year ending June 30, 1912, the total value is estimated by the Department of Agriculture as approximately $950,000,000. The value of poultry and eggs in 1918 is estimated as over one billion dollars.

On November 27, 1912, one of the large New York daily newspapers published the following figures giving the comparative value per annum of leading American farm products for a period of 5 yr.:

Eggs (average price to farmer 22½ c.)..$1,800,000,000
Corn 1,500,000,000
Wheat 625,000,000
Hay 720,000,000
Cotton 685,000,000
Oats 390,000,000
All kinds of farm products............ 8,000,000,000

Accepting this as a fair estimate, we cannot help realizing the immense value of poultry products in the United States.

The rank of the ten leading states in the number and value of fowls produced is shown in the accompanying table.

RANK OF THE TEN LEADING STATES IN THE NUMBER AND VALUE OF POULTRY PRODUCED

Rank	State	Number	Rank	State	Total Value
1	Iowa.........	23,482,880	1	Iowa.........	$12,269,881
2	Illinois.......	21,409,835	2	Missouri.....	11,870,972
3	Missouri	20,897,208	3	Illinois	11,696,650
4	Ohio.........	17,342,289	4	Ohio.........	9,532,672
5	Kansas........	15,736,038	5	New York...	7,879,388
6	Indiana......	13,789,109	6	Indiana......	7,762,015
7	Texas........	13,669,645	7	Pennsylvania	7,674,387
8	Pennsylvania.	12,728,341	8	Kansas......	7,377,469
9	Minnesota ...	10,697,075	9	Texas	4,806,642
10	New York....	10,678,836	10	Minnesota...	4,646,960

This table shows that the wholesale price of poultry in the state of Missouri was greater than in the state of Illinois; that the price of Texas poultry was less than the price in Pennsylvania; that the price in New York was considerably greater than in other states.

The census reports shows that the average wholesale value of live chickens in New England was 74 cents; in the Middle States, 68 cents; in the Southern States, from 38 to 44 cents; on the Pacific Coast and in the mountainous districts the price was from 62 to 82 cents each. These values indicate that the price of poultry increases as the population becomes denser.

The following table shows the egg receipts by months for the years 1913 and 1916 in seven of the largest cities of the country and indicates the months of highest and lowest production. The highest prices are obtained, of course, when the yield is lowest. The seven cities in which the eggs were received were Boston, Chicago, Cincinnati, Milwaukee, New York, St. Louis, and San Francisco.

RECEIPTS OF EGGS IN SEVEN LARGE CITIES
DURING EACH MONTH OF 1913 AND 1916

Months	1913 Cases	1916 Cases
January........	508,673	1,325,131
February......	685,160	551,158
March........	1,281,153	1,802,467
April........	2,218,638	2,844,042
May..........	2,390,427	2,549,954
June.........	1,863,412	1,837,307
July.........	1,344,824	1,317,385
August.......	1,000,157	1,070,635
September....	841,684	814,533
October......	667,834	777,954
November.....	403,146	531,355
December.....	399,277	398,286
Total........	13,604,385	15,820,207

In December, 1913, the total number of cases of eggs received at these seven stations was 399,277. The lowest price for eggs during that month was 35 cents and the highest price for the same month in New York was 63 cents. The lowest wholesale price for eggs in New York during 1913 was 20 cents, the highest wholesale price was 65 cents, which was received in November.

The total importation of eggs into this country during 1913 was 1,367,224 dozens, which amounted to $205,632. Of egg yolks bought by the pound there were 228,305 pounds, which cost $36,892. Ostrich feathers were bought at a cost of $6,252,298; and other kinds of feathers for $1,985,084.

There were exported from this country in the year 1913, 20,409,390 dozens of eggs, for which $4,391,653 was received, and egg yolks worth $57,854 were exported. The value of exported feathers was $690,612.

The total number of eggs received during 1917 and 1918 in the seven cities mentioned is recorded in the following table. Only yearly totals are given, the monthly

records not having been compiled when this table was printed.

RECEIPTS OF EGGS IN SEVEN OF THE LARGEST CITIES DURING 1917 AND 1918

City	1917 Cases	1918 Cases
Boston................	1,501,956	1,604,289
Chicago...............	5,678,679	5,049,743
Milwaukee.............	134,625	180,616
St. Louis.............	1,373,120	934,668
San Francisco.........	715,768	666,845
Cincinnati............	184,022	176,733
New York.............	4,357,061	5,026,548
Total	13,945,231	13,639,442

During the years 1917 and 1918 on acount of the world war, feed and grain of all kinds advanced so much in price as to have an influence on the keeping of poultry. Many who had been engaged in the production of poultry and eggs for market reduced their flocks considerably. Notwithstanding this the production of eggs was remarkably good. The receipts in both these years were in excess of 1913, but not so good as in 1916, which was the banner year for egg production. The world has now returned to near a normal condition, and there is likely to be an increased production of both market poultry and eggs.

It is difficult to state definitely the amount of poultry exports, as the records of these are kept as poultry and game and $1,303,379 worth was reported as having been exported from this country in 1913. The greater part of all the poultry and eggs put in storage and sent from this to other countries is grown in the Western States. They are gathered from many sections into the packing houses at Omaha, Kansas City, St. Louis, and Chicago, where the eggs are selected, candled, and graded for

quality. The best eggs are packed into **new egg** cases. The greater part of these selected eggs **go** into cold storage, only a small portion of them being sent abroad.

Poultry for export is gathered from the West and Northwest into these same packing houses, where it is crate-fattened and made plump and tender. The packers know that to sell poultry in foreign countries it must be the very best, because it must compete with poultry from European countries where the growers have had years of experience in feeding for the London and Paris markets. The packing houses have never been able to supply enough of this quality to satisfy the foreign trade and for this reason very little, if any, has been offered for sale in this country.

This should be a lesson in quality to all who grow poultry for the market. The highest prices for market poultry are paid only for the best. It costs but little more to produce the higher grades and the most profit, of course, will be made from growing and selling the best.

POULTRY HOUSES

ADAPTATION OF HOUSES TO LOCALITY

The many changes and developments in poultry-house construction during the last few years make necessary a careful consideration of all plans, so as to be reasonably certain of having a house that will be suitable for the locality where it is built. It is comparatively easy to designate the type of house best suited for any one locality but when we attempt to choose the style best suited to all localities the selection is difficult. In America alone we require protection from continual ice and snow on the north and from the burning heat of the tropics on the south. Between these two extremes will be found great variation in weather and temperature. During the months of February and March, it may be

so pleasant in Florida that little chicks can run about on the ground. At the same time it may be so cold in the Dakotas as to require unusual effort to keep larger animals sufficiently warm. Notwithstanding this, it is possible through care, management, and proper construction of buildings to use about the same type of house in both localities.

What is known as the **open-front house,** or some modification of it, is best suited for all localities. In Florida and in lower California fully one-half of the front of the house should be open and there should be some arrangement in the rear and perhaps at both ends of the building to clear the house of hot air during the warmest months.

Less open front will be needed in the temperate zones than farther south, and less from the Dakotas to Alaska than in the temperate zones. The greater the number of fowls kept in each house, the more open the front of the house should be, and the fewer kept in each house throughout the temperate and the northern zones, the less open front will be needed. All poultry houses used north of latitude 35° should have both glass windows and open-front or cotton-cloth windows in them. In recent years there has been a practice of putting a window in each end of a house. This is a good plan for the summer, but it is objectionable for the winter unless the windows can be closed so tightly that no cold drafts can enter around the edges.

In temperate zones there should be about 1 sq. ft. of open or muslin-covered windows to each 10 sq. ft. of floor space and about three-fourths as much glass window as muslin window. In the far north, in Winnipeg and in Manitoba, about half as much muslin-covered windows with fully one-third more glass window will answer. The glass windows in all houses should extend from 18 to 24 in. above the floor to near the roof, to permit the sunshine to get into the interior of the building.

Although it is possible to use the same style of exterior construction in all localities, it is necessary to under-

stand climatic conditions where the house is built and follow the kind of construction that seems best suited to that locality. In sections where the winters are of long duration and very cold, there should be no hips or pockets in the roof nor any extra amount of overhead space. The ceiling should be straight and there should be some means of carrying away damp cold air and of keeping an even temperature and distribution of air throughout the entire house. Inside conditions as they exist in the coldest and dampest weather furnish the best means of determining proper housing. If the interior of the house is dry or nearly so when the weather is cold and the air is damp, the conditions inside the building are very nearly ideal for poultry. A sure test for dryness inside of the house is freedom from frost or moisture on the side walls and glass windows and the condition of the litter on the floor. If the litter is damp, it indicates that the floor is damp and that the inside of the building is not as dry as it should be. Dryness inside the house is an absolute necessity for the health of fowls.

One of the best types of house for a very cold climate is one that is not more than 6½ ft. high to the eaves, has a gable roof, and a loft for storing straw overhead. The floor of the loft should be of strong boards to sustain the weight of the straw. It may be made of planks 2 in. thick and 6 in. wide, with the planks laid 4 in. apart. The filling of straw overhead makes the building warm in the winter and the straw will absorb whatever moisture may arise. It may be removed in the spring, thus giving more overhead ventilation and a cool house for summer.

Both glass windows and cloth-covered windows should be used in every locality where the weather is cold. There should be a lining of boards from 1 ft. above the floor, behind the dropping-board and roosts of the back wall, and on the side walls next to the roost. This covering of boards should extend up over the dropping-board and about 2 ft. beyond it, thus affording a con-

tinuous current of air from the floor to the ceiling behind the lining and overhead between the lining and the rafters, making the roosting place much warmer in winter than it would be if there were no lining in that part of the house. This same lining assists in ventilating the house during hot weather. For this purpose openings are cut through the rear of the building so that the air will come in and flow up between the rafters overhead, driving the hot air out of the house through openings very close to the roof in front.

FEATURES OF POULTRY HOUSES OF PROPER CONSTRUCTION

Sufficient advantages are gained through proper construction to warrant some expenditure above what would be necessary if the buildings were less carefully erected. If the poultry houses are perfectly dry inside during the winter, properly ventilated, and kept in a sanitary condition, the hens that are raised in them will be healthy and vigorous, and they will produce more eggs than they would if housed in damp and unsanitary buildings. Perfect health and vitality are of prime importance, and these depend upon proper shelter, ventilation, and care, without which the very best hens will not be profitable.

The principal features of houses of proper construction are floor space sufficient for indoor exercise during inclement weather, convenience of interior equipment for the keepers, window construction that will admit sunshine to all parts of the house, and govern the temperature inside of the house, thus preventing excessive heat in summer and intense cold in winter. The floor should be of a kind that will prevent the entrance of moisture from below and assure protection against the ravages of rats and mice; in addition to this there must be such ventilation and sanitation as to insure a dry interior. Careful practice of these rules will create and maintain vigor, vitality, and health in the fowls.

Floor Space for Fowls.—The best results are obtained in houses where there is at least 4 sq. ft. of floor space for each fowl. One square foot less will answer for the Mediterranean varieties, provided the house is kept perfectly clean; an extra square foot should be provided for the American and English varieties, because they are larger and require more space both for roosting and scratching than the Mediterranean varieties, with the exception of the Minorcas, which will need fully as much space as any of the American varieties.

Poultry-House Floors and Their Construction.—For poultry buildings an earth floor is satisfactory when it can be kept dry and sanitary. For general purposes, the board floor is better and is the cheapest one that can be laid. About the only objections that can be lodged against it are that perfect dryness is not always assured and that rodents can gnaw through it. The best floor, although the most expensive, is the cement floor, because it insures perfect dryness, keeps rodents from digging through, and can easily be kept·in a sanitary condition. A cement floor may be cold and rough for the feet, but these objections can be overcome, if desired, by laying a board on top of the cement.

The floors of poultry buildings should be above the ground level. For the **ground floor,** the most satisfactory way is to lay a foundation of stone, brick, or cement 6 in. high all around, fill it in with dry earth, and pack it down solid.

Board floors should be laid on 2″×4″ joists and the spaces between them should be packed with any kind of filling. If the joists are set in a bed of concrete and concrete is filled in between them level with the top, a perfectly dry floor and the exclusion of rodents will be assured. When the board floor is laid a coating of hot tar should be spread on top of the concrete and covered with a layer of tar paper and on top of this another layer of hot tar. Such preparation makes a perfect underlay for a board floor. The flooring, which should be of grooved . boards, should be laid on the tar while it is warm and

be nailed close together to prevent cracks in the floor. A floor made in this way is an ideal one for poultry.

For a **cement floor,** the foundation should be laid all around at least 18 in. deep and extend at least 6 in. above the ground. The enclosed space should be filled in with dry sand or ashes to within 6 in. of the top and the material should be packed down solid. On top of this should be laid another concrete layer made of 2 parts of sand and 1 part of cement, troweled down very smooth and worked until the moisture comes to the top. A floor made in this way will be smooth and will not hurt the feet of the fowls if the work is carefully done.

Conveniences of Management.—A great saving of time and labor will come through having an interior equipment adequate for caring for the fowls. This equipment may consist of dropping-boards, with roosts and nests beneath them, all of modern construction. In addition to this there should be feed hoppers and watering pans placed up above the floor on platforms, out of the way of litter and dirt. Hopper feeding is a convenient, economical, and labor-saving method that can be practiced by all who keep poultry either in small or large numbers.

Window Construction.—Window construction may well be considered as an interior equipment. When so constructed that they can be opened or closed quickly and easily, they are a great convenience, but when heavy and cumbersome and hard to move, they will make more difficult the changes necessary for controlling temperature, windstorms, and ventilation. Window sash containing glass will be convenient if hung on pivots as in Fig. 1 (a). The cloth-covered windows are best when of small size so that the frames covered with cloth will be light and handled easily and quickly. When of small size, a part of them can be open while the others are closed, thus providing the necessary amount of open front to meet the demands of different kinds of weather.

There are several types of windows well suited to poultry houses. The one most convenient for a small

building is the sliding window, which is simple and cheap to construct. For a house 3 ft.×10 ft., a single sash should slide either to the right or the left. A frame made of wood of the same size as the sash can be covered with muslin and used, when needed, in place of the glass window. The outside of the opening should be covered with heavy ½-in. galvanized wire cloth to prevent birds

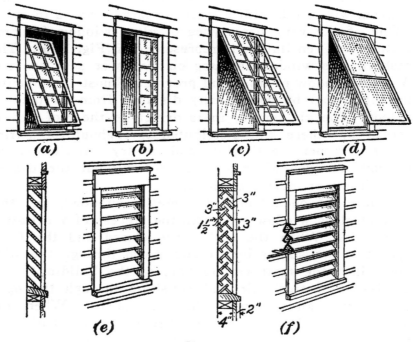

Fig. 1

or fowls from going in or out through the window and to admit air and light when the windows are left open.

The window sash or frame should slide in a groove, as shown in Fig. 1 (*b*). This is made by a 2″×4″ or a 2″×2″ strip, according to the size and needs of the building. The frame for the sliding sash should be sufficiently long to permit the sash to be entirely open, and there should be provision made for replacing or changing the sash by sliding the cloth-covered frame over the opening and leaving the glass-filled sash in the groove.

A sash hinged at the top and opening outwards, as shown in Fig. 1 (c), is a modern construction for ventilation. When opened slightly, a window of this kind will give ventilation and yet turn rain or snow away from the opening. This kind of window serves best when used for the outer covering. Inner protection can be had by fastening a window frame to the inside of the window, this frame to be covered with heavy galvanized wire cloth with a mesh no larger than ½ in.

One of the very best types of glass window for protection and ventilation is represented in Fig. 1 (a). The sash in this window is hung on pivots or sash centers. A glass window of this kind provides almost ideal ventilation; it can be opened any distance from an inch to a foot. The air coming in is driven to the roof and is spread out there and distributed throughout the entire house. Proper ventilation and a dry interior result through the use of these windows without the use of open fronts or muslin windows.

Where the open fronts, the muslin windows, and this type of glass window are used, the process of ventilation is simple. When the sashes are closed and the front open the sun shines bright and warm through the windows into the most remote part of the building. The admission of fresh air and sunshine through the open front dries and tempers the atmosphere. When the weather is cold or stormy or when the wind is blowing fast or cold, or snow is coming into the house, ventilation may be had by entirely closing the open front with muslin-covered frames, as shown in Fig. 1 (d), and opening the glass window a few inches as may be needed.

A wooden shutter or ventilator as a substitute for open windows has been used at the Missouri State Poultry Experiment Station. This ventilator is shown in Fig. 1 (e). It should contain 1 sq. ft. of surface for each 10 sq. ft. of floor space. The strips used in the construction should be 4 in. wide and set at an angle of about 45 degrees, leaving a space of 1½ in. between the strips. Where the weather is extremely cold, thin muslin can

be tacked over the inside of the ventilator and removed as soon as the cold weather is gone.

Considerable attention has been given to poultry-house ventilation, and hundreds of suggestions have been made for different kinds of ventilators. The most recent ventilator is the **Cornell wind baffler,** which differs materially from the Missouri shutter ventilator. The construction of the Cornell baffler is shown in Fig. 1 (*f*). This has **L**-shaped bafflers in place of the flat strips of wood used in the shutter ventilator. It would seem to be almost impossible for rain or snow to pass through the baffler. More glass windows are needed for light in houses where shutters or baffler is used than in houses that have cloth-covered windows.

POSITION FOR POULTRY HOUSES

Position for Poultry Houses.—Houses for poultry should face toward the south; and to meet this condition considerable study in the arrangement and layout of the yard will be at times required. When poultry buildings are erected in the rear of the dwelling house and the front of the dwelling house faces the north, it is easy to have the poultry building in the rear face the south. If the dwelling faces the south, the poultry houses would have to be built facing south, at the rear end of the lot.

In erecting a poultry house at the rear of the lot facing south, the rear of the building should be next to the back fence so that the watershed of the roof will be away from the center of the yard. To have the necessary amount of sunshine and ventilation in a house so placed requires that the south end and a portion of either the east or the west end be of glass and open front, with the roosting place for the hens at the north end of the building. A house so built is shown in Fig. 2. In this illustration the rear part of the poultry building is placed toward the east, the windows facing the south and the west. The reason for locating the

building on the east side is to gain the greatest amount of sunshine inside the house during the winter months.

If the dwelling house faces the south, the poultry building placed at the rear end of the lot can face south. If the house faces the west, the rear of the poultry building can be against the fence on the north side; the same position should be used if the dwelling house faces the east. When the buildings are so arranged, good ventilation and the maximum of sunlight in winter will be assured.

FORM AND ARRANGEMENT OF HOUSES

The most efficient and economical style of poultry house is the straight-front, slant-roof building with open

Fig. 2

front or with glass and cloth-covered windows in the front, constructed according to the needs of the locality where the house is erected. This type of house can be constructed with extreme simplicity, or it can be embellished according to the taste of the builder. Under no conditions, however, should it be built in a way that will detract from its usefulness.

Wide houses are best suited to any locality where the laying hens must be kept inside for a considerable length of time during the winter months. Such houses are warmer, afford better protection from the cold, and are more satisfactory than narrow buildings. Houses from

18 to 20 ft. wide are generally favored, especially where several hundred hens are kept during the winter.

The open-front house should be of close construction, with both ends, back, roof, and floor as nearly air-tight as they can be made, and with a front having the proper arrangement of open and glass windows. Such construction is shown in Fig. 2, which shows a small house, well suited for the side of a city lot. The roosting apartment is to the left and the open runway to the right. This house allows 4 sq. ft. of floor space in the roosting apartment and 6 sq. ft. in the runway for each fowl. That would be 20 fowls for 80 sq. ft. in the roosting house and for 120 sq. ft. in the runway. This house is intended for fowls that are kept shut in. When there is no danger of their injuring the crops, they may be permitted to run about in that portion of the yard used for a garden or for flowers. The runway can always be kept sanitary. When it needs cleaning, the fowls can be shut inside the roosting place, and with a hoe and a rake the filth can be scraped up, carried away, and replaced by fresh earth from the garden.

Houses of this type can be built of almost any size required. If there is plenty of room in the yard, the runway may be made larger or an open runway added to the end of the closed run. A cover of canvas can be spread over the wire front to keep out heavy rains and snow. When the weather is wet or cold the open front in the roosting place should be closed with a frame made of wood and covered with muslin. A covered runway affords dry footing for the fowls, and no opportunity for rain or snow to fall into the runway and make the ground unfit for the fowls to use. Such a runway can be kept sanitary if cleaned frequently, and such yards and houses will be a pleasure to the owner.

For some reasons it may be better for the roof to slope away from the yard rather than toward it. In Fig. 2 a tin water spout is shown that conducts the rainwater to the left of the building down to a cistern from which the stored water may be taken for sprinkling the gar-

den. The water could be so stored even **if the slope of** the roof were toward the north. In that case, however, **the heat** of the southern sun would not serve to keep pipes from freezing or promptly to melt the snow on **the** sloping roof.

The roosting place of the fowls should **be** located at the left in the rear of the building. The latticework shown between the open runway and the roosting place

Fig. 3

affords better ventilation during the warm nights of summer, and it also allows free circulation of fresh air into the roosting place without causing drafts.

It is possible to keep poultry in the most densely populated sections of a town without offense to the neighbors. A suggestion for a model backyard poultry run in shown in Fig. 3. This is taken in part from a photograph made of poultry runs at Cheltenham, England. Two flocks of hens without males can be kept in these runways. The roosting apartment in the rear end is equipped for two flocks; covered runways on each side

are attractive in appearance and furnish plenty of room
for exercise out in the open yet afford protection from
the rain and snow that makes conditions quite unsanitary when permitted to fall in small runways that are in
constant use.

The walks on both sides of the flower garden are made
of cement. The gutters *a* for drainage are laid along
the front of the runways and next to the cement foundation. The cement extends beneath both the runways and
the roosting place. A foot of closely packed earth is
filled in on top of the cement making a dry ground floor
for the runways. This earth can be dug out and replaced
by fresh earth as frequently as necessary, thus keeping
the house and yards sweet and clean and avoiding all
chance of offensive odors or contamination of the soil.

Where there is sufficient room, the runways can be
extended and used for young chicks. Where there is
not space enough for this, pullets for replenishing the
flock must be raised elsewhere. This plan was intended
only for the housing of hens kept for egg production,
but the same construction could be adapted for breeding
pens.

The baseboards as shown in the illustration cover the
cement foundation wall of the runways and the roosting
place. Openings are cut through the rear wall of each
runway; they are covered on the outside with heavy
iron screen and are closed on the inside with shutters or
doors hung on hinges. These doors can be turned up
against the roof during warm weather. The free circulation of air through these openings will reduce the
temperature inside the runways during the warmest
weather. The same kind of ventilation can be applied
to the rear of the roosting place. This would be necessary, however, only in tropical climates or where the
nights are excessively hot.

The front of the roosting house is 9 ft. high and the
front of the runway is 8½ ft. high, affording sufficient
space overhead and better ventilation during hot weather
than a lower house would give. Iron posts are attached

to the rear end of the roof both on the roosting house
and the runways. Heavy barbed wire stretched between
these posts prevents approach from the rear.

The arrangement of house and yards shown in Fig. 4
was evolved in England to meet the food-shortage emergency. The house in the rear is an open-front, scratch-
ing-shed house, in which the poultry can be confined in
all kinds of weather, especially when it rains and the
ground is wet outside. The interior of the house can
be arranged to suit the convenience of the owner. The

FIG. 4

roosts should be placed to the extreme right of the
house and the nests to the left of the roosts, to make
it convenient for those who go into the house through
the door in the center to gather the eggs and to clean
up without disturbing the poultry. The vegetable garden
and poultry yard are alternated yearly. To make the
change, the front fence and the line of fencing along the
pathway should be moved over to enclose the garden
patch for a poultry yard, the other side then being used
as a garden plot. When this change is made, the front
sections at the extreme right and left are changed so

as to transfer the small doorway through which the hens come out into the yard. At the same time, the roosts and the nests are moved from the right to the left end of the building.

HOUSES AND YARDS FOR DIFFERENT VARIETIES

Special arrangements must be made for housing and yarding several varieties of chickens on a limited space.

FIG. 5

They must be kept separate, each variety by itself. To accomplish this, the fences around the enclosure and between the yards must be high enough and so well constructed that the fowls cannot get out of the yards alloted to them. The fences shown in Fig. 5 are 8 ft. high; these yards were used for Hamburgs and Bantams. The lower part of the fence is 2 ft. high, and is made of boards; the upper part is made of 6-ft. wire fencing. Fences 6 ft. high will do for Plymouth Rocks, Wyan-

dottes, Orpingtons, or fowls of equal or larger size. A fence of this height would have wire fencing 4 ft. wide above the boards.

The building shown in Fig. 5 is 12 ft. wide and 100 ft. long, and is divided into twelve compartments. The yards are 8 ft. wide and 24 ft. long and can be made longer when space will permit. One male and six or eight females can be kept in each compartment; more may be kept, but when this is done there is danger of contamination, loss of vitality, and less fertility. The

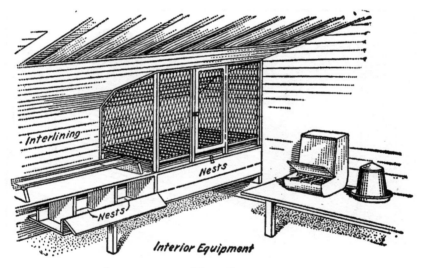

Fig. 6

house is 9 ft. high in front and 5 ft. high in the rear; there is an opening close to the roof in front and one in the rear, which should be left open during hot weather. This permits circulation of air through the house and between the rafters, thus driving out the heat; the rear opening is closed tight when the weather is cool or cold. The one in front is closed in the cold seasons. The house can be built lower, or there can be a lower ceiling to make the house warmer in cold weather.

The doors that lead from one division to another should be hung on self-closing double-acting hinges. The interior equipment of one apartment is shown in Fig. 6.

The nests are under the dropping-board. The coops for broody hens are to the right of the roosts, the feed hopper is fastened against the partition or hung on the uprights, and the shelf for the water pan is to the right of the hopper. The pan goes through or under an opening in the partition, thus providing for two pens of fowl.

A house of this kind will be excellent for bantams, and if not more than five or six of them are kept in each yard, green stuff of some kind can be grown in the yards. Such pens can be used for a male and four or five female bantams of any breed or variety, and the hens should be permitted to hatch their own eggs and raise the brood of chicks in the same enclosure.

HOUSES FOR BANTAMS

A house of small size is most suitable for bantams. The higher the roof and the more extensive the space

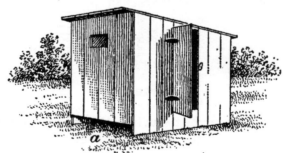

FIG. 7

inside, the colder and less comfortable will be their quarters during very cold nights. The box house illustrated in **Fig. 7** can be built out of packing cases that are 3½ ft. wide, 4½ ft. long, and of the average height, the front elevation of the building being 4½ ft. and the rear elevation 3½ ft. The floor of the house, which is made first, is 4 ft. wide and 5 ft. long, and is elevated 12 in. above the ground by cleats nailed all around on the under side flush with the edge. The walls of the house are nailed to the edge of the floor; the boards in the rear and on the sides reach to the ground and close

the space under the floor on three sides. In front, the boards extend 6 in. below the floor and to within 6 in. of the ground, leaving an open space *a* of 12 in. under the floor. When the siding is in place the roof is put on and covered with roofing paper.

One 8"×10" pane of glass in front admits all the light that is needed; the single-board door admits the bantams and permits the gathering of the eggs and the cleaning of the house. A round roost pole across the rear end and some small nest boxes complete the house. This house will provide quarters for ten or twelve bantams. It can be moved beneath the shelter of a tree during the summer months, placed under a shed or

FIG. 8

moved to the basement during the severe cold weather, or left in the open throughout the entire year. It is, in fact, a comfortable house for bantams in all kinds of weather. The dust bath for the bantams is beneath the house. When the nights are cold the open space *a* in front should be closed. In localities where it is very cold, and where there are spells of severe weather, the outside of the box should be covered with tar paper to close the cracks against the wind.

For Brahama or Cochin Bantams, a low, compact house is the best. These bantams can withstand the coldest weather if they are well protected as are other fowls. The house shown in Fig. 8 is 8 ft. long and 6 ft. wide; it is 6½ ft. high in front and 5 ft. high in the rear; the fence for the enclosure is 5 ft. high. If desired, this

house can be divided through the middle and be used for two separate lots of bantams. When this is done, a division fence should separate the two pens. The interior of the house may be arranged to suit the convenience of the poultryman. The building has a double door, the inner screen door *a* swinging to the inside and the board door swinging to the outside. The outer door should be left open during warm weather and on bright days during cold weather to prevent dampness. The house should have a board floor.

YARDS FOR POULTRY HOUSES

Purpose and Size of Yards.—Fowls are confined in yards to prevent them from trespassing and from going where they may do harm or where they may injure themselves. They are also confined when an effort is being made to secure a large egg yield by intensive methods, and when several varieties of fowls are kept for breeding purposes, in which case the flocks must be kept separate in order that each breed may remain pure.

Yards cannot be too large and are frequently too small. Less than 100 sq. ft. of yard room per head is not enough to secure the best results in producing eggs; a yard 50 ft. wide and 100 ft. long will be sufficient for fifty hens, provided special care is taken to keep the soil in a sanitary condition. If the yard is 100 ft. square, the fifty hens will do much better. Two and one-half acres will answer much better for five hundred hens in one flock than the same space divided into ten yards for fifty hens each. The reason for this is that when the five hundred hens are confined in the space of 2½ A., each one has the free range of the entire area, and when the space is divided into ten yards, each fowl is confined to a space about equal in size to that of an ordinary town lot.

Close confinement causes the flock to become discontented, and overcrowding the yard lessens the egg yield. If either one or both of these conditions is of

long duration, the health and vitality of the fowls is undermined and destroyed. Asiatic fowls can be kept in health and vigor in much less space than can the American varieties; Leghorns must have more than double the space that is necessary for other varieties. These remarks apply to the keeping of laying hens and not to forcing a few fowls to an early maturity for the market on a space so limited that they neither produce eggs nor maintain vitality. The more closely hens are confined, the greater the necessity for cleanliness, care, and proper feeding.

SHADE FOR POULTRY

There is a great need of shade for poultry kept in confined quarters during the summer months. Poultry houses should face toward the south, because the direct rays of the sun are needed inside of poultry buildings to assist in keeping the interior dry and free from germs. But shade of some kind must be provided so that the fowls can be sheltered during warm weather when they are in the yard the greater part of the day.

Shade may be furnished in a way that will add attractiveness to the poultry houses and yards. The fences about the poultry yard should be built straight and strong and attractive in appearance, and they may be overgrown with vines of some kind which will serve as a shade and protect the fowls from the direct rays of the sun.

There are a number of kinds of vines that can be used for this purpose. Throughout Maryland, Virginia, and other states there are honeysuckles that grow profusely and can be trained over the fences and over frames built for the purpose. There are several varieties of the rambler roses which can be trained over the fences and which will beautify the surroundings as well as furnish shade. Sunflowers may be grown along the outside line of the fence. These grow rapidly and provide feed as well as shelter from the sun.

Another vine, commonly known as Dutchman's pipe, is a profuse grower, and is often used as shade for poultry. Hop vines, gherkins, and morning glories also may be grown for the purpose of shelter.

The use of Jerusalem artichokes for shade has been recommended because they grow quickly and come up year after year, affording shade in abundance. It is said that this plant can be grown inside of poultry yards if protected until it gets a good start, and that fowls will not eat the leaves even though no other green stuff is available. Castor-oil plants, where they can be protected from disturbance until well started, will grow profusely and become very large, and will provide abundant shade beneath which the growing chicks may run and be protected during the warmest weather.

Sweet corn makes a splendid shade for poultry. When fairly well up, the mother hens and young chicks may run through it without harming the plants or the ears of corn. When the corn is ready for the table the ears can be removed without breaking the stalks, which continue to furnish shade. Corn fields on farms furnish a most attractive shelter from the direct rays of the sun and the fowls like to wander through them hunting bugs and worms. Some of the best exhibition fowls grown spend the first few months of their life in the corn fields.

When no other shade can be provided, awnings of muslin should be stretched over frames and placed so as to prevent the sun from shining too directly inside of the poultry buildings. Frames made like tables, with the tops of muslin or cloth of some kind, can be placed here and there to protect the fowls from the sun. Tar paper or building paper can be used in place of muslin for the same purpose.

UNIT HOUSE

The demand for houses for large flocks has brought into use a style of house that is called the unit house. A house of this kind may be built in two or more sepa-

rate units 20 ft. long by 16 or 18 ft. deep or wide. This
would be called a connected unit house, meaning that

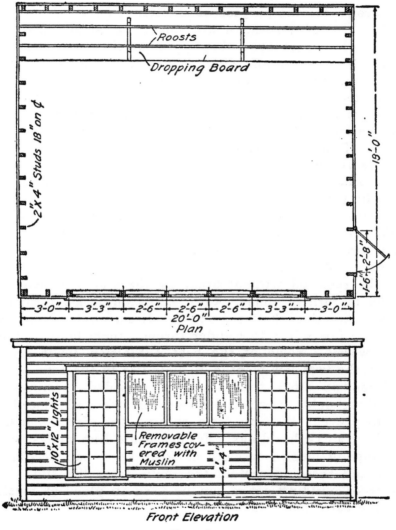

Fig. 9

several units would be built at one time or at separate
times and used as separate houses or as one connected
house.

Such houses are built where laying hens are kept in

large or small flocks. The rule is to build them in multiples of 20 ft. by whatever width or depth may be preferred. Some unit poultry houses have been built 24 ft.
square, with a gable roof. Houses of this width answer

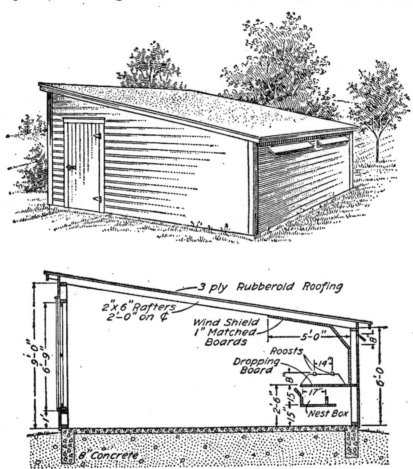

FIG. 10

well for large flocks kept in California or in any other
locality having like temperature. The best width for
general use is 16 or 18 ft.

The most modern type of a unit house is shown in
Figs. 9 and 10. This house is 20 ft. long and 18 ft. wide
and is 9 ft. high in front and 6 ft. high in the rear.

This house has 360 sq. ft. of floor space and will be large
enough for 90 Leghorn hens kept for laying eggs during
the winter months.   This same house will be large
enough for 75 laying hens of the larger kind.   The house
can be divided by partition into two pens 10 ft.×18 ft.

The advantage of this kind of house is that it can be
built section by section as needed.   Two sections like
these might be called a double connected unit house.
Any number of sections can be added to such a house
and all of them connected.   When two or more sections
are used for large floors, the wooden partition between
each 20 ft. should extend about half way forward from
the rear through the house.

As shown in Fig. 9, this house has the modern style
of windows, that is, two glass and three cotton-cloth
windows, which are shown in the front elevation.   These
windows are properly proportioned for a front 9 ft. high
and 20 ft. long.   If two units of 20 ft. each are built, the
cloth-covered windows can begin either to the right or
to the left of the glass windows and thus give a continuous line of glass and cloth windows or they may be
as shown in the illustration.   The house can be built 7
or 7½ ft. high in front and be either 4½ or 5 ft. high in
the rear; the lower the roof or ceiling overhead, the
warmer will the house be during both hot and cold
weather.   The two openings in the rear shown in Fig. 10,
are for ventilation, and should be open continually during the warm weather.   The air passing in through them
will go over the roosts between the inner lining and the
outer covering of the rear wall and the roof.   This will
cool the house by carrying the hot air out overhead.
These openings must be closed during the winter.

The inner lining can be nailed to the uprights; it may
extend from near the floor up the rear and overhead in
front of the roosts and dropping-board.   This protects
the fowls on the roost from the cold that might otherwise be deflected from the rear and overhead onto them.
Such protection is worth much more than it costs.   The
best arrangement for the interior is shown in Fig. 6.

When houses like this are built for large flocks of laying hens, they can be built in sections 20 ft. long and 20 ft. wide. Five sections, or units, of this size, all connected, can be used either for one large open house, which will be 100 ft. long and 20 ft. wide, or it may be divided into five or more separate houses.

Five units of this size will contain 2,000 sq. ft. of floor space, which is sufficient for 500 Leghorn hens; or they may be separated into five units, each house having 100 Leghorn hens. Leghorn hens will do very well with 4 sq. ft. of floor space for each hen. This will provide scratching place for the hens during the winter months. Fowls of larger sizes should have from 5 to 6 sq. ft. of floor space.

HOUSING PROBLEMS IN CALIFORNIA

When considering the climatic conditions of California it must be remembered that in that state, which extends from Oregon on the north to Mexico on the south, great variations in temperature are found. The northern latitude temperatures of California are about the same as those of Denver, Indianapolis, and Philadelphia.

The conditions as they exist in California have been described in the following words by Prof. J. E. Dougherty of the College of Agriculture:

"Abundant ventilation can and should be provided at all times of the year, because the climate is so mild that cold weather does not have to be considered, whereas the intensely hot days of summer represent the California poultryman's most unfavorable season just as the cold winter period is the worst season in other states. Where the temperature reaches the vicinity of 100° F., a house closed on three sides, even though the front is entirely open, becomes a veritable oven. Add to this the fact that a large number of our poultry farms are, under present conditions, supplied with very scant outdoor shade, and the fowls remain largely indoors out of the sun during the hot part of the day, and one can realize

how they can be made to suffer from the heat in poorly
built houses.

"The hot summer sun dries up all vegetation not artificially watered, the ground becomes hot and dry, and
the fowls prefer to stay in and close to the houses where
it is shady. They will not get out on the sun-baked
ground, but live largely in the houses during hot
weather. As a result, a good many fowls are lost every
year from heat prostration. In fact, such mortality rep-
resents a serious loss, and its prevention is a subject
worthy of most careful consideration.

"In order to obviate the hot-box condition, provision
must be made to throw open the rear of the house on hot
days, in addition to the open front, so that every breath
of air may be caught and the air in the house be kept
moving as much as possible. There is invariably at least
a little breeze blowing from one direction or another,
and by having at least two sides of the house open
during the day these breezes circulate through the house
and keep it quite cool."

Very heavy rainfall accompanied with wind prevails
during the winter in California. These storms are frequently so severe as to blow away cloth curtains, and
for this reason they are not recommended as suitable
for that locality.

Mr. Dougherty says further that trees in the runs and
about the houses are of great value in furnishing cool
shade. Deciduous trees of heavy foliage are best, because they furnish dense shade and shed their leaves
in winter. Since evergreen trees do not shed their
leaves, they ought not be located close to the houses, as
they will cut off the sun from the houses in winter. Fig
trees are especially fine for shade in the runs. The use
of two-story houses also makes for coolness, for the
upper story keeps the lower floor cooler than it would
otherwise be, and by hanging windows on all sides of
the lower floor the additional coolness resulting from free
ventilation on all sides is secured.   •

A good type of house for California is a square house,

say 24 ft. square, or one 48 ft. long by 24 ft. wide, according to the number of fowls to be kept in the house. This house should be 9 ft. high all around with a gable roof, and have glass windows on all four sides. All of these windows should be kept open when the days are very warm.

If the wind blows, the windows should be shut tight on the side from which the wind comes. When it rains and blows very hard, all the windows in the house should be closed except those on one side against which the wind does not blow; that is, if the wind blows from the northeast the windows on the north, the east, and the west would be closed and the windows on the south left open. If the wind blows from the southwest, the windows on the north would be left open and the other windows be closed tight.

When a house of this kind is used, the roosts should be placed in the middle of the room lengthwise, directly under the peak of the roof. The dropping-board should be built on legs like a low-set table, the roosts running lengthwise above the table, with the nest boxes beneath it.

Such a house should have ventilators in the peak of the roof; those of galvanized iron with hoods over the top are well suited for this purpose. Such ventilators will work well during all kinds of weather. When it is warm and hot, the air will pass out through them. When the wind blows it causes a current around the hood and the pipe; when the rain falls hard the hood-shaped lid on top will prevent the rain from beating down through the ventilator. Through these ventilators the warm air comes out of the upper end of the pipe and passes through the open space between the top of the pipe and the lower side of the hood.

POULTRY FOODS

COMPOSITION OF FOOD

Food is any substance that a plant or an animal may take into its body and use for building up wasted tissues and maintaining natural conditions. Besides water, which is present in all foods, the different compounds of which solid animal foods are composed have been grouped into four classes; carbohydrates, fats, protein, and ash. All the compounds belonging to these classes of food elements, or principles, are not completely digestible, and the value of poultry food is determined largely by the amount of these food constituents that can be digested by the fowls.

When food is digested it forms blood, which circulates throughout the body and sustains life. By means of the blood the nutritious portions of the food are assimilated, or incorporated into the body of the fowl for the purpose of nourishing it and for renewing wasted tissues. Eggs are composed largely of the same kind of materials that are utilized in the formation of blood and flesh.

All foods contain *water;* dry grains, meals, and hays contain from 7 to 10%, and grasses, green plants, roots, and unripened grains contain from 60 to 70%. The flesh of fowls and their eggs are from 41 to 65% water, 1 doz. new-laid eggs containing almost 1 lb.

The greater portion of the solid part of poultry food is composed of *carbohydrates,* or *nitrogen-free extracts,* as they are sometimes called. Carbohydrates are made up largely of starch, sugar, gums, vegetable acids, and crude fiber. Carbohydrates are used by fowls to supply energy, to produce animal fats and oils, and to maintain the body heat.

The food elements known as *fats,* or *oils,* differ from carbohydrates in being able to produce more heat. For this purpose, 1 part of fat is equal to 2¼ parts of carbo-

hydrates. For this reason, when estimating the heating value of foods, it is customary to multiply the amount of fat in them by 2¼ in order to express its equivalent in carbohydrates.

That portion of the food which contains nitrogen is known as *protein*. The lean meat of the fowl and the white of the egg are composed largely of this principle. As a source of heat and energy, protein is about equal to the carbohydrates, but animal heat obtained from protein is very expensive. Protein is much more costly than the carbohydrates and fats, and no more of it should be fed to fowls than is absolutely necessary to renew waste, make new growth, and furnish the needed quantity for egg formation.

That part of food which would be left if the food were burned is called *ash,* or *mineral matter,* and it contains calcium, magnesium, potassium, sodium, iron, and other elements. When assimilated by fowls, ash enters largely into the composition of bones and the shells of the eggs. There is not enough ash for egg and bone formation in the food usually fed to fowls, and for this reason it is necessary to supply them with such materials as oyster shells, clam shells, limestone, grit, etc.

Foods that contain a large proportion of crude fiber are spoken of as *roughage,* and those that contain little crude fiber and that are nearly all digestible are known as *concentrates*. Clover hay is an example of roughage; corn meal is an example of a concentrate. Although of little direct value as a food for poultry, roughage, or crude fiber, is important in a food because in passing through the digestive organs it distends them and serves as an irritant that stimulates their mechanical action and assists them in digesting their contents.

When feeding fowls it is always best to have a sufficient quantity of ash, fiber, and roughage in their rations to extend the crop and to keep the gizzard actively employed in grinding. During the process of grinding the coarse foods become thoroughly mixed with the concentrated foods and all pass through the intes-

tines in a manner that makes their assimilation much more natural and, therefore, of more real benefit to the fowls than would be the case without them.

Clover and alfalfa hay and bran are very highly considered as roughage for poultry, and they not only well serve the purposes mentioned but are also valuable as food. Clover and alfalfa contain a large percentage of ash and fiber and are among the best substitutes for green food as well; although but little of the bran is digested, it is most valuable as an intestinal irritant.

When feeding clover or alfalfa hay it is well to throw bundles of it into the houses on the litter and permit the fowls to pick the leaves and scratch in the hay as they do in the litter.

Uses of the Food Elements.—After being digested and absorbed into the blood, the different food elements are used by the body for various purposes. From protein are formed the muscles, or lean meat, and this element also enters largely into the composition of the bones and feathers, and, most important of all, the egg. Protein can be more completely utilized than the other food elements and some hens seem to have the power to utilize practically all of the protein contained in the food they eat.

Carbohydrates are mainly used to keep up the body temperature. The utilization of carbohydrates for this purpose is really a slow form of burning, which is just as necessary for the life of the fowl as the fire beneath the boiler is for the running of the steam engine. Carbohydrates are also the source of much of the energy used when the fowl moves itself about and performs other work.

The function of fats is similar to that of the carbohydrates. Fats, however, are a more concentrated fuel, 1 lb. of fat being equal to about 2¼ lb. of carbohydrates. Fats can also be stored for future use in the fowl's body, a thing that cannot be done with carbohydrates.

COMPOSITION OF FEEDSTUFFS

Feedstuffs	Water Per Cent.	Ash Per Cent.	Protein Per Cent.	Carbohydrates		Fat Per Cent.
				Fiber Per Cent.	Nitrogen-Free Extract Per Cent.	
Grains and seeds:						
Barley..............	10.8	2.5	12.0	4.2	68.7	1.8
Buckwheat..........	13.4	2.0	10.8	11.7	59.7	2.4
Corn, dent..........	10.6	1.5	10.3	2.2	70.4	5.0
Corn, flint..........	11.3	1.4	10.5	1.7	70.1	5.0
Emmer..............	8.4	3.9	11.5	11.1	62.9	2.2
Kafir corn..........	9.9	1.6	11.2	2.7	71.5	3.1
Millet seed..........	12.1	2.8	10.9	8.1	62.6	3.5
Milo maize..........	9.0	2.3	10.7	3.0	72.2	2.8
Oats, in hulls........	10.4	3.2	11.4	10.8	59.4	4.8
Oats, hulled.........	7.9	2.0	14.7	.9	67.4	7.1
Peas, Canada........	15.0	2.4	23.7	7.9	50.2	.8
Peanut kernels.......	7.5	2.4	27.9	7.0	15.6	39.6
Rice................	12.4	.4	7.4	.2	79.2	.4
Soybeans............	11.7	4.8	33.5	4.5	28.3	17.2
Spelt...............	8.0	3.9	11.5	11.5	62.9	2.2
Sunflower seed.......	8.6	2.6	16.3	29.9	21.4	21.2
Wheat, whole........	10.5	1.8	11.9	1.8	71.9	2.1
Wheat screenings.....	11.6	2.9	12.5	4.9	65.1	3.0
Meals:						
Bean meal...........	10.9	5.7	23.2	3.8	54.9	1.5
Buckwheat middlings..	12.8	5.0	26.7	4.4	44.3	6.8
Corn bran...........	9.4	1.2	11.2	11.9	60.1	6.2
Corn meal...........	15.0	1.4	9.2	1.9	68.7	3.8
Cottonseed meal......	7.0	6.6	45.3	6.3	24.6	10.2
Coconut cake........	10.3	5.9	19.7	14.4	38.7	11.0
Flour, red dog........	9.9	2.6	18.0	3.0	62.5	4.0
Gluten feed..........	9.2	2.0	25.0	6.8	53.5	3.5
Gluten meal.........	9.5	1.5	33.8	2.0	46.6	6.6
Hominy feed, chop....	9.6	2.7	10.5	4.9	64.3	8.0
Linseed meal, new process..............	9.7	5.5	37.5	8.9	36.4	2.0
Linseedmeal,old process	9.8	5.5	33.9	7.3	35.7	7.8
Oatmeal.............	7.9	2.0	14.7	.9	67.4	7.1

COMPOSITION OF FEEDSTUFFS—*Continued*

Feedstuffs	Water Per Cent.	Ash Per Cent.	Protein Per Cent.	Carbo-hydrates Fiber Per Cent.	Carbo-hydrates Nitrogen-Free Extract Per Cent.	Fat Per Cent.
Meals:						
Oat middlings.........	8.8	4.5	16.2	7.1	56.5	6.9
Peanut cake..........	10.7	4.9	47.6	5.1	23.7	8.0
Pea meal.............	10.5	2.6	20.2	14.4	51.1	1.2
Rice bran............	9.7	9.7	11.9	12.0	46.6	10.1
Rice meal............	10.2	8.1	12.0	5.4	51.2	13.1
Shorts...............	11.2	4.4	16.9	6.2	56.2	5.1
Soybean cake.........	11.3	5.9	42.7	6.0	28.1	6.0
Sunflower-seed cake...	10.8	6.7	32.8	13.5	27.1	9.1
Wheat bran..........	11.9	5.8	15.4	9.0	53.9	4.0
Animal foods:						
Blood, dried..........	8.5	4.6	84.4			2.5
Bone and meat meal ..	6.0	37.4	39.5		6.3	10.8
Bone, fresh cut........	34.2	22.8	20.6		1.9	20.5
Buttermilk...........	90.2	.7	4.0		4.0	1.1
Fish, dried...........	10.8	29.2	48.4			11.6
Meat scrap...........	10.7	4.1	71.2		.3	13.7
Milk, whole..........	87.1	.7	3.6		4.9	3.7
Milk, skim...........	90.6	.7	3.1		5.3	.3
Hay and vegetables:						
Alfalfa hay...........	6.8	10.6	15.4	33.3	32.5	1.4
Beet pulp, dry........	8.4	4.5	8.1	17.5	60.8	.7
Beets	88.5	1.0	1.5	.9	8.0	.1
Carrots..............	88.6	1.0	1.1	1.1	7.6	.4
Clover hay...........	10.0	8.1	16.32	17.84	45.99	1.75
Potatoes.............	79.1	.9	2.1	.4	17.4	.1
Pumpkins............	90.9	.5	1.3	1.7	5.2	.4
Sweet potatoes........	68.3	1.1	1.9	1.2	26.8	.7
Turnips..............	90.1	.9	1.3	1.2	6.3	.2

The preceding table gives the average composition **of** various poultry foods.

SEEDS AND THEIR BY-PRODUCTS

Foods the quality of which is unquestionably good are the most economical for poultry. Shriveled, immature, or imperfect grains do not contain the full amounts of digestible nutrients, and such grains are likely to be deficient in protein. When the best results are desired none except good, plump, mature grains are used. The same principle applies in selecting the by-products of grains.

The relative value of poultry foods can best be estimated when the food value of each is well understood. It is usually more profitable to buy the foods rich in protein than those lacking in this valuable principle.

WHEAT

Whole Wheat.—A grain of wheat is made up of an outer shell, an inner lining, and a food center, its structure in a general way resembling that of an egg. The shell of the wheat kernel is composed largely of crude fiber; the central part contains some protein, but consists mainly of starch. The protein, or gluten, of the wheat is the most valuable part of it, and no other grain will fill the place of wheat as a food for the production of lean meat and eggs by fowls. Wheat is rich in both protein and the fat-forming principles, but it is a better food for making blood, flesh, and feathers than for fattening purposes; hence, it is a better food for egg-producing hens than for those intended for the market. Wheat is commonly one of the several grains used in making up a ration for fowls. Although the best whole grain for hens, it does not form a perfect ration when fed alone.

Second grades of wheat can be purchased at a lower price than the higher grades. If they are sound and have good feeding qualities, these second-grade wheats can be used to advantage; but if they are shriveled or blighted, they have little value. Burned, wet, musty, or

otherwise damaged grains are not fit for feeding **to** poultry.

The accompanying table shows the digestibility of the various food principles found in wheat of good quality. Although about 20% of its dry matter is indigestible, wheat, on account of its palatability, is the best possible whole-grain food for fowls.

DIGESTIBLE MATTER IN WHEAT

Parts of Wheat	Per Cent. Digest- ible	Parts of Wheat	Per Cent. Digest- ible
Organic matter	81.86	Crude fiber.........	None
Protein............	77.12	Carbohydrates......	86.59
Fat................	39.67		

Wheat Screenings.—The value of wheat screenings as a food depends on the quantity of weed seeds and other materials that are mixed with the wheat of inferior quality. Good wheat screenings have a food value equal to that of oats; screenings of poor quality have a food value that may be less than that of oat hulls or straw. Although fowls will eat a large portion of the weed seeds in screenings, many of them have no food value. Wheat screenings as a food for poultry are used in connection with an animal food and corn.

Wheat Bran.—The amount of gluten contained in wheat bran, which is a by-product in the manufacture of flour, determines its value as an egg-producing food. If the bran has the appearance of being kiln-dried, it probably contains so little digestible material that it is worthless as a food for hens. As dry bran free from gluten is practically all crude fiber, it is valuable only as a bulky substance for distending the intestines so that concentrated foods may be digested.

Middlings and Shorts.—The terms middlings and shorts are applied to by-products of the manufacture of flour. Wheat middlings are made from the membrane that lies between the outer shell and the starchy interior of the wheat kernel; they contain some gluten, a substance composed largely of protein. Shorts as usually sold are made up of small, or ground, bran and wheat sweepings. Thirds, or fine shorts, are middlings of good quality. Middlings are worth more than bran and are much used in making dry-mash rations.

Flour.—When it can be cheaply obtained, the lower grade of dark flour is sometimes used for feeding to poultry. This flour is rich in protein and other food principles, and can be mixed with middlings and corn meal. The resulting mixture may then be baked like bread and fed to young or growing chicks. A small quantity of this flour mixed with mash forms a crumbly mass.

OATS

Whole Oats.—The determination of the value of whole oats by their appearance is exceedingly difficult. Good oats rank next to wheat as a poultry food, but the one objection to oats is that they vary widely in the proportion of hulls, or husks, which are indigestible. Some oats are two-fifths husks, which are of no value as food. The weight of oats varies from 25 to 50 lb. per bu. Light oats are unfit for food for fowls; heavy oats with full, plump kernels are one of the very best. Hulled oats are preferable for feeding poultry; heavy-weight clipped oats stand next in value; ground oats of the best quality are also an excellent food for poultry.

Oatmeal and Hulled Oats.—In the manufacture of both oatmeal and hulled oats, which have the same nutritive ratio, the hulls are removed; consequently, the food value of both oatmeal and hulled oats is greater than that of whole oats. Oats thus prepared are extensively used in making rations for young or growing chicks. Whole oats have a nutritive ratio of 1 to 6; hulled oats and oatmeal, 1 to 4. (By nutritive ratio is meant the ratio

between the protein and the total of fats and carbohydrates.) Consequently, prepared oats are better than
whole oats as food for young chicks and laying hens.
Either hulled oats or oatmeal is one of the best single-
grain rations for fowls.

Oat Hulls.—As a poultry food, oat hulls, apart from
their value as manure, which is small, are worth no
more than sawdust. Ground oat hulls are liberally used
as an adulterant to lessen the cost of other foods in
preparing poultry feeds, and the presence of much of
this adulterant may so reduce the value of the feed as
to make it useless.

CORN

Whole Corn.—The structure of the corn kernel is
similar in a general way to that of the wheat grain.
Corn is the grain that is ordinarily the most attractive
to poultry. Some corn is almost a necessity for successful poultry feeding, but an all-corn ration is
injurious because it is too fattening. Corn alone, however, will not fatten a fowl in the best way, nor will
it produce a good yield of eggs. Corn is rich in carbohydrates and fats; it provides heat for the body, and
oil and fat for the feathers, for the yolk of the egg, and
for the flesh. Corn contains too little protein and ash
for successful egg production, and to produce the best
results is combined with other grains. A balanced
ration is formed by the use of corn and some other
grains and meat.

Corn Bran.—The outside of the grain, or the shell,
from which corn bran is made, is removed from corn
when it is made into food products for human beings.
This shell is hard and dry and has almost no food value,
being composed almost entirely of indigestible fiber and
a little ash, and is, therefore, of no use in poultry
rations.

Gluten Meals and Feeds.—Gluten, a by-product of corn-
starch manufacture, is sometimes sold as gluten meal,
and is a very important food for dairy cows. Good

gluten meal that does not contain corn hulls or other waste products is also useful as a part of the meal ration for poultry. Gluten meal is a concentrated food, rich in protein, nearly all of which is digestible. Not more than 10% of a ration should consist of this meal.

The germ of the corn is rarely sold separate from the other by-products. Like gluten meal, it should be fed sparingly to fowls.

Gluten feed, which is much more commonly sold than either gluten meal or the corn germs, is made by grinding the germs, hulls, and gluten together. Gluten feed, although not so rich in protein as either the gluten meal or corn germs, should not be fed too liberally to poultry.

Hominy Chop.—Hominy is made from the hard or flinty part of the corn. The hulls, corn germs, and some gluten left after the hominy is made, are ground into coarse meal and sold as· hominy chop, which, if of good quality, is fully equal in value to corn meal as a poultry food. Like the value of all grain by-products, the value of hominy chop depends on its quality, and it should not contain too much crude fiber.

Corn Cobs.—The coarse meal made from corn cobs cannot be prepared in any way that fits it· for food. It has about the same chemical composition as straw, and as food for poultry both corn cobs and straw are valueless.

MISCELLANEOUS GRAINS AND SEEDS

Kafir Corn.—Both Kafir corn, or dari, and broom corn belong to the sorghum family of plants. The fact that Kafir corn is used largely as food by people of Africa and in other countries is evidence of its nutritive value, Kafir corn being, in this respect, about equal to barley or buckwheat. Kafir-corn grains are very ·hard; tests made by the feeding of old, very dry grains to fowls show that many of them passed through the fowls without being broken up. The same grains resisted for a time an effort to soften them by boiling. When broken into bits, however, the small pieces could be eaten and

digested by young chicks. In some localities where bugs and worms are plentiful, the entire grain ration for the summer months is Kafir corn, a plentiful supply of insect food with this kind of grain making a nearly balanced ration. Kafir corn can be used with safety in the ration for the full-grown fowls, and, if broken into small pieces, for chicks as well.

Broom Corn.—The seed of broom corn as a food for poultry is about equal in value to sunflower seed. Broom corn is fed sparingly; a ration containing more than 10% of this grain cannot be fed with safety to fowls. In order to avoid fermentation and mildew, the heads of the grain are spread out and kept in a dry place. Cryptogamic poisoning is liable to be produced by the eating of moldy grain or seed of any kind.

Rye.—The use of rye as a food for poultry should be avoided; fowls do not relish it and bad results may come from its use.

Barley.—The grains of barley, if plump and of good quality, contain almost as much protein as oats, more than corn, and more of the carbohydrates than oats but not so much as corn. Good barley is about 15% hulls; poor barley may have a much larger percentage of hulls, and the grains themselves may be so shriveled as to be valueless as food. Good barley meal is useful for forming a part of the meal ration for fattening fowls. It is one of the best meals for this purpose; but the ordinary barley meals are likely to be made of a mixture of barley and waste products, which tend to deprive the meal of its feeding value.

Buckwheat.—Fowls have to acquire a liking for buckwheat; they are not naturally fond of it, and as the hull, which forms a large percentage of this grain, is indigestible, buckwheat is not good as a single-grain ration. Buckwheat whitens the flesh and improves its flavor when fed liberally to fowls. The yolks of eggs from hens fed freely on buckwheat are light in color. Although a small quantity of buckwheat may be used

as a part of an all-grain ration, it is not classed as a desirable grain for fowls.

Buckwheat Middlings.—The hulls of buckwheat have no feeding value, but in some localities they are used as litter in buildings and brooders. Buckwheat middlings are superior to wheat bran and wheat middlings as a food for fowls, and this fact brings into the market buckwheat bran, which is largely broken hulls mixed with buckwheat middlings. Although the floury middlings of buckwheat are fit for poultry food, the bran of this grain contains no nutriment and is useless for food purposes.

Peas.—Although fowls relish pea vines, they must acquire a liking for peas themselves, which are very good food. The field pea, or Canada pea, as it is sometimes called, is largely used as food for pigeons, and on the whole is probably the best pea for other kinds of poultry. Low-priced, broken peas, if cooked, can at times be used to advantage. When they have been thoroughly softened by boiling, wheat bran is added to them to make a crumbly mass; a little flour put with the bran will help to make the mass stick together. A mixture prepared in this way is greedily devoured by hens, and is an excellent egg-producing ration. Pea meal is a concentrated food that should be sparingly used. Peas or pea meal added to a fattening ration improve the quality of the lean meat.

Beans.—As a food for poultry, beans are more nutritious than peas. Bean vines are not so well liked as the pea vines, nor will the fowls eat beans as long as they have other food before them. Soybeans contain much protein and ash; because of this fact they are valuable food for fowls. Beans should be boiled to a soft mush and mixed with corn meal and bran; this preparation makes an egg-producing ration. If sufficient corn meal is added, a fat-forming ration that will produce a good quality of table meat is made. Fowls are naturally attracted to a mixture of this kind. Like other cooked foods, boiled beans may be fed to fowls while warm, but never while hot.

Rice.—Rice is a fat-forming food that is little used for poultry. Small or broken rice, however, may be used in chick feed to advantage. Boiled rice is a good food for bantams because it produces so little bone and size; it satisfies hunger but does not produce growth to any extent. It is an expensive food for fowls.

Millet.—The seed of the foxtail millet is a rich grain that should not be fed liberally to poultry. When thrown into litter, the small, bright-colored seeds attract the fowls. A ration made up entirely of millet will destroy young chicks and injure old fowls. This seed is used to a limited extent in chick feeds, and also in scratching foods for hens. Millet is a fattening food and when hard, dry millet seed is liberally fed, it may clog the intestines or pass through them undigested.

Sorghum Seed.—The food value of the seed from sugar-producing sorghum is about equal to that of the seed of broom corn, but sorghum seed is more fattening than the broom-corn seed, and contains a little less protein than that seed. Sorghum plants that make good green food for fowls are grown from sorghum seed sown broad-cast or drilled into the ground.

Sunflower Seed.—Sunflower seed has a nutritive ratio of 1 to 7, about the same as wheat; but the digestibility of sunflower seed has not yet been accurately determined. It is likely that the larger part of sunflower seeds are indigestible. The kernels have a pleasant flavor and contain considerable fat, but when dry and shriveled their food value is small. Fresh, plump sunflower seeds are used to advantage by sparingly feeding them to fowls in molt; if these seeds are liberally fed, the digestive organs of fowls soon become clogged with indigestible fiber.

Flaxseed.—Of all the grains and seeds fed to poultry, flaxseed is the richest in oil and protein. Its use is seldom necessary, because equal benefit can be derived by using by-products of seeds that are much less expensive. Flaxseed is a laxative, but contains so much gluten that it may clog the digestive organs.

Linseed Meal.—There are two kinds of linseed meal —old process and new process. The latter contains less protein and is more fattening than the former. There is very little old-process meal made at the present time. Linseed meal contains the feather-forming elements to a large extent and is valuable during molt; it can be cautiously fed at all times. Fowls do not favor it as a food; it is laxative, concentrated, and contains so much gluten that it will clog the crop if used too liberally. The quantity of linseed meal used should not exceed 5% of the entire ration.

Cottonseed Meal.—Even when fed sparingly, cottonseed meal is not relished by fowls. Neither cottonseed nor any of its products should ever be fed to fowls, as these foods act as irritants to the digestive organs, and if fed liberally cause death.

LIGHT BRAHMA MALE

Peanut Meal. — Meal made from peanuts after the oil has been extracted is a good food for poultry. It is a palatable food and can be used in small quantities with other fattening meals. An ounce and a half of peanut meal has about the same food value as 1 oz. of the best meat scrap. There is so little of this meal that it cannot often be used as food for poultry.

Hemp Seed.—Hemp seed contains more fat and less fiber than sunflower seed; for this reason, it is more easily digested and gives better results than sunflower seed. Hemp seed is a stimulating, fat-forming food, and is fed in small quantities and only to fowls that are slow to molt. A small quantity of this seed is also fed to exhibition fowls during cold weather to improve the gloss on their plumage. Hemp seed is too expensive for general use.

Canary Seed.—The best known balanced ration for cage birds is canary seed; young chicks also enjoy a little of this seed, on which they will thrive when they do not do well on other grains. All waste canary seed should be fed to chicks, but this feed is too costly to use except in an emergency or to save the waste from cage birds.

Rape Seed.—German rape seed, or bird-seed rape, is a better food than millet seed for young chicks. It is a fattening food, rich in protein, and dark or chestnut brown in color. Rape-seed grains are smaller than millet seeds. For ailing or weakly chicks, rape seed is boiled for 5 min., turned into a fine, funnel-shapel sieve, and left to drain overnight. A small quantity of this food is given in the morning and evening. Only the true German rape seed is fit for this use. .

VEGETABLES

Mangels.—Of all the vegetables and roots that are fed to poultry as substitutes for green foods, mangels are the best; they are fine-flavored, sweet, and nutritious, and impart these qualities to the meat and eggs of the fowls. No objectionable flavors are introduced into either the flesh or the eggs as a result of feeding mangels liberally. Mangels are rank growers, keep well throughout the winter if protected from frost, are easily fed, and are freely eaten by fowls.

Beets.—There are many kinds of beets, all of which are eaten freely by poultry. If too many raw beets are fed, however, the bowels of the fowls may become so loose that diarrhea will result, especially if the use of beets is long continued. Raw beets should be sparingly fed, but if they are cooked they make a valuable addition to a ration.

Turnips.—As a poultry food, turnips are not so desirable as beets. If turnips are fed raw, they taint the flavor of the eggs and do not improve the meat of market

poultry. The rutabaga is the best variety of turnip for poultry, but even this turnip will taint the eggs if fed freely. Turnips, parsnips, and carrots, when boiled to a pulp and mixed with the mash feeds, make good rations for all kinds of poultry. A very little salt should be put in the water in which the vegetables are boiled. Too much salt will kill poultry; fowls require much less salt than men.

Potatoes.—When they are plentiful and cheap, potatoes are used as poultry food; 5 lb. of potatoes are about equal in feeding value to 1 lb. of corn meal. Potatoes fed to laying hens are thoroughly boiled, drained, and mixed with wheat bran, middlings, and ground oats; the same mixture will do for growing chicks, but if it is to be used for fattening purposes some corn meal is added to this ration. Meal that is made from small potatoes is used as a fattening food; this meal contains all the solid food of the potato and only a small percentage of the original moisture. The meal is an easily digested food, and it is used where potatoes are more plentiful than grain. Raw potatoes are not fit food for poultry.

Onions.—Although onions are wholesome food for all kinds of fowls, their flavor is imparted to the eggs and meat of the fowls that eat them; for this reason onions should not be used when their flavor will prove objectionable. Turnips, onions, and potatoes may be boiled together and used in mash food for all kinds of poultry without harm, provided none of the mixture is fed for 2 wk. before killing the fowls for market or selling their eggs for food. All of these vegetables can be safely used for hens when their eggs are to be used for hatching and not for food.

Cabbage.—Although not the best thing for them, cabbage is a favorite food of fowls, and is often quite liberally fed. Cabbages are laxative, especially when they have been frozen. They also impart an odor to eggs that detracts from their quality. If cabbages are permitted to freeze and are carelessly fed they may reduce the egg yield materially, and may also cause

so much looseness of the bowels of the fowls that their
health will be injured. Kale and Swiss chard can be
used in the same way as cabbages.

Apples.—No other fruit is more plentiful nor so generally eaten as are apples. They are liked by poultry,
and little chicks may be taught to eat them raw. Wher-
ever sweet apples abound they can be cut up into small
pieces and fed raw to little chicks. They may be sliced
in root cutters and fed to fowls of all ages. When
cooked and mixed with meals they are eaten greedily
by livestock of all kinds. Apples and apple peelings
cut into small pieces, cooked into a thin sauce, and
mixed with meals are good feed for laying hens.

Carrots.—For feeding of poultry, there is no more
desirable root crop than carrots. The tops are relished
by the fowls; and they are a succulent green feed for
them. The roots may be fed raw to fowls of all kinds,
both young and old. Raw carrots fed freely to laying
hens are likely to impart color to the yolk and flavor to
the egg. When cooked before feeding they impart but
little color to the yolk and no flavor to the egg. Carrots
contain a large percentage of water. The solids contained in them are mostly digestible. Boiled carrots
mixed with meals are an excellent mash feed for laying hens.

Pumpkins.—For some reason there is an impression
that pumpkins are not good feed for cows, hogs, or
poultry. There does not seem to be any good reason for
such a belief. Although pumpkins are not an excellent
ration alone either for milk or egg production, they can
be used for feeding to poultry of all kinds and to laying
hens to good advantage. Pumpkins that are frozen or
partly frozen are detrimental to the health of poultry if
eaten raw; if cooked and mixed with meal they may
be safely eaten but they are not so good for feed as
when they are in good condition. For feeding to poultry,
the pumpkins should be thoroughly cooked, stirred into
a mash, and dried off with meals, in which condition
they can be fed plentifully.

GREEN FOODS

Green, or growing, plants are valuable as food for poultry on account of the natural juices they contain. The tender blades of grass and other forage plants impart new life to fowls that feed on them in the spring. Chicks can be grown and fowls sustained without green food, but the difference between those that have it in abundance and those that do not is so marked that all question of its value is removed.

Green food is at its best when gathered by the fowls from the field where it grows, but good results may be obtained by substituting clover hay or other dried forage for the green portion of the ration. This practice is necessary when the fowls cannot range extensively and whenever there is no available green food owing to climatic or other conditions.

The green food consumed by fowls or chicks should not to be considered as a regular portion of the nutritive ration, but rather as a supplement to the grain and animal food. The composition and nutritive ratio of different kinds of green foods, that under various circumstances and in different places have been found to be of more or less value for poultry food, are given in the table which appears on the following page.

Vegetable Tops.—Poultry relish the tops of vegetables as green food. Trimmings from vegetables and the waste from fruit, cabbage, and roots, cut into small pieces, boiled to a pulp, and mixed into a mash of meal, make an excellent food for all kinds of fowls, both old and young.

Grass.—Nearly everywhere grass of many kinds grows naturally or is cultivated for feeding, grazing, and hay making; none of the green foods is better for poultry. Where grass is naturally abundant, a supply of green food is always at hand during the growing season. But green food for winter use must be grown

COMPOSITION AND NUTRITIVE RATIO
OF GREEN FOODS

Food	Dry Matter Per Cent.	Digestible Nutrients			Nutritive Ratio
		Protein Per Cent.	Carbo-hy-drates Per Cent.	Fat Per Cent.	
Alfalfa............	20.0	3.7	7.3	.6	1 : 2.4
Alfilerilla.........	20.0	2.1	8.5	.7	1 : 4.8
Barley............	21.0	1.9	10.2	.4	1 : 5.8
Red clover........	29.2	2.9	14.8	.7	1 : 5.7
Crimson clover....	19.3	2.2	9.3	.4	1 : 4.6
Corn.............	20.7	1.0	11.6	.4	1 : 12.5
Cowpeas..........	16.4	1.7	8.8	.3	1 : 5.6
Blue grass........	34.9	2.7	17.8	.7	1 : 7.2
Hungarian grass...	28.9	1.9	15.6	.4	1 : 8.7
Orchard grass	27.0	1.9	15.9	.6	1 : 9.1
Oats.............	37.8	2.4	17.9	.9	1 : 8.3
Rye..............	23.4	2.5	14.1	.4	1 : 6.0
Rape.............	14.3	2.2	8.6	.3	1 : 4.2
Red top..........	34.7	2.6	21.2	.6	1 : 8.7
Soybeans.........	28.5	2.8	11.8	.6	1 : 4.7
Timothy..........	38.4	2.1	21.2	.6	1 : 10.8
Kafir corn........	27.0	.8	13.8	.4	1 : 18.4
Lettuce..........	4.1	1.0	2.7	.8	1 : 4.5
Artichokes	20.0	2.0	16.8	.2	1 : 8.7
Beets............	15.7	1.6	11.9	.1	1 : 7.6
Beet leaves.......	11.3	1.7	4.6	.1	1 : 2.8
Cabbage..........	15.3	1.8	8.2	.4	1 : 5.1
Carrots..........	11.4	.8	7.8	.2	1 : 10.4
Mangels..........	9.1	1.1	5.4	.1	1 : 5.1
Parsnips..........	11.7	1.6	11.2	.2	1 : 7.3
Potatoes..........	21.1	.9	16.3	.1	1 : 18.3
Pumpkins.........	9.1	1.0	5.8	.3	1 : 6.5
Rutabagas........	13.0	1.2	7.5	.2	1 : 6.7
Sweet potatoes....	19.7	1.5	24.7	.4	1 : 17.1
Turnips..........	9.5	1.0	7.2	.2	1 : 7.7
Apples...........	15.9	.4	14.2	.3	1 : 37.3
Onions...........	12.4	1.4	9.4	.5	1 : 7.5

and stored, and in some places the supply for the entire year must be grown.

Clippings of grass from the lawn are also good food for poultry that is confined in yards; or, if dried and stored, these clippings will be good for winter use. Either fresh or dry, they are valuable as litter for the floor of the brooder or brooder house.

Fodder Corn.—Corn that is sown broadcast or drilled in rows produces tender, green stalks called fodder corn, which is relished by fowls that are confined; it is not preferred by fowls having their freedom, nor should it be fed after it has passed beyond a succulent or juicy condition.

Alfalfa and Clover.—The tender leaves of all the clovers and of alfalfa are in much demand by fowls. They probably prefer alfalfa, or lucerne, to clover. After it has become well established, alfalfa will continue to grow for many years and will produce heavier yields of green forage and hay than any of the clovers. To raise alfalfa successfully, the soil must be adapted to the needs of the plant, and in many localities clover can be raised more easily than alfalfa.

During winter months, clover hay can be used as a substitute for green food. Hay made from Red clover is most frequently used for this purpose, although hay made from any of the clover plants is good winter food for fowls. It may be used as litter on the floor, from which the fowls will help themselves, or the hay may be cut into small pieces and placed in a box for the fowls to work over. They eat all the leaves of clover hay. Bright, clean, early-cut hay is preferable to a dark hay made from cured plants. Ground clover and clover meal may also be used as food for poultry.

Hay made from alfalfa is extensively used for poultry, and it may, like clover, be cut into pieces or ground into a fine meal before feeding. All forms of alfalfa are freely eaten both by old and young fowls, and alfalfa is not equaled by any other hay as a substitute for green food for fowls. Meadow hay may

be ground and mixed with alfalfa meal, but alfalfa **is** best fed without mixture or adulteration.

Miscellaneous Green Crops for Winter Feeding.—In addition to those already mentioned, many other green crops are grown for winter feeding. A mixture of oats, peas, rape, and clover planted on the same ground and cut while green makes a good forage crop for fowls. First, sow 3 bu. oats and 2 bu. peas per acre and harrow into the ground; then, seed over the oats and peas with a mixture of 6 qt. clover seed and 1 qt. German rape seed.

___

ANIMAL FOODS

MEAT AND MEAT PRODUCTS

Marked success in producing eggs and in growing poultry for the market cannot be obtained without the use of some animal food.

Insects and worms form an important part of the food of wild birds and of domestic fowls whenever they are permitted to range.

Lean Meat.—Meat is an acceptable substitute for insects and worms. Lean meat is especially useful in the feeding of laying hens, for by using this food much protein may be added to the ration without increasing its bulk or using concentrated foods that impair digestion. The carcasses of horses and cows are composed mainly of lean meat and are used as poultry food.

Meat Scrap.—There are two kinds of meat scrap, fat and lean. The latter kind contains twice as much protein as carbohydrates, while the former contains more fat than protein and very little ash. The best lean-meat scrap should be selected for laying hens; the more protein and the less fat the scrap contains, the better it is for the hens. Fat-meat scraps and fat or tallow are used in fattening special grades of table poultry.

Animal Meal.—One of the numerous by-products of the slaughter houses is animal meal. The feeding value

of animal meal is higher than that of cut green bone; but better results are obtained from the use of cut green bone than from animal meal, because the former contains a larger percentage of ash than of protein—presumably because the meal is made from both bone and meat. Good meat meal is rich in protein but contains less ash than animal meal, and can only be used sparingly in making an egg-producing ration. Because of its cost and richness in protein, meat meal is used only when good meat scrap cannot be obtained.

Dried Blood.—Dried blood and blood meal are sometimes used to supply protein in foods for poultry. These blood products are concentrated foods and a small quantity of either mixed with other foods will make a narrow ration. Dried blood and blood meal are not generally economical or profitable foods for poultry.

Cut Green Bone.—The food commonly called cut green bone is made by cutting fresh bones into small pieces by means of a bone mill. Being fresh meat, bone, and fat, its composition closely resembles that of bugs and worms, the natural food of fowls. About ½ oz. of cut green bone per day for each fowl, mixed with wheat bran, will make a balanced ration well suited to fowls.

Tainted Meat.—Tainted meat that is not fit for human food should not be fed to fowls. The taint of such food may sometimes be removed by boiling it in water containing baking soda, in which case the meat can be safely fed to fowls.

Bone Meal.—Bone meal consists of bones of animals cleaned of all meat, fat, and marrow, and reduced to meal. It is used to supply any deficiency of lime, ash, or bone-forming material that exists in the ration. Bone meal can be fed to young chicks to produce a strong growth of bone. The particles in this meal vary in size from those that are very small to those of the size of whole wheat or even corn; the largest sizes are not desirable for poultry food.

Fish.—Fish that are handled for their oil are reduced in presses until little of their flesh remains. The bone and other residue are then ground into a meal. This fish meal and dried fish are sometimes fed to poultry. Fish products are liable to transmit a disagreeable flavor to the eggs or meat, and for this reason are not desirable.

MILK

Milk is a valuable poultry food, more valuable than its commercial analysis indicates. Nothing excels warm milk direct from the cow as the first ration for chicks. The use of whole milk as a chicken feed, however, will rarely prove profitable, for even when carefully handled it is not worth more than 2c. per qt. for this purpose. The most profitable method of feeding milk to fowls is to use it in moistening mash feeds.

Some persons prefer sweet milk for poultry, but G. A. C. Wyllie, of the British Dairy Institute, Reading, England, says that sour milk has been found to give better results, as the acid produced by the bacteria present causes more rapid action. He states: "Soured milk also prevents scouring, and makes the food easier digested. The acid formed from the milk sugar also prevents sickness and stimulates the appetite. It keeps the digestive organs in proper activity, which saves feeding so much green food. When fed to all kinds of poultry it produces a fine white flesh, due to the amount of phosphates, with extra good flavor. It is without doubt one of the best foods we have both for young and old stock, and is becoming more popular every day. I may say it also increases the egg supply and hastens the molt."

Skim-milk, sour milk, and buttermilk, may be improved for feeding purposes by scalding; but care should be taken not to boil, as boiling destroys the value and palatability. The whey of milk is of no value as a poultry feed. In the accompanying table is shown the composition and nutritive ratio of whole milk and of various milk products.

Food	Water Per Cent.	Ash Per Cent.	Protein Per Cent.	Carbohydrates Per Cent.	Fat Per Cent.	Nutritive Ratio
Whole milk	87.2	.7	3.6	4.9	3.7	1 : 2.4
Skim-milk	90.6	.7	3.3	5.3	.1	1 : 1.9
Sour milk	90.6	.7	3.3	5.3	.1	1 : 1.9
Cottage cheese (milk curds)	72.0	1.8	20.9	4.3	1.0	1 : .3
Buttermilk	90.3	.7	4.0	4.5	.5	1 : 1.4
Whey	93.4	.5	.8	5.0	.3	1 : 7.0

COMPOSITION AND NUTRITIVE RATIOS OF MILK AND MILK PRODUCTS

MINERAL MATTER

Grit.—The food eaten by fowls goes first into the crop, where it is softened by water; it then passes into the gizzard, and by the action of small sharp stones, or grit, is there ground into a pasty mass. The best grit is sharp, irregular pieces of hard limestone about the size of corn kernels.

Mineral matter is necessary for the good health of the fowls and for eggshell-forming material. A deficiency of this in the regular ration may be supplied by grit, limestone, plaster, broken oyster shells, or shells of any kind. Granulated bone and bone meal serve the purpose fairly well, but the lime in shells is more quickly dissolved by the action of grit and gizzard, and hence is better than the bone.

Charcoal. — Charcoal is one of the necessities of poultry feeding and should be kept constantly before poultry; it assists digestion, sweetens the crop, gizzard, and intestines, and prevents ailments of the

digestive tract. The charcoal, which should be broken into small pieces, should be supplied with the oyster shells and grit.

Salt.—The use of salt in poultry food is not a necessity; but when a forcing ration is fed to fowls either to produce broilers, to fatten fowls, or to produce eggs, some salt may be used to assist digestion; 8 oz. of salt to 100 lb. of meal is enough to use; much more than this will injure the digestion of grown fowls, and it is positively unsafe to feed more to young chicks.

POISONOUS FOODS

Fowls sometimes die from ptomaine poisoning. For this reason putrid meat, spoiled grain, and other fermented or spoiled foods should not be fed. Foods that are otherwise wholesome may be made unwholesome if exposed to dampness, due to the development of molds.

Excessive quantities of salt, salt meat, or the brine from which the meat has been removed, salt fish, salt from ice-cream freezers, and in fact, salt of any kind consumed in large quantities is very destructive to poultry.

Solutions of sulphate of iron or of sulphuric acid, carelessly used, are very destructive to poultry.

Decayed vegetables or fruits, fermenting waste, waste from cider mills or canning factories, and slops from distilleries are not suitable for feeding to laying hens, because they flavor the eggs. Tainted meat eaten by a fowl will also influence the flavor of eggs.

Moldy bread is detrimental to poultry. It may be freed from mold by toasting or baking it dry and hard, but when so prepared it is not fit food for chicks under 6 wk. old.

INTERNAL ORGANS OF FOWLS

The process of digestion in poultry differs materially from that in animals that chew their food. Fowls have no teeth, the functions of the teeth being performed by the gizzard, in which, by the aid of grit, the food is

Fig. 1

ground into pulp. The greater part of the food eaten by poultry is swallowed whole and passes in that condition to the crop, where it absorbs considerable moisture before it passes to the other digestive organs. A general view of the internal organs of a hen is shown in Fig. 1. After being picked up by the bill, the

food passes through the upper part of the esophagus *a* into the crop *b*; from the crop the food passes through the lower part of the esophagus into the gizzard *c*; and from there through the other organs of the digestive system.

Crop.—In fowls and other granivorous, or grain-eating, birds, the crop is relatively larger than the crop of birds that feed largely on grass. Within the crops are juices that moisten the food and hasten its passage into the gizzard.

Gizzard.—The gizzard *c* may be looked on as a powerful grinding machine in which the whole grain and other foods of poultry are ground, oftentimes finer than they would be ground by the teeth of chewing animals. The grinding is accomplished by means of the powerful muscles of the gizzard, which keep the mixture of sand, grit, and food within it constantly in motion. In the gizzard the food is also acted on by digestive juices before being passed into the intestines.

Intestines.—The intestines as applied to fowls means all of the alimentary canal beyond the gizzard. The intestines of the fowls, although different in many respects from those of other animals, present a somewhat similar appearance and have functions nearly identical with those of the other domestic animals. In fowls, the intestines are made up of the *duodenum,* and the rest of the *small intestines d,* the *caeca e,* and the *large intestines* and the *rectum g.* Inside of the intestines the food is acted on by various digestive fluids, and digestible nutrients within the food are taken from it and eventually converted into blood. The inner walls of the intestines are covered with minute projections known as *villi,* which absorb the digested material from the contents of the intestines. The indigestible part of the food passes into the rectum *g* and out of the body through the vent *h.*

Liver.—The liver *i* is a large, two-lobed organ of peculiar cellular structure. It has two offices, one of them being to purify the digested material brought to

it by the capillaries, and the other to secrete the bile, an important digestive fluid. The liver must be kept in a healthy condition or the blood, and consequently the entire system, will speedily become poisoned.

Gall Bladder.—The gall bladder *k* serves as a reservoir for the bile secreted by the liver, to which it is closely attached. The bile is passed, as needed, from the gall bladder to the intestines, where its special office is to break up the vegetable fats and oils and convert them into soluble animal fat, which is readily made a part of the fowl's body.

Spleen.—The spleen *s* is located near the liver and is an organ whose use is not definitely known. It is thought, however, that it is useful in producing certain modifications in the blood.

Pancreas.—Situated among the folds of the small intestines is the pancreas *l*, a small organ of insignificant appearance. This organ is of vital importance, for in it is secreted the pancreatic juice, which flows from the pancreas into the intestines, where it acts directly on the starchy portions of food, and to a limited extent on protein; it also aids in the absorption of fat. The juice from the pancreas unites with the bile and they together flow over the foods as they come from the gizzard.

Heart and Lungs.—The heart *m* and the lungs *n* are vital organs. The work done by the latter, like that of the liver, consists in purifying the blood. The office of the heart, as is well known, is to pump the blood to all parts of the body. The heart, lungs, and liver may be considered as the most important organs of the body, and care should be taken to keep them in good working order, for when the action of one of these organs is faulty, the effect is soon apparent on the others. The air is supplied to the lungs through the windpipe *w*.

Kidneys.—The kidneys *o* are located in cavities in the pelvic bone. They act on the blood and separate from it liquid waste material, which is eventually passed from the body through the vent.

Ovaries and Oviduct.—The ovaries *p* and the oviduct *q* are shown enlarged in Fig. 2. The ovaries *a* (Fig. 2) are attached to the under side of the backbone, usually on the left. The ovaries and the oviduct are the female organs of reproduction. The yolk of the egg attains its full size within the casing of the ovaries, which, in good laying hens, contain yolks varying in size from that of a small pin head to that of the full-grown yolk. As soon as the yolk has reached its full development, the casing of the ovary, or *ovisac,* as it is sometimes called, opens and the yolk passes into the oviduct *c.* The yolk may or may not be fertilized by the male element before or just after entering the oviduct.

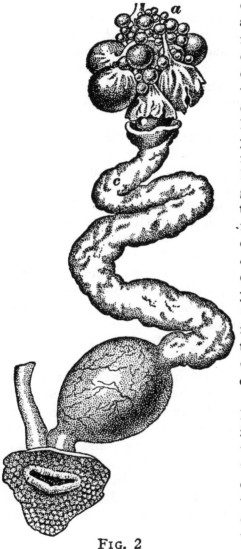

FIG. 2

The oviduct varies in length, and in some cases it is nearly 2 ft. long. As the yolk passes through the oviduct it becomes covered with albumen, of which the white of the egg is composed, and with a double membrane, or the lining to the egg-shell. After the egg has reached its full size the shell is formed about it in the oviduct. The passage of the egg through the oviduct requires from 6 to 18 or 20 hr.

FEEDING OF FOWLS

In poultry feeding it is necessary not only to provide fowls with a ration properly balanced in the food elements, but the ration must also be of a character most suitable to the digestive organs of the fowls. In addition to this the fowls must be forced to take sufficient exercise so that their bodily functions will demand a plentiful supply of food, be in a condition to secure the best results from the food that is eaten, and be able to eliminate readily all waste materials.

When fowls take sufficient exercise, the only secret of keeping their digestive organs in the best condition will be found in feeding them a plentiful supply of coarse feed like bran, or some of the succulent green foods, such as cut clover, cut grasses, vegetables, or fruits. These foods will distend the intestines and aid in distributing the concentrated foods that are necessary for upbuilding the tissues of the body and for egg production. To induce fowls to take considerable exercise, a certain part of their grain food should be scattered in the litter of the houses and on the ground of the ranges so that they will be compelled to scratch to get it.

When kept actively exercising, fowls will not eat more than their digestive organs will be able to handle easily, provided fattening foods are not fed in excess and the ration is well balanced for egg production.

Despite the necessity of a certain quantity of coarse food to regulate their digestive organs, fowls must be fed as little indigestible matter as is consistent with the maintenance of their health and of a well-balanced ration. For instance, hens cannot thrive on a ration made up entirely of even the best grade of oats, and when oats are fed that are three-fourths husks, all the hens can possibly stuff themselves with will do little more than barely sustain life and will produce but few eggs. Chick feed and feed for full-grown fowls

that is largely indigestible will 'seriously injure those that eat it. It is possible for chicks and full-grown fowls to dwindle away with their crops stuffed full of indigestible material. The fact that a fowl's crop is distended with food is no proof that it has been well fed. Hence, the only actual proof of the value of any particular feed for fowls lies in the results that are obtained from it.

BARRED PLYMOUTH ROCK FEMALE

As a part of the daily ration, water is equal in importance to grain. Without water, the food would not be softened in the crop and digestion would not go on. Blood, eggs, and meat are all largely water; even the bones and muscles are dependent on moisture for growth. Pure water is an absolute necessity for poultry; if the drinking water is tainted, putrid, or contaminated with germs, disease is sure to follow its use. A gallon of fresh water each day is not too much for 2 doz. hens. A plentiful supply of pure water from which they can help themselves must be constantly kept within reach of fowls.

The composition of fowls and fresh eggs is shown in the accompanying table. The large percentage of water

COMPOSITION OF FOWL AND EGG

	Water Per Cent.	Ash Per Cent.	Protein Per Cent.	Fat Per Cent.
Hen..................	55.8	3.8	21.6	17.0
Pullet................	55.4	3.4	21.2	18.0
Capon................	41.6	3.7	19.4	33.9
Fresh egg............	65.7	12.2	11.4	8.9

in them emphasizes the necessity for a plentiful supply of water.

WEIGHT OF POULTRY FOODS PER QUART

Food	Weight Pounds
Alfalfa meal	1.0
Barley, whole	1.5
Barley meal	1.1
Beans	1.9
Beef	1.5
Buckwheat	1.3
Corn, whole	1.7
Corn meal	1.5
Corn bran	.9
Corn and oat food	.7
Cottonseed meal	1.5
Gluten feed	1.3
Gluten meal	1.7
Hemp seed	1.4
Hominy chop	1.1
Kafir corn	1.7
Linseed meal, new process	.9
Linseed meal, old process	1.1
Millet	1.6
Oats, whole	1.0
Oats, ground	.7
Peas	1.9
Rice	1.7
Rye, whole	1.7
Rye, ground	1.5
Sunflower seed	1.4
Salt	2.5
Shorts	.6
Wheat, whole	1.9
Wheat, ground	1.7
Wheat bran	.5
Wheat middlings (standard)	.8
Wheat middlings (flour)	1.2

Weight of Poultry Foods per Quart.—In the mixing of rations for poultry the weights of poultry foods per quart as given in the preceding table are useful.

FEEDING OF YOUNG CHICKS

No food is given to young chicks for the first 48 hr., but grit of some kind is supplied to clean out their digestive organs. Beginning with the third day, they may have stale bread moistened with sweet milk and pressed until nearly dry. For the next 2 or 3 da. a mixture of stale bread crumbs and fine oatmeal makes a good ration, and is better fed in small quantities at frequent intervals.

For chicks that are a week or more old, a simple ration can be made of 4 parts, by weight, of cracked corn, 2 parts of broken wheat, 2 parts of oatmeal, and 2 parts of granulated meat scrap. The corn should be broken into small pieces and the meat scrap must be of good quality, rich in protein, and of small size; meat scrap that contains fat is not fit to use in this ration. After the chicks are 6 wk. old, a ration made of cracked corn, whole wheat, hulled oats, and meat scrap can be used. In addition to the grain and meat ration, grit, green food, broken sea shells, or bone meal are necessary for young chicks. All food fed to chicks should be in small particles to avoid disorders in the crop and digestive organs.

Green stuff of some kind should be fed continually after the chicks are 3 or 4 da. old. Sprouted oats, lawn clippings, vegetable tops of any kind, and lettuce may all be fed. It is best to cut them into very small pieces before feeding. There is no danger of poultry of any age having too much green feed. Partly-grown chicks and older fowls will get a plentiful supply of this if given free range where it is abundant. When kept in confinement, they should have a plentiful supply of green stuff fresh every day.

One of the most successful poultry growers and exhibitors of New England feeds his little chicks for the first day or two on a baked cake made of 2 parts of bran, 2 parts of corn meal, and 1 part of wheat middlings, with just enough sweet milk or water to make a dry, crumbly

mass. This is baked in the oven until thoroughly done. When cool, this cake is rubbed into crumbs and fed to the chicks, a little fine grit being sprinkled on the board where the cake is spread. This is fed to the chicks every 2 hr.; they should have only as much as they will eat up clean. After the second day, hoppers containing a dry mash composed of 2 parts of wheat bran and 1 part of corn meal should be placed where the chicks can help themselves. A hopper filled with charcoal, grit, and very fine oyster shell is also used.

After the first week the same feeding is continued, with the addition of some grain, chick feed being scattered in the litter for the chicks to scratch for. After the second week but one feed a day of the baked cake is given to them, the remainder of the ration being composed of the grain chick feed. After the second week some hard-boiled egg chopped up very fine and mixed with the cake is given to the chicks. This is fed once a day for 2 or 3 wk.

After the third week the chicks are fed very small size cracked corn in place of the chick feed, and the baked cake is omitted, the hoppers of dry mash being kept before them all the time. In addition to this they should have sprouted oats fresh each morning. Sprouted oats is considered of equal importance with the other feeds.

Until they are well grown the chicks are fed continually with some broken grain composed of wheat, corn, and hulled oats, which is scattered in the litter to furnish plenty of exercise. As soon as the chicks can run out of doors there is less need of feeding the sprouted oats, provided they can get growing greens on the outside.

CORNELL FEEDING SCHEDULE

The Poultry Department of Cornell Agricultural College recommends that chicks be fed from the first to the fourth day with rolled oats, 8 parts; bread crumbs, 8 parts; sifted beef scrap, 2 parts; bone meal, 1 part.

This is moistened with sour skim-milk, and fed five times daily. Cracked grain mixture should be left before the chicks in a shallow tray containing a little dry mash like that given in later feeding. This grain mixture is composed of finely cracked wheat, 3 parts; finely cracked corn, 2 parts; pinhead oatmeal (steel-cut oatmeal), 1 part. Fine grit and charcoal mixed with grain, and a little finely shredded green food, should be scattered in the trays. Plenty of clean water should be supplied at all times.

For subsequent feeding, the following mash moistened with skim-milk should be gradually substituted for the first mixture: Wheat bran, 3 parts; corn meal, 3 parts; wheat middlings, 3 parts; sifted beef scrap, 3 parts; bone meal, 1 part. The moist mash should be fed two or three times daily. Cracked grain should be given at least twice daily, scattered in light litter as soon as the chicks are able to find it. Mash in dry condition should be kept in shallow trays before the chicks. Grit, charcoal, and fine cracked bone should be fed in separate trays or hoppers. When 4 wk. old, the chicks should be receiving two meals of mash and three of grain.

After 4 wk. the number of meals should be reduced, first to two of mash and two of grain, then to one of mash and two of grain; the grain should be fed morning and night and the dry mash should be constantly accessible. As soon as the chicks will eat larger grains, the wheat need not be cracked; hulled oats may be used in place of pinhead oatmeal, and the corn may be coarsely cracked. When the chicks are 8 wk. old, the grain ration may be changed to the following: Large cracked corn, 3 parts; wheat, 2 parts. If it is desired that the chicks shall develop slowly, the moist food may be gradually discontinued after 3 wk. Beef scrap may be fed in the mash up to one-fourth by weight, in quantity, or, after the chicks have become accustomed to it, may be kept constantly before them in hoppers. This method of feeding has been proved to be good where all feeds are to be purchased. Farmers having certain prod-

ucts of their own may modify it to advantage. Soured
skim-milk and table scraps will largely replace beef
scrap, particularly if chicks are on free range. Bread
moistened with milk is a good food for the first day or
two. Scalded clover leaves, either alone or mixed with
other feeds form a valuable addition to the rations, and
chicks a week old will eat wheat screenings. Buckwheat, barley, or rye should not be fed to young chicks.

FEEDING OF LAYING HENS

There has been so much written relative to feeding
laying hens that one is at a loss to know just where
to begin and what method to adopt. However, it may
be said that a ration for laying hens is not suitable
unless it contains enough of the food principles to maintain the bodily growth and to supply sufficient material
for the production of eggs; that is, protein, fats, carbohydrates, ash, and water must be plentifully supplied
and in the proper proportions.

A few suggestions that might be followed as a guide
for selecting a ration to be fed to hens are given here.
Never feed a ration containing any considerable amount
of fattening feed during the summer months, nor in a
climate that is continually warm. An all-corn ration
will not produce many eggs in winter, neither will a
ration composed entirely of wheat and oats do much
better. It is not necessary nor advisable to feed many
different kinds of grain, and, above all, a grain mixture
should not be fed unless its grain content is such as will
produce eggs.

The most rapid assimilation and transformation of
feed into table products is accomplished by the hen and
the cow; the former is most active and when in good
producing condition transforms the food consumed into
eggs even more quickly than the cow transforms her
food into milk. Doctor Jordan, of the New York Agricultural Experiment Station, says: "If you will con-

sider the dry matter of the hen and compare it with the dry matter of the eggs she lays in a year, there will be figured 5½ times as much dry matter in the eggs as in her whole body. The weight of the dry matter in a cow's body will be to the weight of the dry matter in the milk as 1 is to 2.9. In other words, based on the dry matter, the hen does twice as well as the cow." This indicates more. activity and a greater amount of assimilating power by the hen than by the cow. .

The hen that lays 150 eggs per year will, if these eggs weigh 2 oz. each, have laid 300 oz. of eggs. Of this, approximately 10% is protein; that is, 30 oz. of protein is extracted from her feed. The hen will need more than three times as much protein as her egg yield contains to sustain her body during the year, which would be in all 120 oz. of protein, or 7½ lb. If the entire grain ration of the hen were composed of wheat, and if she should eat 100 lb., which is the average ration for a year, there would be only a little more than 9 lb. of digestible protein in her year's supply. If the hen should extract 7 lb. of protein from the 9 lb. of protein contents in the wheat, she would be doing remarkably well. To accomplish this she would need to gain 70% efficiency from the food consumed.

Professor Patterson, of Missouri, has advanced the theory that the best egg yield will be secured from hens that are fed a ration that contains about equal proportions of yolk-forming material and white-forming material. He believes that if the hens are fed in this way they will produce more eggs than if fed otherwise. These suggestions might be called experimental. The only way of knowing to a certainty whether or not this is true will be through practical experience or from giving the suggestion a fair trial and noting the results. The grain ration suggested is a mixture of 150 lb. of cracked corn and 150 lb. of wheat. For a dry mash, 20 lb. each of wheat bran, wheat middlings, corn meal, ground oats, and gluten meal, with 30 lb. of beef scrap, 5 lb. of alfalfa meal, and 5 lb. of linseed meal, is recommended.

For a ration for laying hens that have free range, Professor Patterson suggests 150 lb. of cracked corn, 150 lb. of wheat, and 25 lb. of beef scrap. - The beef scrap, of course, would need to be fed from the hopper.

Another suggestion for feeding laying hens that have free range is a mixture of 100 lb. of wheat, 100 lb. of corn, and 50 lb. of oats or buckwheat. A dry mash to be used with this is composed of 20 lb. of bran, 10 lb. of corn meal, 10 lb. of wheat middlings, 10 lb. of beef scrap, and 10 lb. of gluten meal. The difference between these two rations is that the grain ration contains 50 lb. of buckwheat and the beef scrap is fed in the mash. This ration may be obtained in almost every locality, and the hens that are fed with it may do fairly well at egg production.

MODERN METHODS OF FEEDING

The most modern method of feeding laying hens has been established as a result of the egg-laying contests that have been held in several parts of the world. The information gained from these experiments has established the feeding of a double ration, or a ration composed partly of whole or broken grains and partly of a dry-mash mixture. In some cases, the grain mixture is fed from self-feeding hoppers; in other cases, the grain is hand fed into the litter. In all cases the dry mash should be fed from hoppers.

An excellent ration for laying hens which can be fed in all localities—north, south, east, and west—for 12 months of the year, and which will produce a satisfactory egg yield, is as follows:

Dry Mash	*Scratch Grain*
Wheat bran, 100 lb.	Cracked corn, 30 lb.
Corn meal, 50 lb.	Whole wheat, 30 lb.
Gluten feed, 50 lb.	Heavy white oats, 20 lb.
Ground oats, 50 lb.	Barley, 10 lb.
Wheat middlings, 35 lb.	Kafir corn, 10 lb.
Beef scraps, 35 lb.	Buckwheat, 10 lb.
Low-grade flour, 12 lb.	

Mix the beef scraps with the flour. After this has been thoroughly done mix them into the other meals. Put the dry mash in a self-feeding hopper, and keep it before the fowls constantly so that they can help themselves. Feed the scratch grain in deep litter so that the hens must scratch and dig for all they get; feed it twice a day, morning and afternoon, giving for each hen about 1 oz. of grain in the morning and 2 oz. in the afternoon. The hens must have a plentiful supply of green food, all they will eat of it; also grit, oyster shell, and plenty of water.

Another method of feeding is to give no grain at all until after 2 o'clock in the afternoon, thus compelling the hens to eat freely of the dry mash from daylight; at 2 o'clock scatter in the litter 3 oz. of the grain mixture for each hen. Where self-feeding grain hoppers are used they can be locked at night so that no grain can be worked out, thus forcing the hens to eat dry mash all day until 2 o'clock, at which time the self-feeding grain hoppers can be released so that the hens can feed themselves on grain from 2 o'clock until dark. The dry-mash mixture is a 1 to 3.1 nutritive ratio; the scratch-grain mixture is a 1 to 7.7 nutritive ratio. If the hens eat as much of one as they do of the other during the day they will have a ration the nutritive ratio of which is 1 to 5.4.

Other rations recommended by experiment stations have been successfully used; the most prominent among them being what is known as the Maine ration. In this method, cracked corn is fed in the litter early in the morning. About noon a grain ration composed of equal parts of wheat and oats is fed at the rate of 2 qt. to each 50 hens. The dry mash, which is kept constantly before the hens in hoppers, is composed of wheat bran, 50 lb.; corn meal, 25 lb.; gluten meal, 25 lb.; meat scraps, 25 lb.; linseed meal, 12 lb.; low-grade flour, 25 lb. The meat scraps should always be mixed into the flour, when flour is used; this is done to coat the meat scraps and to separate them for feeding. A plentiful supply of green

feed with grit, oyster shell, and water is a prominent part of this ration.

The Missouri ration, as it is called, is highly recom-mended by the Missouri poultry experimental farm. It is composed of a grain mixture of 200 lb. of coarse cracked corn with 100 lb. of wheat. For dry mash, ground oats is continually before the hens in open hoppers. When the ground oats cannot be obtained, a mixture composed of 50 lb. of wheat bran, 25 lb. of corn meal, and 25 lb. of shorts or middlings is used. It is recommended that some of this dry-mash mixture be moistened with water or with sour milk or with buttermilk and fed to the hens during the afternoon of each day. A plentiful supply of green feed, shell, and grit has a prominent place in this ration.

A ration recommended by the Ontario (Canada) Experiment Station is composed of whole wheat and whole corn. A liberal feeding of wheat is thrown into the litter morning and noon and a plentiful supply of whole corn fed at night. A dry mash is used with this grain mixture, the mash being composed of 100 lb. each of wheat bran, low-grade flour, and barley chop or meal. Some of this dry-mash mixture is fed in the middle of the afternoon as a wet mash. Boiled vegetables, waste bread or kitchen scraps, and 10-per-cent. beef scrap are included in the afternoon mash feed. A plentiful supply of green feed of some kind with grit, oyster shell, and charcoal are considered as a prominent part of this ration.

Quantity of Food Required by One Hen in a Year. The figures for the quantity of food required by one hen in a year given in the accompanying table were derived from careful records of the food eaten by several hundred hens in a year. They show a total average of about 4.86 oz., or a little less than 4 oz. of grain and meal and about 9/10 oz. of other material per day for each hen. Another test of 4,800 hens shows a food consumption of 3.96 oz. of grain per day for each, besides green food and grit.

QUANTITY OF FOOD REQUIRED BY ONE HEN IN A YEAR

Food	Quantity Pounds
Grain of all kinds and meal..................	90.0
Oyster shell and bone.......................	6.4
Grit..	2.0
Charcoal....................................	2.4
Green food and clover hay...................	10.0
Total.....................................	110.8

FEEDING OF FOWLS DURING MOLT

Fowls that are molting should have good nourishing food in order properly to nourish their bodies while they are under the unusual strain of replenishing the plumage. Foods rich in fat and protein are best for the the purpose; hence, during molting, a mash that contains a large proportion of linseed-oil-cake meal and meat is particularly desirable.

In the morning, molting fowls should have a moderate meal, composed of equal parts, by weight, of cracked corn and whole wheat.

At noon they should have all they will eat of mash composed, by measure, of the following:

Food	Parts
Wheat bran	4
Wheat middlings	3
Ground oats	3
Meat scrap	4
Corn meal	3
Linseed-oil-cake meal	4
Low-grade flour	1
Alfalfa meal	2

During the first week of the molting period this ration should contain only 1 part each of meat scrap and lin-

seed-oil-cake meal; after the first week the quantities of these materials should be increased at the rate of ½ part per day every other day until the quantities given in the table have been reached. In case such a ration proves to be too laxative, the quantity of meat and lin-seed meal is lessened and ½ part of fine charcoal is added to the mixture.

At night all the cracked corn and wheat they will eat is fed to the fowls.

This method of feeding should be continued until the molt is complete, after which a laying ration is fed to the hens.

Attempts to force molting are occasionally successful, but the advantages derived from the practice do not usually pay for the trouble caused. To force molting, fowls are confined in a small house for about 3 wk., are fed very sparingly, but all the fresh water they will drink is given to them. The quantity of food given should be gradually reduced until at the end of the first week they are receiving only about ⅓ of the usual food supply. During the second and third weeks not more than 1 oz. of grain, or ¼ of a ration, should be fed per day to each fowl. This partial starvation will reduce flesh and fat and dry the oil from the feathers, causing them to drop very readily. At the end of the third week the fowls should be liberated and the food supply gradu-ally increased. By the end of the fourth week they should receive full rations.

FEEDING OF CHICKS FOR BROILERS

One of the most difficult problems in the rearing of poultry is the feeding of the cockerels for squab size and larger broilers. A good plan is to feed a bread made of meals, the meal mixture to contain 2 cups of wheat middlings, 2 cups of corn meal, 2 tablespoonfuls of meat meal, 1 raw egg, 1 tablespoonful of baking pow-der, and sufficient water or milk to give a proper con-

sistency to the baking. The mixture should be put into a pan the same as is corn bread and be baked until thoroughly done. This should be fed plentifully to the chicks for one week; thereafter, feed them all the wet mash they will eat. This mash should be composed of equal parts of ground oats, corn meal, and wheat middlings, into which 1 pt. of beef scraps should be mixed for each 3 qt. of the meal mixture. The mash should be moistened with milk or water and the chicks should have all they will eat of it morning and noon. For night feeding they should have all the cracked corn they will eat. The main feature of importance is that the chicks shall have all they will eat three times a day without any being left to sour. If either sour milk or buttermilk can be used for moistening the mash, better results will be obtained than will come from feeding the mash moistened with water, yet water will do for the purpose when milk is lacking.

The English method of feeding broilers differs from the methods used in this country. One broiler plant in England feeds almost exclusively ground oats, boiled rice, and boiled wheat. The broilers are very fond of the boiled rice and wheat, and it is thought that such feeding is most profitable. The ground oats are moistened with milk and fed early in the morning. The second feed is composed of either cooked rice or cooked wheat; the third feeding is ground oats mixed with milk, and the fourth, either the cooked rice or the wheat. If the rice is fed in the morning, cooked wheat is used for the fourth feeding. For the last feeding at night they have all of the cooked rice and cooked wheat they will eat. While this method of feeding is very exacting, it is said that the best small size broilers sent to London market are fed in this way.

SPECIAL FEEDING MIXTURES

It not unusual to have in every flock some chicks that grow their feathers very slowly. This may come from lack of mineral elements in the system. Mineral matters compose about 5 per cent. of the body weight of birds, and for the most part they enter into the formation of bone and feathers. All feed rations should contain sufficient of these substances, which are largely lime, potash, and calcium phosphate. Calcium phosphate from bone is most beneficial, although both bone and meat scraps are necessary for a well-formed ration. A dry-mash mixture containing these elements can be made of wheat bran, 20 lb.; ground oats, 10 lb.; gluten meal, 5 lb.; corn meal, 5 lb.; alfalfa meal, 5 lb.; meat scraps, 3 lb.; low-grade flour, 1 lb.; bone meal or granulated bone, 3 lb.

Mix the meat scraps into the flour. This is for the purpose of coating them thoroughly so as to keep the particles separated for better mixing into the meals. The greater part of all the husks should be sifted out of the ground oats and the larger particles should be sifted out of the meat scraps. The alfalfa meal should be pure and ground fine. Meat scraps should be of excellent quality.

This dry mash mixture is fine for growing chicks, as it hastens the growth of the feathers, bone, and muscle. It contains the elements that satisfy the growing chicks and to some extent prevents feather pulling and the eating of their toes. This same dry mash can be used for all fowls kept in confinement. It should be fed in hoppers.

Bread-and-Milk Mixture.—Moisten stale bread with milk, either sweet milk, sour milk, or buttermilk. The milk may be warmed a little, but not enough to boil or to set the curds. After the bread is thoroughly softened with the milk and mixed almost to a liquid, add ground oats and corn meal in equal parts, making the mixture into a crumbly mass. Add salt, not more than a stroked teaspoonful to 100 chickens. This mixture is excellent

for feeding to growing cockerels or pullets that are not doing well. It is equally fine for feeding to pullets within a month of laying. When fed plentifully to young stock it will fatten them quickly for market. When feeding for quick growth for market, feed all they will eat of it twice a day, with a heavy feeding of cracked corn at night. When feeding for growth of pullets, feed all they will eat of it at noon. This mash should be fed as an extra meal; in all cases feed all they will eat up clean. A plentiful supply of green feed must be fed with bread-and-milk mixture.

Cleansing Mixture.—Laying hens that are plentifully fed on concentrated feed should occasionally have a cleansing mixture of some kind fed in their ration. A mixture may be made of 8 oz. of Epsom salts and 8 oz. of flowers of sulphur mixed thoroughly; this should be added to 6 qt. of dry mash and all mixed thoroughly. Sufficient of this for one feeding should be moistened with milk or water and fed to the laying hens once every two or three weeks or after a spell of very hot or very wet weather. It will relieve the intestines and expel intestinal worms, if any are present. The mixture should not be fed oftener, nor should more be used, than is here recommended.

FEEDING OF TURKEYS

Poults should have nourishing food in small particles so that they will be able to digest it properly. No sour or fermented food, chopped green bone, raw meat, or large quantities of millet seed, cottage cheese, or wet or sloppy foods should ever be fed to poults. Poults require plenty of grit and fresh water.

A ration of stale bread crumbs and a ration made up of equal parts of stale bread crumbs, finely chopped hard-boiled eggs, and dandelion leaves, fed alternately, is a good method of feeding poults.

Turkeys on a range plentifully supplied with natural foods that they like will need much less feeding than

turkeys that are compelled to live on a range where the natural food supply is scanty. Turkeys should have plenty of corn, wheat, and some oats, the quantities and proportions varying with the character of the food on their range.

FEEDING OF GUINEA FOWLS

Like poults, young guinea fowls should be fed on finely divided foods, and water should be given to them in very shallow vessels to prevent the young birds from drowning in them. Grit and plenty of fresh water should be supplied.

A ration suitable for young guinea fowls is composed, by measure, as follows:

Food	*Parts*
Very fine oatmeal	2
Finely cracked wheat	2
Rape seed	2
Canary seed	1
Ant's eggs, or very small particles of cooked meat, or finely chopped hard-boiled eggs	1

Guinea fowls for market can be fattened on milk curds, steamed hulled oats, and warm mash. If these feeds are not available, guinea fowls can be satisfactorily fattened on a ration composed of equal parts of ground oats, barley meal, and table scraps.

FEEDING OF PHEASANTS

The first food of young pheasants should be composed, by measure, as follows:

Food	*Parts*
Very small bread crumbs	1
Canary seed	1
Fine grit	1
Very fine corn grits	1

If the pheasants are 2 da. old, about 10% of cooked lean meat may be added. Stale bread softened in sweet milk and a custard of eggs and milk put together with enough stale bread crumbs to soak up the greater part of the moisture, are good foods for young pheasants. A certain quantity of meal worms may be fed to mature pheasants, although a ration composed by measure, as follows, is preferable:

Food	Parts
Finely chopped hard-boiled eggs.......	1
Crushed hemp seed	1
Stale bread crumbs	1
Oatmeal	1
Finely chopped cooked lean meat.....	½
Finely chopped green food should also be fed.	

FEEDING OF DUCKS

During the fall, in addition to green food, ducks should have twice a day as much as they will eat of a mash consisting, by measure, of the following:

Food	Parts
Corn meal	4
Wheat bran	12
Low-grade wheat flour	1
Fine grit	¼

A small quantity of meat scrap may be added to this ration if desired.

During the winter, ducks should have a liberal supply of chopped green feed. Twice a day they should have all they will eat of a mash feed composed, by measure, as follows:

Food	Parts
Wheat bran	5
Corn meal	6
Low-grade wheat flour	1

A small quantity of meat scrap may be added to this ration if desired.

During the laying season ducks will eat about 1 pt. of food each per day. Their food should always consist of at least 2 or 3% of grit, ground oyster shells, or some similar material.

A suitable feed for laying ducks, when they have an ample supply of green food, is a mash food composed, by measure, as follows:

Food	Parts
Wheat bran	3
Ground oats	3
Corn meal	3
Low-grade wheat flour	1
Meat scrap	1

Many rations are used for fattening broiler ducks for market. A good one to use for the 10 da. or 2 wk. previous to killing is composed, by measure, as follows:

Food	Parts
Corn meal	10
Wheat bran	4
Wheat middlings	4
Meat scrap	3
Low-grade wheat flour	1
Green feed	2
Coarse sand	1

No green stuff should be fed during the last week of fattening, but a plentiful supply of water must always be furnished.

Ducklings intended for breeders are fed on a ration composed, by measure, as follows:

Food	Parts
Wheat bran	10
Wheat middlings	6
Corn meal	3
Low-grade wheat flour	1
Meat scrap	1
Sand	1

This is mixed into a crumbly state by the addition of milk or water and fed three times daily. In some cases, instead of wheat bran 6 parts of bran and 4 parts of ground oats are substituted.

Another ration for ducklings intended for breeders is composed, by measure, as follows:

Food	Parts
Corn meal	6
Wheat bran	6
Wheat middlings	6
Meat scrap	1

All meal fed to ducks as a mash feed must be moistened with either water or milk, and must be mixed dry enough so that the ducks can shovel it up with their bills. They cannot do this well if the mash is sticky.

FEEDING OF YOUNG DUCKLINGS

There are several methods of feeding young ducklings; one is to give either a mixture of rolled oats and bread crumbs in equal parts with a little fine grit mixed into it, all moistened either with water or milk, preferably milk. The meals should be moistened slightly so that they will scatter about and not stick together. The little ducklings can shovel up this kind of a mixture from a flat board. Beginning on the third day, add some bran and corn meal in about equal parts by measure with the bread crumbs and rolled oats. When the ducklings are a week old, feed them with a mixture of equal parts of wheat bran, wheat middlings, ground oats, and corn meal, with some green stuff and some beef scraps mixed into the meal. The green stuff should always be cut into very small pieces and be mixed into the meal, which should be moistened with water or milk. Never moisten the feed for ducklings so that it will stick together or be sloppy; have it only slightly moistened so that it will be easily shoveled up by the ducks.

One rule that must be observed when feeding ducklings is to have drinking water continually before them

and yet not where they can run through it. It is a habit of ducklings to take a mouthful or two of feed, then some water. They will run backwards and forwards from the feed trough to the water, eating and drinking alternately until they have finished. If ducklings are fed on dry grain or dry food of any kind without plenty of water they will frequently choke, stagger, fall over, and in some cases die.

Another good plan for feeding ducklings is to teach them to take from a trough cracked corn, whole wheat, and any other kind of grain without husks, these grains to be submerged in water. After being fed in this way for several weeks, they can be gradually taught to eat dry grain or even whole corn without injury, provided they have water to go to at will; but they cannot stand such feeding when very young.

Dr. Prince T. Woods, of Massachusetts, recommends the following formula for feeding ducklings less than 4 da. old: Mix 4 qt. of wheat bran, 1 qt. of corn meal, 1 qt. of low-grade flour, 4 oz. of grit of small size; moisten some of this mixture with cold water and feed the ducklings four times a day all they will eat of it in a short period of time. After the ducklings are 4 da. old they may be fed from this same mixture of meals with 12 oz. of beef scraps of small size added to the mixture. When feeding beef scraps to young ducklings it is always a good plan to scald the beef scraps separately, stir them up, mix them into the meal; but when feeding, add sufficient cold water to moisten the whole of it slightly, so that it is of a proper consistency for the ducks. After the ducklings are a week old, green stuff of some kind should·be cut up very small and mixed in with the feed. After the ducklings are 3 wk. old, continue to feed them from the same meal mixture, adding double the quantity of beef scrap and giving them more green feed.

FEEDING OF GEESE

A simple ration for goslings is composed, by measure, of the following:

Food	Parts
Corn meal	1
Wheat bran	1
Ground oats	1
Table scraps	1

This should be slightly moistened with either water or milk.

Geese are by nature grazing birds, and the greater part of their living consists of green food. Because of their lack of a crop, geese should be fed on ground corn in the form of a slightly warmed mash. During the winter, in addition to green food, the matured geese should have once a day all they will eat of a ration composed, by measure, as follows:

Food	Parts
Corn meal	3
Wheat bran	3
Ground oats	3

This should be moistened into a crumbly mass.

During the winter this same ration with 4 parts of steamed clover added is suitable.

The following rations are suitable for fattening geese for market:

They should be fed liberally three times a day. The morning and noon feeds should consist, by measure, of the following:

Food	Parts
Corn meal	6
Ground oats	6
Meat scrap	1

This mixture should be slightly moistened and mixed until it assumes a crumbly state. During the last 10 da. of feeding the quantity of meat in the ration should be doubled.

In the evening the geese should be fed all they will eat of a ration composed, by measure, as follows:

Food	Parts
Cracked corn boiled until soft........	1
Corn meal	1
Wheat middlings	1

FEEDING OF WILD WATER FOWLS

Where wild water fowls have the freedom of a large enough pasture, they will graze the greater part of their living, but it is always advisable to keep near at hand covered hoppers where the fowls may help themselves at will. For mature ducks and geese, the hopper should be kept filled with a dry mixture composed, by measure, as follows:

Food	Parts
Ground oats	1
Cracked corn	1
Wheat bran	1

FEEDING OF PIGEONS

The grains most suitable for feeding to pigeons are wheat, corn, buckwheat, barley, peas, vetch seed, hulled oats, millet, rice, hemp seed, and canary seed. No large quantity of buckwheat, barley, hulled oats, or Kafir corn, should be fed to pigeons, because these grains contain a large percentage of crude fiber.

Pigeons that are not feeding their young may consume as little as 2 oz. of grain each, per day, but those feeding their young will require perhaps as much as 4 oz. per day.

A suitable ration for pigeons is composed, by measure, as follows:

Food	Parts
Corn	2
Wheat	1
Peas	1

During the fall and when the pigeons are molting, a good ration for them is composed, by measure, as follows:

Food	*Parts*
Corn	4
Wheat	4
Peas	4
Millet	2
Vetch seed	1
Flaxseed	1
Hemp seed	¼

A ration for the hand feeding of pigeons, that is, for scattering on the floor of the house, is composed, by measure, as follows:

Food	*Parts*
Canada peas	3
Cracked corn	1
Wheat	1
Kafir corn	1

INCUBATION

In poultry, the reproductive process is accomplished in two stages. The egg is first produced, developed, fertilized within the body of the hen, and laid. Then the egg is subjected to a certain temperature (100° F. or a little higher) for about 21 da., during which time the embryo develops and hatches out of the shell as a chick. The process of developing the embryo within the egg by means of heat is called *incubation*. When this is carried on by a hen, it is known as natural incubation; when incubation is accomplished by means of a machine, oven, or other device, it is known as artificial incubation. Man has little control over the reproductive process in its first stage except so far as the selection of the breeders is concerned; in the second stage, however, if artificial incubation is practiced, he

can, by his methods of conducting the process, greatly influence the development and future well-being of the chick.

Fertilization of the Egg.—In order that eggs shall hatch, the hen that lays them must have been mated with the male. The actual fertilization of the egg probably takes place as the yolk enters the oviduct. In the process of fertilization the germ from the male comes in contact with the germ cell, or blastoderm, and causes it to develop, provided that it is exposed to the right temperature. Hatchable eggs are those that are fertilized and have vitality enough to insure the production of a living chick.

Eggs are usually fertile up to and including those laid the ninth day after the hens are separated from the males, and fertilization is impossible after the sexes have been separated for 12 da. or more. Eggs may safely be counted as fertile after the males have been with the hens for 9 da. or more.

The eggs of all kinds of fowls are more apt to be fertile during the spring and early summer than at any other time. Fertility begins to decline with the commencement of molting, and during the fall and winter the production of fertile eggs is at the minimum. The average production occurs in January or soon after.

NATURAL INCUBATION

The poultryman very naturally prefers the incubator to the hen for hatching chicks. This preference has brought incubators into general use and so few chicks are hatched by hens as to have made this process nearly a lost art. Yet those who give the most thought to poultry culture know that the best chicks grown are hatched and reared by the mother hen. Chicks hatched and reared artificially do better during the cold weather than chicks hatched and reared naturally. As soon as spring arrives, a brood of chicks with the mother hen

will do much better than chicks hovered under the heated brooders. Although incubators are so generally used, there are some farms where a large number of chicks are hatched and brooded by hens.

Where but few chicks are reared, and where there is no necessity for early hatching, it would be quite as well and less troublesome to hatch and rear chicks with broody hens. The chicks so hatched and reared will, if properly cared for, be more vigorous than chicks hatched artificially.

The question is frequently asked, "How do fanciers hatch and rear their chicks?" One of the most ardent fanciers says that fanciers unquestionably produce their best specimens by natural incubation. He says also that artificial incubation has absorbed the attention of our investigators and others to such an extent that little is written or taught of the old-fashioned but trustworthy, natural method. In view of the fact that most flocks raised by amateurs are hatched by hens, some instruction bearing upon this particular method is necessary.

To hatch eggs successfully it is well to follow the following precepts: "Select a quiet hen; discard one that uses her voice constantly. Have the nest ready before removing her from the laying coop. Set the hen in such a manner that she may walk on the nest and not be obliged to jump up or down to reach the eggs, for such a procedure means broken eggs or crushed chicks. Before setting and between hatches, paint all the wood-work with kerosene. This is particularly important in warm weather. Dust the hen thoroughly with insect or lice powder before placing her on the nest. Repeat this 4 da. before hatching time."

Such words of encouragement for natural brooding might well be considered by all those who rear but a few chicks, and even by those who rear several hundred of them. Since it is always well to hatch part of the chicks and rear them with mother hens, these directions should be valuable to all persons engaged in raising poultry.

Box Nest.—Nests for sitting hens can be made from boxes from 14 to 16 in. square. A box ·from 9 to 12 in. deep and from 15 to 18 in. wide and long has about the correct dimensions. Deep nests protect the eggs from the cold below. The entire box should be lined with hay, as shown in Fig. 1. The nest, shown in Fig. 2, should be sufficiently deep to incline the eggs slightly toward the middle and flat enough to avoid crowding or piling the eggs. Several nests like this can be placed on the floor of a room with each nest occupied by a sitting hen. When this is done, hens that are accustomed to being together should occupy the nests, other-

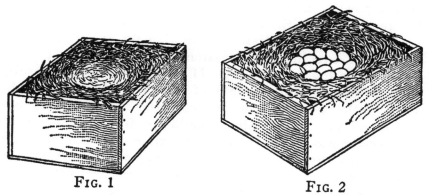

FIG. 1   FIG. 2

wise, they will fight. If hens are strangers, their nests must be enclosed to keep them from coming together and the hens should be carefully watched when they leave their nests.

Hens for Sitting.—Broody hens that are quiet and tractable should be selected for hatching purposes. Those that are wild and unmanageable are not suitable for sitting or for mothers after the chicks are hatched. The use of hens with scaly legs should be avoided, as this ailment is liable to be transmitted to the chicks. Hens that are to be set in the same room should all come from the same flock. Before the hen is placed in position, the nest should be thoroughly dusted with insect powder and the body of the hen covered with it. The powder should be well worked in down to the skin and

the work should be done with especial care about the vent, under the wings, and around the neck. This operation should be repeated on the seventh and fourteenth days of the incubation period. In this way only are vermin kept from the hens and the chicks saved from their ravages. Non-fertile, or clear, eggs should be placed under the hen for 2 or 3 days to test her. If she is faithful and attentive to these she may be trusted with selected eggs. If she pushes them under her body with her head, it is a sign that she will be a good sitter and a good mother.

Care of Nest and Hen.—To dust the hen and nest with insect powder is fatal to body lice, and red mites may be kept away with kerosene oil or turpentine; 1 oz. of naphthalene flakes dissolved in 3 gills of kerosene oil makes an excellent application to keep the latter pest away from the nest boxes. If this solution is liberally used in cracks and crevices of nest boxes, there will be very little trouble from mites; and where mites are abundant this preparation should be freely used on all the woodwork of the nest every time a hatch is taken off. When the day of hatching arrives the nest is flattened out in order to make more room, for if the eggs are crowded too close together the chicks are liable to be smothered as they emerge from the shell. The hens and chicks should not be removed from the nest until the beginning of the second day after hatching, nor should the chicks be fed until the third day after the hatch begins. If the nest is to be used again, all the old nesting material should be removed and burned, and the nest box itself should be well cleaned before making another nest of new material.

Number and Arrangement of Eggs.—A setting of eggs should consist of an odd number. Thirteen eggs are generally considered as a setting, and they are arranged in the nest as shown in Fig. 2. The eggs should be uniform in size, for if some are small and others large the body of the hen will not come close to the smaller ones and the temperature of the eggs will not be uni-

form. Eggs of irregular size are unfit for incubation.
Eggs of this kind seldom, if ever, produce perfect chicks.
Eggs set under hens gain a smooth gloss from contact
with the body of the hen. By this means, as the process of
incubation advances, the pores of the eggshell are closed.

Moving the Broody Hen.—Broody hens of quiet dis-
positions can be moved anywhere and may be actually
placed on the nests if they are properly handled. To
move a sitting hen, place the left hand gently under
her breast bone, and take the shanks in the right hand
with one finger between them. Clasp her firmly but
gently; raise her from the nest, holding her against the
body with the head toward you and the tail away from
you. Do not carry her by the shanks, head hanging
down. Place the hen gently on the nest, in which
should be a few test eggs; settle her quietly with one
hand on her back, the other smoothing her head—just
a little of this—then remove the hands and cover or
close the hen in the nest. If she settles down at once
on the nest and turns the eggs with the motion of her
body and wings, moving has been successful; if she is
restless, shut her in the nest and do not disturb her until
morning. It is always best to move broody hens at
night. If the hen takes quietly to the nest and eggs,
as she is apt to do during the night, let her remain
undisturbed until an hour before sundown, then permit
her to come from the nest for food and water. If she
refuses to sit during the night and day, she had best
be returned to the flock of hens.

Care of Sitting Hens.—If the hen is quiet and willing
to sit, dust her body with insect powder as already
described and let her stay the second day on the nest,
permitting her to feed before noon of the second day.
If she returns to the nest herself, all is well; if she
does not, place her on the nest again. After 2 da. of
proper behavior on the part of the hen, dust the nest
and the hen's body again with the insect powder, and
place an odd number of eggs in the nest. Some hens
can cover 13 eggs, others only 9 or 11. Do not crowd

too many eggs into the nest, for the best returns come from too few rather than from too many eggs in the nest.

Broody or sitting hens must be kept quiet and undisturbed, except at feeding time, which should occur at the same hour each day. This statement refers to hens that are confined to their nests. Hens that come and go at will should have food and water close at hand, from which they may help themselves at any time. Corn and wheat with grit and shell are perhaps the best foods for sitting hens. Fresh water should also be provided each day. A dust bath is a necessity for health and cleanliness. If any eggs are broken in the nest, they should be removed without delay, and the nest should be cleaned. If the eggs in the nest become soiled, they should, if possible, be cleaned without washing them. This cleaning may be done by scraping them with a dull knife or with the thumb nail; if washing is indispensable, the eggs must be immersed in water the temperature of which is 90° F., or a little less—not more; the dirty coating on the shell should be softened and removed with as little rubbing as possible. When the nest and eggs have been cleaned, the eggs should be replaced under the hen. Eggs that have been washed do not hatch as well as those that have not been so treated.

Feeding the Sitting Hen.—Hens that are sitting must be regularly fed on good, solid grain. They should have at each feeding grain enough to last 24 hr. Whole corn that is dry and hard, wheat, and some shell and grit must be supplied. Hens that cannot come from the nest at will should be liberated or taken from the nest to feed. Their crops should be felt each day. If they are not sufficiently fed, they will lose fat and their temperature will decrease, so that the eggs will not be properly warmed. When the hens come and go from the nest at will, food grit, and water must be placed where they can help themselves and at the same time be out of the reach of other hens. Looseness of bowels at this time should be avoided, as such a condition weakens the hens and lowers the temperature of the body. In returning

the hen to the nest she should be placed on the edge of the nest and be permitted to settle on the eggs as she will; she should never be forced or hurried.

Period of Incubation.—Fresh-laid eggs hatch in fewer hours than eggs that are kept 2 wk. or longer before incubation begins. After eggs are 4 wk. old, their vitality will probably be insufficient to produce chicks that will grow to maturity. In some instances, eggs more than 3 mo. old have produced chicks that grew to maturity. These eggs, however, were unusually strong in vitality and were cared for in the most careful manner prior to being placed under hens for hatching.

Fresh-laid eggs, if placed for incubation within 24 or 48 hr. of laying, will hatch in from 8 to 12 hr. less time than eggs that were older when placed for incubation. Eggs for hatching may be safely kept for 2 wk., provided they are kept where the temperature is even and about 55° F. Such eggs should be moved about a little each day. The more vigorous the hens that lay the eggs, the stronger will be the vitality of the eggs. Such eggs will keep longer for hatching and will produce stronger chicks than eggs laid by less vigorous hens. The average period of incubation of eggs of several kinds is as follows:

	Days
Fowls of medium and large-sized breeds..	21
Bantams and other small breeds...........	19 to 20
Ducks	28
Muscovy duck	35
Muscovy duck crossed with Pekin or other drake	32
Geese	28
Turkeys	27 to 29
Guinea fowls	28 to 30
Pheasants	24 to 25
Peafowls	27 to 29
Pigeons	17
Swans	35 to 40
Ostriches	40 to 42

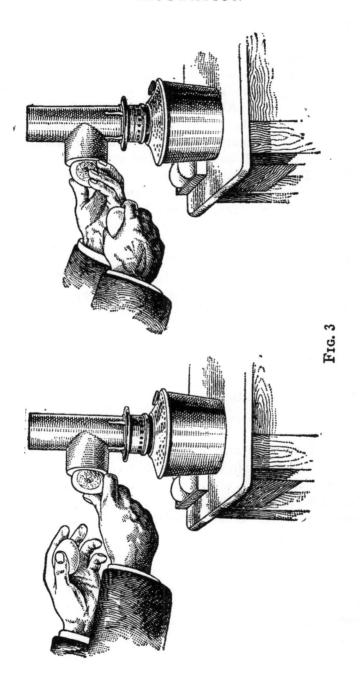

Fig. 3

The Best Sitter.—Cochin, Orpington, Plymouth Rock, Rhode Island Red, and Wyandotte hens are the best sitters. The quiet hen that will sit contented on the nest until her work is finished and will then care for her chicks properly is the kind to be depended on both for raising utility fowls and fowls for exhibition.

The most unsatisfactory hen for hatching is the nervous hen that fusses and fights all who move about her; that will spring quickly from the nest when any one approaches her, thus breaking her eggs and disturbing those left in the nest. A good motherly hen that will rear two broods in one season is the kind to be depended on.

Testing Fertility of Eggs.—After eggs have been incubated for some time, it is usually desirable that they be examined for fertility. This examination may be best made during the seventh day of incubation. The work of testing the eggs can be done in daylight. To do the work well, however, requires that it be done after dark or in a darkened room. An appliance called an egg tester is used for this purpose.

Many kinds of egg testers are offered for sale. An excellent one is the kind that has a bull's-eye lens like those used for bicycle lamps. A tester of this kind is shown in operation in Fig. 3. The tester is placed over the flame of any kerosene oil lamp, in a room that is dark. The eggs should be placed against the opening so that the light may shine through the egg; both live and dead germs may then be clearly seen.

Development of the Embryo.—To one well trained in the testing of eggs, the first material change will be visible in about 48 hr. after incubation begins. The head and the lines of the body can be seen by the trained observer. The stages of development of the embryo are shown in Fig. 4. To become expert in the testing of eggs, one should compare the successive steps in the development with the day on which it should occur as recorded in this chart, which includes all the phenomena from the first to the twenty-first day.

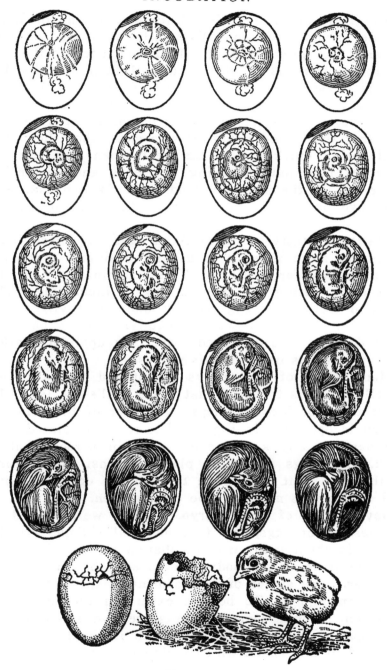

Fig. 4

ARTIFICIAL INCUBATION

During recent years there has been a large increase of market poultry, resulting from the practice of artificial incubation. The incubator operator can control production by artificial means, but with hens a desire to hatch cannot be hastened. The artificial methods of hatching and rearing chicks bring alike to the farmer and to the small grower the choice of the day of production and of the number of chicks produced.

The results obtained from artificial incubation depend primarily on the vitality of the eggs; but the handling of the incubator, surrounding influences, and the general efficiency of the incubator itself are other conditions of fundamental importance. The vitality of eggs depends on the constitutional vigor of the fowls that produce them; superior vigor must come through several generations of strong and healthy fowls. It follows therefore that, in order to have embryo c h i c k s of marked vitality, eggs must be used that come from strong, vigorous, well-bred fowls.

WHITE PLYMOUTH ROCK MALE

The *per cent. fertility* is an expression that is frequently misleading. More than 9 0 % o f t h e e g g s may be fertile and yet no living chicks may come from them, because the germ is so lacking in vitality that it dies before incubation is completed. The per cent. fertility is increased by proper feeding and the vigor of both male and female is also increased, but there is a pronounced difference between fertility and vitality. The former may exist to a marked degree even though

the vitality of the germs or the egg be lacking, but the latter obviously cannot be present without the former. Chicks that are not strong and of abundant vitality when hatched should never be raised for breeders, but such fowls may be used for market poultry.

There is a marked difference between the production of fowls for exhibition or for beauty and the production of those fitted for egg yielding and for table meat. Where exhibition fowls are desired, the producing stock must be yarded to avoid the mixing of breeds or varieties. This is necessary only during the breeding season. At other times the old and young stock may have free range. Where egg producers and market poultry are desired, it is best to give the breeding stock all possible liberty. It is best to keep only one variety, and the flock should have free range if possible.

The records of artificial incubation are derived from experiments with different makes of incubators.

The hatch from hens ranged as high as 83.3% and as low as 50%, and that of the incubator from 77.1% to 32.5%.

Selection of Eggs for Incubation.—Eggs for hatching in an incubator should all be of one kind, size, and color; for only when eggs of such character are incubated together can uniform hatching be secured.

Eggs from Leghorns and Brahmas do not hatch well if both are together in the same incubator, for the eggs of the Leghorns usually hatch during the twentieth day, and the hatching of the Brahma eggs may be delayed to the end of the twenty-first day. If eggs from Leghorns, Plymouth Rocks, Wyandottes, and Brahmas are all together in the one incubator the hatch is irregular. Eggs but 1 da. old hatch a day sooner than eggs that are 2 wk. old. Leghorn eggs placed in an incubator on the day they are laid may hatch in 480 hr.; eggs of Asiatic fowls placed in the same incubator when 2 wk. old may hatch for 516 hr., a difference in time that makes poor results inevitable if the eggs of both breeds are incubated together. The eggs of ducks and of chickens

cannot be successfully hatched together in the same incubator, nor do the eggs of any two or more kinds of fowls hatch well if placed together in the same incubator or under the same hen.

If the eggs are of uniform size, the temperatures of all are equal or nearly so; if large and small eggs are in the same machine the temperature may not be the same in all.

Eggs with white shells hatch in fewer hours than do the dark-shelled eggs, for white shells are thinner and transmit heat more freely to the germ within. Under the same conditions, eggs with white shells will have larger air cells than those with heavier shells.

Only smooth and well-formed eggs should be used; eggs with uneven surfaces, bad form, rough shells, or mixed colors should be discarded, as well as eggs that are abnormally large or small.

Care of Eggs for Hatching.—The best hatch is obtained from eggs placed in the incubator the same day on which they are laid. Eggs keep in prime condition for hatching up to the tenth day; if 2 wk. old they are safe for incubation; but if older than this they seldom hatch well, although some eggs that have been kept a month will hatch. Eggs keep the best in a uniform temperature of about 55° F. in an atmosphere free from oil and other bad odors. The vitality of eggs that are exposed for any length of time to a temperature below 40° F. is impaired.

Eggs for hatching are shifted at least every other day so that the yolks will not settle to one side, stick to the shell, and thus destroy the germ. Preferably, the eggs should be stored small end down, either in a regular packing crate or any suitable receptacle.

Eggs for hatching are injured if they are washed; washing removes the natural glaze from the shell, and such eggs do not hatch well. Though it is not advisable to hatch dirty eggs, such eggs hatch better in soiled condition than they would if washed.

INCUBATORS

An incubator is an apparatus by means of which eggs may be artificially kept at the proper temperature for hatching. Many different styles and sizes of incubators are now in use, some of them being adapted for all sizes of eggs from those of the bantam to those of an ostrich. Incubators range in size from those the capacity of which is limited to a few dozen eggs to those that are

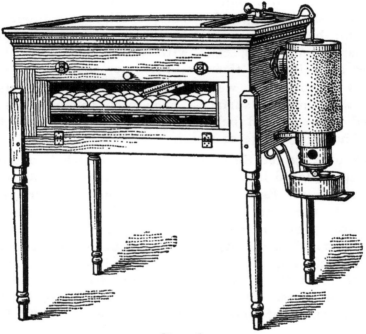

FIG. 5

capable of incubating many thousand eggs. The machines most commonly used have capacities that range from 5 to 30 doz. hen's eggs or a smaller number of any eggs that are larger than hen's eggs.

Though many different types of incubators are made, with but few exceptions in outward appearance they resemble the one shown in Fig. 5.

The essential parts of an incubator consist of a heating apparatus that is controlled by a regulator, and an egg

chamber that can be held at the required temperature. Incubators are also supplied with thermometers and means of ventilation.

In the various incubators heat is brought into contact with the eggs either by diffusion or radiation. In *diffusion incubators,* hot air is evenly distributed throughout the egg chamber. In *radiation incubators,* the heat is radiated from pipes or radiators that are heated either by hot air or by hot water. A large part of the incubators in use are of the diffusion type, in which the air is heated by an oil lamp. In these machines the heated air passes directly into the egg chamber and throughout the interior of the machine. The eggs in the tray are thus surrounded with air at the required temperature. Incubators in which the heat is both radiated and diffused are also used. The more evenly the egg chamber is warmed the greater will be the success in hatching.

The most satisfactory source of heat for incubators of all kinds is that obtained from oil lamps. Some incubators are heated by circulating hot water. Some incubators require particular care and attention, and their efficiency depends on the proper circulation of the water, the distribution of the pipes, and the lasting qualities of the entire heating system. Illuminating gas, electricity, and alcohol lamps are also used to some extent as sources of heat for incubators.

Incubator manufacturers prefer *thermometers* specially made to suit each kind of machine. There is usually a reason for such preference, and the thermometer recommended by the manufacturers should be favored. If this instrument cannot be obtained, the best that is made must be selected. Incubator thermometers are scaled from 90° F. to 110° F., and are marked *low* at 100° F. and *high* at 105° F., and the scale is crossed at 103° F. by an arrow or a heavy line. It is thus easy to make an accurate reading between the low and the high marks, provided the thermometer is correctly graduated.

Before being used, incubator thermometers are tested in the following manner: An instrument known to be

correct is stirred about in warm water until the degree
of heat is 105° F. or a little higher. Other thermometers
are then held in the same hand with the one known to
be correct and all are stirred about in the water so that
the reading of all may be taken under like conditions.
Any instruments that fail to mark the temperature correctly are rejected. It is best to test all thermometers
in use at least once a season.

The printed directions that come with each incubator,
giving instructions for its operation, also tell where
the thermometer is to be placed in the machine, and to
secure the best results such directions should be followed to the letter. The thermometer is usually placed
in or near the center of the egg tray.

Temperature and Moisture.—An expert who has had
more practical experience with the use of incubators
than any other man has said: "Briefly stated, all that
is required to hatch eggs artificially is a temperature
of 100.5° F. at the center of the eggs, which is 101° F. to
103° F. by contact; at the same time, the eggs should
be immersed in still air containing moisture of a relative
humidity of from 45 to 70 per cent., this moisture to be
changed sufficiently often to carry off the waste gases
eliminated by the eggs. Any excess of ventilation beyond this is deleterious."

Professor Lamson, of the Connecticut State Agricultural College, has said that the chief factors in the artificial incubation of good fertile eggs are "temperature,
turning the eggs, moisture, and ventilation." The meaning of this would be that when eggs are hatched in the
incubator, the temperature as usually taken by a thermometer should range from 101° F. to 103° F. and that
when a thermometer is used that would indicate the
temperature at the center of the egg the temperature of
that position should be 100.5° F. The thermometer used
for taking this particular test is known as the "In-Ova
Thermometer." This is a thermometer the bulb of which
is inside a celluloid egg, the bulb resting in the center
of the egg. When such a thermometer is used it indi-

cates the temperature at the center of the egg, which should be 100.5° F. When the ordinary or regular type of thermometer is used, and when the bulb rests at or near the upper outside of the egg, the temperature should not go below 101° F. and not much above 103° F.

The statement made that the atmosphere should be changed sufficiently often to carry off the waste gases refers to proper ventilation. In writing of this, Professor Lamson says that by the use of specially constructed apparatus it was shown that the ventilation required in the incubator to secure the best results in living chicks consisted in a change of 5 cu. ft. per hr. for each 50 eggs. Where the change of air exceeded 10 cu. ft. per hr. for each 50 eggs, the hatch began to run down, and when the air change was reduced to ¼ cu. ft. per hr., only a very small percentage of chicks were hatched.

As a result of many experiments, it has been shown that hen-hatched chicks weigh 1.258 oz.; that incubator-hatched chicks with maximum moisture weigh 1.184 oz.; that chicks hatched in incubators with a medium amount of moisture weigh 1.159 oz.; and that chicks hatched in non-moisture machines weigh 1.072 oz. It has also been shown that the minimum moisture in the incubator might be 45%, while the maximum might be 70%.

The weight of these chicks seems to indicate that to have the greatest possible vigor in chicks a greater quantity of moisture is required during incubation than is present in the average incubator. For these reasons, considerable effort has been made to find some means of introducing moisture into machines during the period of incubation. Among the devices used are pans of water or pans of sand moistened with water and placed under the egg tray. Another way is by sprinkling the eggs with water morning and evening during incubation as clothes are sprinkled with the hand or by means of sprays such as are used by druggists or florists.

An excellent method of applying moisture is to have pads made of burlap or felt, and cut to fit under the

egg tray. These pads are saturated with hot water, wrung out almost dry, and then placed under the egg tray. Pieces of outing cloth or cotton flannel of sufficient size to cover the top of all eggs may be soaked in hot water, wrung out until they are almost dry, placed on top of the eggs, and left there. This is an excellent method of providing moisture for the eggs from the twelfth to the eighteenth day.

The rules sent out with each incubator should always be strictly followed; yet it must be remembered that in some latitudes the air is much drier than in others. Sometimes, therefore, it is necessary to supply moisture, a need indicated by the size of the air cell. If this cell is larger than normal, moisture must be supplied and the rate of air change must be reduced. The water pan, sand tray, or the moistened felt, or the wet outing flannel should be used when it is necessary to supply moisture.

Turning and Cooling.—It is necessary that the eggs in the incubator tray should be turned and cooled at regular intervals. Turning every 12 hr. is practiced by some; turning once in 24 hr. when the eggs are cooled is practiced by others. Some experts insist that eggs will hatch better if turned and cooled more frequently. They advise that the trays of eggs be taken from the machine and cooled for a short time, three or four times a day, and each time the eggs are turned they will be cooled slightly. This practice has not yet been tested sufficiently to warrant its acceptance; however, it might be experimented with to advantage.

Some operators of considerable experience insist that the cooling of eggs is useless. The common practice is to cool and turn the eggs twice a day, never turning them over entirely, but just moving them slightly in the egg tray so that each egg will be moved a little. When the weather is cool, the eggs need not be kept out of the egg chamber longer than 4 or 5 min.; when the weather is warm and the incubator room is at a temperature of 70° F. or more, the eggs should be cooled fully 30 min.

Chicks Dead in the Shell.—The prevailing question as to artificial incubation is, "Why do chicks die in the shell?" In answer to this, one of the most expert in incubating says: "The best of incubators add nothing to the vitality of the developed embryo. When the vitality of the embryo is impaired or the eggs are old, the hen will not hatch a higher percentage than any incubator ever constructed, yet to find dead chicks in the shell is a very common experience, even when the most faithful hens are employed." This would indicate that we must look beyond the hatching machine for the cause of the dead chicks in the shell. The causes for chicks dying in the shell are several. The most prevalent of all is inexperience in the handling of the incubator; another is lack of vitality in the eggs. This, being due to low vitality in the hen that laid the eggs, can be remedied only through several years of careful breeding of the parent stock for greater vigor.

Another writer has said that a successful hatch begins with the fowls that lay the eggs. Immature pullets will not furnish eggs desirable for incubation. The best eggs for this purpose will be laid by hens in their second year that have great vigor and have been fed and cared for with the object of procuring eggs for hatching. There will be no dead chicks in the shell when the hens laying the eggs are full of vitality and when the person that handles the incubator has had sufficient experience to act quickly and properly as each emergency comes.

Rules for Hatching.—The manufacturers of incubators assume that the treatment of eggs during incubation is an exact science, and that the directions that they have formulated are faultless. One of the largest manufacturers of incubators has printed a bulletin on the handling of incubators to get the best results. In this bulletin he says that the eggs should be turned every 12 hr. beginning on the third day and ending on the night of the eighteenth day. It is better, however, to keep on changing the position of the trays as usual until the eggs begin to pip. Never turn the eggs with oily

hands or with hands that have any substance on them which might adhere to the shells.

Test the eggs on the sixth and the seventeenth days, but do not turn or cool them while testing them. Cooling and ventilating should be done according to the instructions given in the book of directions that accompanies each machine. Cooling helps to soften eggs.

Be sure that the thermometer is accurate. If your machine is supplied with a suspended thermometer, see that the bulb is just 2 in. above the wire of the egg tray. Do not allow the thermometer to go above 103° F., except when the chicks are coming out lively, at which time it may go as high as 105° F. without injury.

Do not open the door of the incubator after the eggs begin to pip. Close the ventilator when the chicks begin to come out and keep it closed until the hatch is completed, unless the hatch is very large and the chicks are crowded, in which case the ventilators may be opened when the hatch is two-thirds off. Open the ventilator and wedge the door slightly ajar after the hatch is over and the trays containing the shells have been removed. Allow the chicks to remain in the incubator for from 24 to 36 hr. Do not feed or water the chicks while they are in the incubator.

FACTORS THAT INFLUENCE SUCCESS IN INCUBATION

The factor of prime importance in incubation is the vitality of the eggs, and this depends on the vitality of the fowls that produce them.

Eggs for hatching should all be of one kind, size, and color.

Only smooth and well-formed eggs should be used for hatching. Eggs of bad form or with rough shells should be discarded.

The best eggs for hatching are those that are placed in an incubator on the day they are laid; eggs are in good condition for hatching up to 10 da. after they are laid; after they are 2 wk. old they are unreliable.

Clean eggs are the best, but eggs should not be washed. Washed eggs do not hatch well.

The incubator must be set up perfectly level and kept so for the best results.

The directions given by the manufacturers for the operation of their machines must be closely followed.

The thermometers recommended by the manufacturers of the incubators should be used, and they should be placed in the machine exactly where directed.

Incubator eggs should not be handled with hands soiled by dirt or oil. Oil will kill the germ within the egg.

Avoid jars of the incubator while hatching. This ruptures the egg and destroys the embryo.

The incubator room should be kept free of drafts and bad odors of all kinds.

Keep the flues of the incubator clean and free from soot. A coating of soot prevents the proper amount of heat from reaching the egg chamber.

Keep the lamps clean and free from oil. Oil odors affect the eggs, and may even destroy the embryos.

When the eggs are first placed in the incubator, they should be warmed gradually. If they are heated too fast the germs will be destroyed.

Do not neglect to turn and air the eggs in an incubator.

When the eggs are taken out of an incubator to air, the door should be closed so that the egg chamber will not cool off. The eggs should not be kept out of the chamber until they become chilled. This kills the embryos.

Be sure to have the brooders prepared for the accommodation of the chicks when they are ready to be taken from the incubator.

When the incubator is not in use, keep it in a place where it will not become infested with vermin. When it is again put in use, it should be examined, thoroughly cleaned, and run for several days before the eggs are placed in it.

BROODING OF CHICKS

NATURAL BROODING

The brood coop that will house three or four hens and their broods is quite convenient for natural brooding.

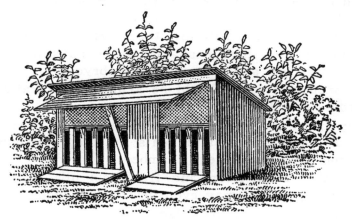

Fig. 1

A coop for two hens and their chicks is shown in Fig. 1. Another coop well suited for wet, cold, or stormy weather is shown in Fig. 2. After the chicks are well dried off,

Fig. 2

and have been in the nest with the mother hen for at least 12 hr., the hen and the brood, or two or more hens and their broods can be removed to the brood coops. Three or four hens that are remarkably quiet will brood their chicks in one large open coop. If they are quarrelsome, they should be placed with their broods in separate coops.

The chief factors of caring for the mother hen and her chicks are cleanliness inside of and about the coop. The coops should be placed where the chicks can run out on the ground, and where they can have a dry spot under foot when the ground is damp. They should always be sheltered from wet and rain until they are 2 or 3 wk. old.

ARTIFICIAL BROODING

Chicks that are hatched from eggs put in the incubator on Monday evening do not need to be removed until Wednesday morning of the third week thereafter. This leaves the chicks in the incubator two nights and one day after they should be hatched. If from any cause the hatch is completed 12 or more hours ahead of time, the chicks may be removed an equal number of hours earlier. Chicks that are hatched on Monday need not be fed until Wednesday; they may, however, if removed from the incubator, be fed 12 or 15 hr. earlier than this. When the chicks are removed from the incubator to the hover or brooder, they should be protected from the cool or cold air by being covered with woolen cloths that have been warmed for the purpose.

Chicks in the Brooder.—From 50 to 100 chicks may be placed under each hover, according to the kind of hover or brooder used. The sizes of the brooders vary from a 50-chick size to a hover that will care for 500 or more. The most satisfactory results will be obtained through the use of hovers that will care for from 50 to 100 chicks. Considerable experience and natural ability are necessary to succeed with brooders and hovers of larger size.

Management of Hover.—Each separate kind of brooding appliance must be cared for according to its needs. The average heat required beneath the hover is from 80° F. to 95° F. These differences in temperature are necessary, not because the floor of the nursery needs to be any warmer or any cooler in one kind than in another, but because the placing of the thermometer is not alike in all of them. Each manufacturer recommends a heat basis suited to the placing of the thermometer in that brooding system. The chicks on the floor should be in a temperature ranging from 85° F. to 92° F. When the chicks are first placed in the hover, the temperature should be about 92° F.; the presence of the chicks beneath the hover will raise the temperature to at least 95° F. After the chicks have been for 3 or 4 da. under the hover, the temperature can be gradually reduced. In winter it may be dropped to 90° F. and kept there until the chicks are fully 2 wk. old or more, at which time 1° or 2° less will answer.

Always have sufficient heat under the nursery to satisfy the chicks and keep them contented. The one sure evidence of contentment of the chicks under the hover is the gentle peep of satisfaction which they give when properly brooded. Whenever there is not sufficient heat they will sound a cry of alarm or distress which every poultryman should learn. This call should be answered immediately and the cause of the cry discovered and remedied at once.

Some authorities say that the temperature should register 95° F., running up fully to 100° F. when the chicks are placed in the brooder, and that this temperature should be maintained for the first week, after which it may be gradually reduced. This temperature may answer very well when the weather is cold, but in warm weather it is too high. The temperature should be kept as low as practicable, depending on the time of year and the age of the chicks. One safe rule is that the chicks should always have heat enough to obviate the danger of becoming chilled.

No matter where the hover may be placed, whether in a coop made for the purpose, or in a box, a small house, or an outbuilding, the floor should be covered with dry sand over which should be scattered a coating of 2 or 3 in. of cut straw, hay, alfalfa, or chaff of some kind. There should be sufficient of this on the floor to protect the chicks from the cold during severe weather, and enough of it so that the curtain of the hover will rest

FIG. 3

on it. Cleanliness, care, and proper. feeding are always necessary for success in the growing of chicks.

A brooding coop well suited for one or two hovers is shown in Fig. 3. This coop was made from two piano boxes placed together, the roof being covered with ordinary roofing paper. There are two doors in front; one is a frame door covered with wire cloth, the other a glass door, which is. kept open when the weather is warm and the sun shines bright; but on very cold days and at night it should be closed. A brood coop of this kind can be safely used during the winter months. It

is not unusual to have one or two hovers each for fifty or a hundred chicks running inside of such a coop when the thermometer is nearly zero.

POINTS IN SUCCESSFUL BROODING

Brood coops should be perfectly sanitary and free from vermin, and should be painted with liquid insecticide at least a week before they are occupied. They should also be sprayed with insecticide every 2 wk. while in use, and the floors must be cleaned frequently.

Brood coops should be ready a day in advance of the time when the chicks are to be placed in them, and the temperature should be about 90°. This temperature should be maintained for 7 da., after which it should be gradually reduced to 80°.

If newly hatched chicks become chilled they will be seriously injured, and if they are overheated they will lose vitality. The proper heat must be maintained with regularity.

The directions given by the manufacturers for the operation of brooders should be strictly followed, and the particular kind of thermometer recommended should be used. Temperature readings are taken at different heights, according to the construction of the brooder, and if the thermometers used are too long or too short the temperature readings will be misleading.

Overcrowding in brooders should be avoided. When a brooder is overcrowded the air becomes impure, and this will result in a loss of vitality.

As soon as chicks are able they should be allowed to run in the open, but they should be protected from predatory animals by covered runways.

During inclement weather, chicks should be induced to take exercise by scattering small grains in the litter.

After each meal, unconsumed food should be removed from the floor of the brooder. If it is left to be trampled over and becomes sour, it will cause bowel troubles.

Chicks that contract ailments of any kind should be isolated immediately.

A critical stage in the life of chicks is when they are feathering, and at this time they should be supplied with an abundance of nitrogenous foods.

MAMMOTH INCUBATORS AND BROODERS

The Mammoth system of incubating and brooding has been so well developed that it can now be used with perfect safety. Incubators are built in sections and have a capacity of from three thousand to many thousand eggs. It is not unusual to see one Mammoth machine containing 15,000 eggs in operation. These incubators are heated by self-regulating coal-burning furnaces, the heat from which is distributed by means of hot water that passes through a system of pipes so adjusted as to keep a continuous flow, or circulation, from the furnace, through the pipes, and back to the furnace again. The heat in the egg chamber is regulated through the raising and lowering of the egg trays and by an automatic or thermostatic regulator. In writing of this system, one familiar with it says that the simplicity, economy, and safety of this type of heater is now universally recognized.

A system of hot-water heating is used with the Mammoth brooder. This system can be used with either a single- or a double-row brooding house. The system for heating is much the same as has always been used in hot-water brooding systems. The one great difference is that by using the self-regulating coal-burning furnace better service can be obtained at less cost than when boilers are used. Complete information regarding this system of incubating and brooding can best be obtained from those who manufacture the apparatus.

EGGS

Food Value of Eggs.—Eggs are a cheap food. They are less costly than most meats. One dozen eggs will better serve a family of six than 1½ lb. of meat. The average value of these is about equal.

Composition of Eggs.—About 11% of hens' eggs consist of shell, 32% of yolk, and 57% of white. The white and yolk are made up of 72% of water. The table shown on pages 116 and 117, adapted from a bulletin of the United States Department of Agriculture, gives the composition and fuel value of eggs of the common domestic poultry, and, for purpose of comparison, the composition and fuel value of some of the more common foods other than these.

Uses of Eggs.—In addition to their use as food, eggs are used to a limited extent for other purposes. The white of an egg is a remedy for burns, and if taken in time it is an effective antidote for poisoning by corrosive sublimate. Food or bones lodged in the throat can sometimes be dislodged by swallowing a raw egg. The oil extracted from the yolk has healing properties, and the inner lining or membrane of the shell can be used as an adhesive plaster. Eggshells, on account of the purity of the carbonate lime of which they are largely composed, are used in compounding medicine and for several other purposes.

There is a limited demand for rotten eggs for the finishing of some kinds of leather. They may be used as fertilizer, and in many instances they are used in the manufacture of calico. The supply, however, is much greater than the demand, and such eggs bring but a few cents a dozen. Often the price paid for them is not sufficient to cover the cost of transportation, which in most cases is paid by the shipper.

Color of Eggshells.—Fowls of European origin lay white-shelled eggs; those of Asiatic origin lay dark-shelled eggs, as a rule. The eggs of different varieties

of the same breed may differ slightly in color. **For** example, the eggs of dark-plumaged fowls have darker-colored shells than those of the lighter-plumaged fowls.

A cross between two breeds, one of which lays brown-shelled eggs and the other white-shelled eggs, results **in** fowls that lay eggs of a color intermediate between the brown and the white. There is also considerable variation in the color of eggs from different hens of the same variety. The color of the shell is more pronounced in the eggs first laid than in those laid later in the season. All fowls having the least amount of Asiatic blood show this influence in the tinted shells. The more of Asiatic blood a fowl has in its veins the darker will be the color of the eggshell. The eggs with the darkest color of shell are laid by the Langshans.

The New York market pays the highest prices for white-shelled eggs, and the Boston market pays the highest prices for brown-shelled eggs. In other markets the matter of color of shell is one of small importance.

The color of shell produced by the most popular egg-producing breeds is given in the following list:

Brown Shells	*White Shells*
Brahmas	Anconas
Cochins	Adalusians
Dorkings	Crévecœurs
Dominiques	Campines
Faverolles	Games (some have a tint)
Indian Games	Hamburgs
Javas	Houdans
Langshans	Leghorns
Orpingtons	La Flèche
Plymouth Rocks	Minorcas
Rhode Island Reds	Polish
Wyandottes	Redcaps
	Spanish

Weight of Eggs.—Marketable eggs should weigh **not** less than 2 oz. each. At this weight, a crate of 30 doz. eggs will weigh 45 lb., exclusive of the crate, and such eggs will bring much better prices in the market than eggs of smaller size. Eggs much larger than 2 oz.

COMPOSITION OF EGGS AND CERTAIN OTHER FOODS

Food	Refuse Per Cent.	Water Per Cent.	Protein Per Cent.	Fat Per Cent.	Carbo-hy-drates Per Cent.	Ash Per Cent.	Fuel Value per Pound Calories
Hen egg:							
Whole egg as purchased........	11.2	65.5	11.9	9.30		.9	711
Whole egg, edible portion......		73.7	13.4	10.50		1.0	802
White......................		86.2	12.3	.20		.6	338
Yolk.......................		49.5	15.7	33.30		1.1	1,825
Whole egg boiled, edible portion.		73.3	13.2	12.00		.8	860
White-shelled eggs as purchased..	10.7	65.6	11.8	10.80		.6	771
Brown-shelled eggs as purchased..	10.9	64.8	11.9	11.20		.7	791
Duck egg:							
Whole egg as purchased........	13.7	60.8	12.1	12.50		.8	851
Whole egg, edible portion......		70.5	13.3	14.50		1.0	968
White......................		87.0	11.1	.03		.8	298
Yolk.......................		45.8	16.8	36.20		1.2	1,977
Goose egg:							
Whole egg as purchased........	14.2	59.7	12.9	12.30		.9	864
Whole egg, edible portion......		69.5	13.8	14.40		1.0	977

	Refuse	Water	Protein	Fat	Carbohydrates	Ash	Fuel value
White..........		86.3	11.6	.02		.8	311
Yolk..........		44.1	17.3	36.20		1.3	1,990
Turkey egg:							
Whole egg as purchased.....	13.8	63.5	12.2	9.70		.8	736
Whole egg, edible portion.....		73.7	13.4	11.20		.9	831
White.....		86.7	11.5	.03		.8	309
Yolk.....		48.3	17.4	32.90		1.2	1,854
Guinea fowl egg:							
Whole egg as purchased.....	16.9	60.5	11.9	9.90		.8	736
Whole egg, edible portion.....		72.8	13.5	12.00		.9	868
White.....		86.6	11.6	.03		.8	312
Yolk.....		49.7	16.7	31.80		1.2	1,788
Miscellaneous foods:							
Cheese as purchased.....		34.2	25.9	33.70	2.4	3.8	2,158
Sirloin steak as purchased.....	12.8	54.0	16.5	16.10		.9	1,121
Sirloin steak, edible portion.....		61.9	18.9	18.50		1.0	1,286
Milk.....		87.0	3.3	4.00	5.0	.7	348
Oysters in shell as purchased.....	81.4	16.1	1.2	.20	.7	.4	53
Oysters, edible portion.....		86.9	6.2	1.20	3.7	2.0	284
Wheat flour.....		12.0	11.4	1.00	75.1	.5	1,710
Potatoes as purchased.....	20.0	62.6	1.8	.10	14.7	.8	319
Potatoes, edible portion.....		78.3	2.2	.10	18.4	1.0	397

are not profitable to sell, because they bring very little,
if any, higher price in the general market, and hens do
not lay so many. For a special market, however, it is
sometimes possible to get a premium on eggs that
average about 2½ oz.

The weight of eggs depend to a large extent on the
breed of fowls that lay them and also on the peculi-
arities of individual fowls. The following, however,
gives the average weight of various eggs:

Eggs	*Ounces*
8 hen's eggs, average	16
11 guinea eggs	16
1 duck egg	3
1 turkey egg	4
1 goose egg	6 to 7

Washing of Eggs.—Eggs that are so badly soiled as
to need washing to fit them for market may be cleaned
with a solution made up of 1 oz. of ammonia to 2 qt. of
water. Soiled eggs may also be washed in warm water
and rubbed dry with a piece of cotton cloth or flannel.
Deep stains may be removed by rubbing with dry, coarse
salt. When cleaned in this way they should be rinsed
in lukewarm water. Stained eggs are sometimes cleaned
in lukewarm water that contain a small quantity of soap.

After soiled eggs have been cleaned their appearance
is improved by rubbing them with a cloth that has been
moistened with a solution made up of 4 oz. of salt to
1 pt. of vinegar; this treatment, however, is not necessary for eggs that have been washed in a solution containing ammonia.

Percentage of Loss of Total Egg Crop.—According to
the United States Department of Agriculture, about 17%
of the total egg crop of the country is lost, because of
improper handling, or because of unsanitary conditions
where the eggs are laid. The following table shows the
percentage of loss of the total egg crop due to various
causes:

PERCENTAGE LOSS OF TOTAL EGG CROP

Class	Per Cent.
Dirty eggs...............................	2
Broken eggs..............................	2
Chick development........................	5
Shrunken or held eggs....................	5
Rotten eggs..............................	2½
Moldy and bad-flavored eggs..............	½
Total...................................	17

Relation of Weight of Eggs to Egg Production.—As a general rule, the larger the number of eggs laid by a

RELATION OF WEIGHT OF EGGS TO EGG PRODUCTION

Variety	Number of Hens	Number of Eggs Laid	Weight per Dozen Ounces	Average Number of Eggs
Andalusian..........	72	11,883	26.85	162.26
Single-Comb Black Minorca.............	156	23,910	26.72	146.85
Langshan..............	108	17,766	26.03	164.50
White Leghorn........	984	173,939	26.00	176.75
Ancona...............	42	5,883	25.94	140.00
Black Orpington.......	954	162,623	25.61	170.45
Buff Orpington........	234	35,199	25.25	150.42
Buff Wyandotte.......	66	10,479	24.71	157.85
Silver Wyandotte......	834	139,694	24.50	167.49
Brown Leghorn........	180	32,593	24.47	181.08
White Wyandotte.....	90	14,066	24.45	156.25
Golden Wyandotte	108	16,902	24.38	156.50
Rose-Comb White Leghorn...............	66	11,578	24.31	173.90
Black Hamburg.......	30	5,554	24.19	185.00
Rose-Comb Brown Leghorn..............	72	13,155	22.74	182.70
Total, all varieties.....	4,362	732,082	25.28	167.50

fowl, the lighter in weight the eggs will average. This is shown in the table on page 119, which is a summary of the egg record of 4,362 hens of fifteen different varieties that laid a total of 732,082 eggs, the records of the different lots of fowls being taken over a period of 5 yr. In the table, the fowls are arranged with those laying the heaviest eggs per doz. at the top and those laying the lighter eggs coming in their proper order. The Black Hamburgs and the Rose-Comb Brown Leghorns that produced the two highest average egg records produced the lightest-weight eggs, and though the results obtained are not all exactly in accordance with this statement, a careful inspection of the table will show that on an average hens with high egg records produced light-weight eggs, and that the hens with the lowest egg records produced somewhat heavier eggs. Since little attention is paid in the market to the weight of eggs, it is obvious that the best egg producers are the most profitable.

Relation of Egg Production to Season.—In spite of the many assertions that hens lay more prolifically at one time of the year than at another, an inspection of the egg records of a large number of fowls fails to show any uniformity in regard to this point, but rather tends to indicate that egg production is more a matter of individuality than of season. The egg records given in the table on page 122 have been taken from laying hens in America, England, and Australia. The records of some exceptionally high egg producers have been selected and also the average production of a large number of fowls where it was possible to obtain authentic records of this character. It will be noted that the individual fowls that make high egg records lay consistently throughout almost every month in the year, and that the only time when they fall off in egg production is during the molting period or when they are broody.

The single hens that do not make such high egg records usually lay very well for certain months in the year, but are unable to stand the strain of heavy

egg laying ˍand fail, sometimes almost completely, in other months.

When the average egg production of a large number of fowls is taken, it will be seen that there is a certain similarity between their rates of monthly production, but if the record of the 80 White Leghorn hens in America is compared with that of the 28 American Wyandottes and the 6,771 hens of assorted varieties in America, it will be seen that the egg production in the cold months was fully as large as in the spring months, and that the production declined only in the fall when the fowls were molting. Some hens that are prolific egg producers in their first year prove very unsatisfactory in their subsequent years, as for instance, the Australian Silver Wyandotte shown in the table. To be sure that no such hens are selected for breeders, it is necessary that careful egg records be kept.

BLACK ORPINGTON

In all localities the fewest eggs are produced during the season of molt and the period immediately following that season. In the United States, the molt occurs during the months that intervene between July and Jan. Naturally, eggs will sell for the highest prices at this time. Hens should be encouraged to lay during these months. The greater profit will be made when a prolific yield of eggs during the winter months has been secured.

Pullets that are hatched in the early spring lay at an earlier age than do late-hatched pullets. March-hatched pullets frequently lay in July, while those hatched in July seldom lay before the following March.

MONTHLY EGG RECORDS SHOWING ABSENCE OF UNIFORM PRODUCTION

Laying Hens	Jan.	Feb.	Mr.	Apr.	May	June	July	Aug.	Sep.	Oct.	No.	Dec.	Total
American records:													
White Leghorn, single hen													
First year of laying..........	20	19	25	25	23	23	25	26	23	19	12	17	257
Second year of laying.........	0	10	17	23	19	24	25	27	23	21	0	0	189
White Leghorn, av. of 80 hens..	15	19	21	21	17	16	11	4	3	3	5	11	146
Rose-Comb Rhode Island Red, single hen													
First year of laying..........	30	27	23	27	19	25	18	13	15	1	15	28	241
Second year of laying.........	16	24	17	14	14	13	14	13	7	2	10	29	173
White Wyandotte, average of 28 pullets..........	15	17	22	17	20	17	15	13	14	9	10	12	183
Assorted varieties, average of 6,771 hens and pullets ...	8	11	16	18	16	14	13	10	6	4	4	7	127
English records:													
Single hen													
First year of laying..........	24	23	29	10	0	22	24	22	18	15	24	18	229
Second year of laying.........	21	21	23	12	0	23	19	26	24	12	0	10	191
Australian records:													
White Leghorn, single hen													
First year of laying..........	19	15	22	12	19	17	14	26	26	27	24	22	243
Second year of laying.........	18	14	15	15	3	0	18	21	23	20	24	21	192
White Leghorn, single hen													
First year of laying..........	13	2	7	5	7	4	13	22	21	19	19	19	151
Second year of laying.........	8	1	0	2	0	0	0	13	22	23	22	22	113
Silver Wyandotte, single hen													
First year of laying..........	16	16	17	12	13	13	20	24	21	21	21	23	217
Second year of laying.........	10	7	12	3	6	8	13	14	15	6	8	9	111
Assorted varieties, average of 524 pullets..........	16	13	10	11	12	13	14	20	22	20	19	19	192

STANDARDS FOR EGGS

Eggs are graded in many ways. The number of grades varies in different markets. In general, it may be said that eggs are graded according to their size, shape, color of shell, finish of shell, and general condition.

The rules for the classification, grading, and packing of market eggs as adopted by the New York Mercantile Exchange are as follows:

RULE 1—CLASSIFICATION AND GRADING

1. Eggs shall be classified as "fresh gathered," "held," "refrigerator," and "limed."

2. There shall be grades of "extras," "extra firsts," "firsts," "seconds," "thirds," "No. 1 and 2 dirties," and "checks."

RULE 2

1. All sales of all grades of eggs shall be at mark.

QUALITIES

2. *Fresh gathered extras* shall be free from dirty eggs, of good uniform size, and shall contain reasonably fresh, reasonably full, strong bodied, sweet eggs, at the discretion of the Egg Committee, as follows:

A—90%.

B—80%.

C—65%.

The balance—other than the loss—may be slightly defective in strength or fulness, but must be sweet. The maximum total average loss per case permitted in "extras" shall vary with the requirement of reasonably full, strong bodied eggs as follows:

A—90% full, 1 doz. maximum loss.

B—80% full, 1½ doz. maximum loss.

C—65% full, 2 doz. maximum loss.

When sold "storage packed," extras must not contain an average of more than 12 cracked or checked eggs per case.

3. *Fresh gathered firsts* (or extra firsts) shall be reasonably clean and of good average size, and shall contain reasonably fresh, reasonably full, strong bodied,

sweet eggs, at the discretion of the Egg Committee, as follows:

A—75%.

B—65%.

C—50%.

D—40%.

The balance—other than the loss—may be defective in strength or fulness, but must be sweet. The maximum total average loss per case permitted in "firsts" or "extra firsts" shall vary with the requirements of reasonably full, strong bodied eggs as follows:

A—75% full, 1½ doz. maximum loss.

B—65% full, 2 doz. maximum loss.

C—50% full, 3 doz. maximum loss.

D—40% full, 4 doz. maximum loss.

When sold "storage packed," fresh gathered firsts (or extra firsts) must not contain an average of more than 18 cracked or checked eggs per case.

4. *Fresh gathered seconds* shall be reasonably clean and of fair average size, and shall contain reasonably fresh, reasonably full eggs, at the discretion of the Egg Committee, as follows:

A—65%.

B—50%.

C—40%.

D—30%.

The balance—other than the loss—may be defective in strength or fulness, but must be merchantable stock. The maximum total average loss per case permitted in "seconds" shall vary with the proportion of reasonably full eggs required, as follows:

A—65% full, 2 doz. maximum loss.

B—50% full, 3 doz. maximum loss.

C—40% full, 4 doz. maximum loss.

D—30% full, 5 doz. maximum loss.

5. *Fresh gathered thirds* shall be reasonably clean and of fair average size, and shall contain reasonably fresh, reasonably full, sweet eggs, at the discretion of the Egg Committee, as follows:

A—50%.

B—30%.

C—20%.

The balance—other than the loss—may be defective in strength or fulness, but must be merchantable stock. The maximum total average loss per case permitted in "thirds" shall vary with the requirements of reasonably full, sweet eggs, as follows:

A—50% full, 4 doz. maximum loss.

B—30% full, 5 doz. maximum loss.

C—20% full, 6 doz. maximum loss.

6. *Held firsts* shall be reasonably clean, of good average size, and sweet. At least 40% shall be reasonably full and strong. The balance may be defective in strength and fulness, but not badly shrunken, excepting the loss. There may be a total average loss of 2 doz. per case, but if the loss exceeds that by not more than 50% the eggs shall be a good delivery upon allowance of the excess.

7. *Held seconds* shall be reasonably clean and of fair average size. May be defective in fulness, strength, and flavor, but must be merchantable stock, not musty. There may be a total average loss of 4 doz. per case.

8. *Refrigerator extras* shall be free from dirty or small eggs, reasonably full, strong, sweet, and free from mildew or foreign taste or odor.

The maximum loss shall be, at the discretion of the Egg Committee, as follows:

A—1½ doz.

B—2 doz.

Cases, fillers, and packing shall be as required for "storage packed."

9. *Refrigerator firsts* shall be reasonably clean and of good average size; they must be reasonably full, strong, and sweet, and free from mildew or foreign taste or odor.

The maximum loss shall be, at the discretion of the Egg Committee, as follows:

A—2 doz.

B—3 doz.

Cases, fillers, and packing shall be as required for "storage packed."

10. *Refrigerator seconds* shall be reasonably clean and of fair average size; they must be reasonably full, strong, and sweet, and free from mildew or foreign taste or odor.

The maximum loss shall be, at the discretion of the Egg Committee, as follows:

A—3 doz.

B—4 doz.

Cases shall be substantial, and fillers and packing reasonably sweet.

11. *Refrigerator thirds* shall be of fair appearance and may be off-flavored to some extent.

The maximum loss shall be, at the discretion of the Egg Committee, as follows:

A—5 doz.

B—6 doz.

Cases shall be substantial.

12. *Limed extras* shall be of uniformly good size, well cleaned, strong bodied, and reasonably full and sweet.

The maximum loss shall be, at the discretion of the Egg Committee, as follows:

A—1½ doz.

B—2 doz.

Cases, fillers, and packing shall be as required for "storage packed."

13. *Limed firsts* shall be of good average size, well cleaned, of good strength, reasonably full and sweet.

The maximum loss shall be, at the discretion of the Egg Committee, as follows:

A—2 doz.

B—3 doz.

Cases, fillers, and packing shall be as required for "storage packed."

14. *Limed seconds* shall be of fair average size, well cleaned, of good strength, and reasonably full and sweet.

The maximum loss shall be, at the discretion of the Egg Committee, as follows:

A—3 doz.

B—4 doz.

Cases shall be substantial, and fillers and packing reasonably sweet.

15. *Limed thirds* shall comprise stock which is rusty, weak, or shows hot weather defects, but must contain at least 50% of fairly useful quality.

The maximum loss shall be, at the discretion of the Egg Committee, as follows:

A—5 doz.

B—6 doz.

Cases shall be substantial.

16. *No. 1 dirties* may be offered in the classes of Fresh Gathered, Held, and Refrigerator. They must be of good, useful quality, sweet in flavor.

The maximum loss shall correspond with the requirements for "firsts" in the class, at the time when offered.

When sold "storage packed," No. 1 dirties must not contain more than 18 cracked or checked eggs per case.

17. *No. 2 dirties* may be offered in the classes of Fresh Gathered, Held, and Refrigerator.

The quality, if fresh gathered, shall be the same as specified for No. 1 dirties.

If held, or refrigerator, may be off-flavored, but not musty.

The maximum loss shall correspond with the requirements for "seconds" in the class, and at the time when offered.

Checked eggs may consist of blind checks and cracked eggs (not leaking). They must be sweet in flavor, and the loss must not exceed 3 doz. per case.

18. Loss, as used in these rules, shall comprise all rotten, spotted, broken (leaking), broken-yolked, hatched (blood-veined), and sour eggs. Very small, very dirty, cracked (not leaking), badly heated, badly shrunken, and salt eggs shall be counted as half loss in all grades excepting dirties and checks. * * *

19. At the discretion of the Egg Committee it may put in force two grades of firsts at the same time, one requiring a higher proportion of reasonably full, strong-bodied eggs than the other, and when this is done, the higher of the two grades shall be designated as "extra firsts."

All requirements for grades determined upon by the Egg Committee must be chosen from those specified under Rule 2.

20. The classification provided in this rule shall apply equally to hen eggs, duck eggs and goose eggs, but in the case of duck and goose eggs the maximum loss shall be pro rata with the number of dozens contained in the packages.

RULE 3.—PACKAGES AND PACKING

1. All grades of eggs not storage packed, shall be in new or good second-hand substantial egg cases, of uniform size.

Fillers shall be of substantial quality, sweet and dry, with flats or other suitable substitutes under bottom layers and over tops, and sweet, dry excelsior or other suitable packing under bottom and over tops.

Any grade of eggs not storage packed, which shall inspect in quality according to these rules, but be deficient, not to exceed 10% in flats or other suitable substitutes and tops and bottoms, shall be a good delivery.

2. *Storage packed.* When sold as "storage packed," all grades must be in new 30 doz. cases, well seasoned, smooth, clean, and substantial, fillers dry, sweet, medium, No. 1, or other good substantial straw board, flats under bottom layers and over tops. The packing shall be dry, sweet excelsior under bottoms and over tops, unless otherwise specified.

3. To be a good delivery, all eggs must be packed in 30 doz. cases except goose eggs, which may be packed in any style of packages containing not less than 10 doz. each, and duck eggs, which may be packed in any style of packages containing not less than 15 doz. each.

CARE AND PRESERVATION OF EGGS

CARE OF EGGS

The Bureau of Chemistry of the United States Department of Agriculture has given marked attention to investigations the results of which it is thought will add considerably to the value of egg products by saving many millions of dollars as the result of more care in handling them.

Eggs contain a large percentage of moisture, which will evaporate through the shell. The evaporation is more rapid when the eggs are exposed to heat or variations in temperature. Mr. Greenlee, of the Food Research Laboratory of the government, says that chemical analyses of eggs by various investigators are fairly numerous, but that little has been done to correlate the change in moisture content with the age or condition of the egg.

One investigator, who has made an extensive study of eggs, has found that eggs kept for a year show a loss of weight equivalent to 10% of the total weight, which loss is largely water evaporated from the whites. He found also that when fresh eggs are boiled a loss in weight occurs, whereas storage eggs gain in boiling. Apparently the whites lose more water than the yolks, and consequently gain more in boiling. The boiled yolks, when fresh, contain less than 50% of water; when cold-stored, this percentage is increased, the figures reaching 64% in the last examination. This would indicate that the yolks of eggs in storage gather moisture from the whites and that the whites evaporate moisture through the shell.

Other experiments made by the government chemists do not indicate definitely that water passes from the white to the yolk. The same results, they say, would be obtained if the white took up solids from the yolks. They say further that the phenomena of a transfer of water from the white to the yolk may easily be ex-

plained by the simple process of osmosis. The yolk, which contains a very high percentage of solids, is surrounded by a membraneous tissue called the vitelline membrane, which, in turn, is surrounded by the egg white, a liquid much more dilute than the yolk. By osmosis, the water passes through the membrane from the more dilute to the more concentrated solution until a constant equilibrium is obtained. This process continues until the vitelline membrane becomes so weak that it breaks, when the white and the yolk begin to lose their identity.

Professor Lamson writes that the egg is complex chemically, and, like milk, it is one of the best places for bacteria to multiply. The work of these organisms is to simplify or decompose the white and the yolk until the egg is seemingly worse than useless; though even rotten eggs find a place in the market for polishing leather, and are sold by the large packing houses for that purpose.

Fresh-laid eggs will be contaminated if left even for a short time under unfavorable conditions. A case of eggs that are perfectly good may be taken from cold storage on a hot day in summer, hauled from the storage house in a wagon to the retail store, be opened immediately and the eggs placed in baskets for sale. The exposure of the eggs so quickly to a heated temperature causes moisture to gather on the surface of the shell. This is called sweating. The moisture that gathers on the egg dissolves the coating of albumen that partly fills the pores of the egg; thus, the heated atmosphere works through into the interior of the shell and in a very few hours the eggs begin to change in quality. By the time they are carried home and prepared for the table, they are not nearly so good as they would have been if they had been properly cared for.

When the eggs are taken from cold storage or from a refrigerator car they should be kept in the store or the storehouse away from the cold-storage room for from 12 to 24 hr. without opening the case. This will temper

the eggs and bring them to or near to the temperature of the room. When the case is opened after this wait, the eggs will be dry and will be much better for selling and for table use than they would be if treated in the other manner. The greater part of all the deterioration in eggs is directly blamable on careless handling.

Eggs that are perfectly fresh when put in cold storage will, if packed in clean cases and properly stored, be quite as good as when removed from cold storage as they were when placed there. More cold-storage eggs are injured between the time they are removed from storage and are sold than are injured while in the cold-storage room. If low-grade or inferior eggs are placed in cold storage, they will be worse when taken out of storage than they were when placed in storage.

Eggs that are fresh and good and poultry that is fresh, good, and properly dressed will, if carefully packed, keep in cold storage for many months, and be nearly or quite as good for food as they were when placed in storage. Eggs that have been heated in transit or that have not been cared for properly prior to being placed in storage, will have deteriorated when taken from storage. Such eggs are the kind that call down condemnation on cold-storage eggs. The same is true of dressed poultry. If it is good when placed in storage, it will be good when it comes out; if it is inferior when placed in storage it will be less fit for food when taken out than it was when it was placed in storage.

Most fresh-laid eggs are a typically perfect food, but they may be infected almost immediately after being laid. For example, the filth of nesting material may adhere to the moist surface of fresh-laid eggs and so infect them as to render them unfit for food. Such contamination will speedily spoil the eggs in spite of the most careful later handling. Eggs left in the nest for a few hours when the weather is very hot may be injured. It is not unusual for the temperature at noon to be 98° or 100° inside of some poultry houses. Eggs that are laid in infected nesting material and left there

a few hours in such a temperature will, within an hour or two, show blood spots and decomposition.

Laying hens should be kept apart from the males during the summer months, because infertile eggs will keep good much longer at summer temperatures than fertile eggs. There is no reason whatever for the males to run with the hens at any other time than during the breeding season.

Quality of Eggs.—Eggs that are old and undesirable may be called stale, decomposed, or rotten, according to their condition. Any deterioration in eggs brings them and their vendor into disfavor. Consumers partial to eggs that are perfectly fresh will turn in disgust from eggs served in soiled shells. This is reason sufficient for the greatest care in safeguarding egg production by means of clean houses, clean nests, and clean and healthy hens. Eggs should be gathered frequently, at least three or four times daily, in both cold and warm weather. All eggs the shells of which are the least bit soiled or off-colored should be placed by themselves to be cleaned and sorted or graded before they are sent to market.

No other food product will gain in price from proper grading so greatly as eggs. They can be graded in size, shape, color, and cleanliness, with the result of always enhancing the price.

Freshness and internal conditions may be determined by candling. The process of candling is simple. A lamp is placed inside a pasteboard box having a hole in the top through which the heat of the lamp may escape, and a hole two-thirds the diameter of the egg in the side of the box just opposite or even with the flame of the lamp. By placing the egg against the hole in the side of the box the interior of the egg can be plainly seen. If the contents are perfectly bright and clear, the egg is fresh and fit for food. If spots, shades, or lines are visible through the shell, the egg is more or less deteriorated. Eggs must be tested in a dark room. There are several kinds of egg testers sold for very moderate prices. Persons who sell eggs should have one

of these testers and test all their eggs before sending them to market.

Eggs differ considerably in size, shape, and color. When eggs are packed for market, either in dozen cartons or in egg cases of large size, those of one size and one color should be packed by themselves. The standard size for market eggs is 24 oz. per doz., each egg averaging 2 oz. Eggs smaller than this are under size; those that are larger are over size. Over-sized eggs all of one color packed in clear cases will bring the highest prices in the markets. Eggs that vary in size, shape, and color, even though perfectly fresh, sell for lower prices. It is not unusual to see fresh-laid eggs all of one size, shape, and color selling for 25 to 40 per cent. higher than eggs equally fresh, but of miscellaneous sizes, shapes, and colors.

Eggs selected for hatching should be the finest obtainable. Never hatch an egg that is small in size or inferior in shape and color. If this rule is closely adhered to for a few years, the egg product of a poultry farm will almost double in value. The same rigid selection and grading should be followed and continued year after year, for both hatching and selling, until no poor eggs, or at least very few, are produced.

The shells of all eggs should be smooth and free from indentations and unevenness. The surface of the shell should be finished and have a polished appearance. If the shells are white, they should be perfectly white and free from any tint or shade whatever; if brown or tinted, they should have an even shade of color. When the shells are irregular in form or color they are classed as seconds, thirds, or miscellaneous in quality. No eggs of this kind should ever be found in the first selection, because they will lessen the value of the entire lot.

Not all of the fowls of any one breed lay eggs of proper size, shape, and color, but some hens of all breeds and varieties lay such eggs. By proper selection of eggs for hatching, all breeds and varieties might within 10 or

12 yr. be so developed as to produce eggs of the size and color proper for the various breeds. No one breed excels all others as layers; there are good layers in all breeds and varieties. The production of many eggs of proper size,. shape, and color may be accomplished with any breed by proper breeding, selection, and care.

The color of the yolk may be influenced largely by feeding plenty of green stuff. Experiment has shown that the eating of dried alfalfa leaves by the hens will produce eggs of good yolk color. White beets or mangels eaten plentifully will produce eggs having a very pale yolk. Carrots, kale, spinach, green clover, and many other kinds of green feed will influence the color of the yolk. A plentiful supply of grass will always insure eggs with yolks of good, rich color and fine flavor.

Green clover, alfalfa, rye, grass, or young corn are all good for feeding to laying hens, because they impart fine color and flavor to the eggs. The feeding of green rape, millet, or mustard is apt to make both the color and flavor undesirable. No kind of green stuff is better for feeding to hens in confinement during the summer months than short lawn clippings when perfectly fresh. Carefully selected feed of all kinds is most desirable, because of the tendency of the feed to flavor the eggs.

PRESERVING EGGS

It is quite as necessary to have eggs well selected as it is to have them properly preserved for keeping. That is, eggs that are to be kept should be fresh, infertile, if it is possible to have them so, and all of them should be laid in April, May, or the early part of June. No eggs should ever be stored that are laid when the maximum temperature is above 60°. When eggs are gathered they should be kept in a cool place where the temperature averages between 40° F. and 55° F. They should never be put in the preservative until they have been cooled thoroughly. The eggs that are used for pickling or preserving should have smooth, strong shells. Eggs with shells that are rough or porous are not well suited for storage.

The eggs should not be washed or exposed to the heat of the stove or sun. Never keep eggs, either in or out of storage, where they are in danger of contamination from potatoes, onions, kerosene oil, or anything that will impart an odor which may be absorbed by the eggs.

The best method of keeping the eggs good for food for any length of time is that of cold storage. The ideal cold storage for eggs is that which has a temperature ranging between 32° F. and 36° F. The atmosphere should be dry or nearly so, yet there should be sufficient moisture in the air to prevent evaporation of the eggs. The requirements for success in keeping eggs are that they shall be protected from evaporation and that there shall be no penetration which makes possible the destruction of the eggs through the presence of bacteria and molds.

Eggs may be kept for a longer or shorter time, according to their condition and the method used to preserve them. Eggs packed in bran, oats, or perfectly dry sand will keep longer than eggs exposed to the air. Eggs packed in salt and kept in a temperature of 50° F. or 55° F. where it is perfectly dry will keep good for a number of months. Eggs coated with shellac, varnish, vaseline, or tallow, and stored in a dry cool place will keep for a number of weeks.

The most successful method of storing eggs at home is by the use of liquid preparations made for the purpose. The use of lime water for this purpose has been general throughout the world. In France a solution with from 8 to 10% of unslaked lime or 20% of slaked lime in pure water is used. In the United States a solution containing both salt and lime is in common use.

Eggs laid during the month of April should, if possible, be selected for storing; they keep better than eggs laid at other times. Eggs laid in May and June are next best. The reason for this lies in the fact that April eggs are usually very choice, because the fowls can have a plentiful supply of fresh-grown green food, which adds a rich color to the yolk and a delicate flavor

to the egg. Some eggs do not keep well, however, no matter when they may be laid. Hens that have the free range of barnyards, cow barns, and pig pens gather food that is liable to spoil the flavor of the eggs. Besides, such food may transmit properties to the eggs that will prove detrimental to their keeping. When eggs are perfectly fresh they will keep very well, provided they are gathered, as has been stated, during weather that is not warm and are put into the preservative as soon as the animal heat has left them.

The success obtained from preserving eggs depends largely on the care in selecting them, the preparation of the preserving liquid, and the temperature of the place of storage. Eggs of bad flavor will not improve from this or any other method of preserving. Eggs with a bad odor before being put into the preserving liquid will deteriorate rather than improve. Eggs of poor quality will not be made better, but good eggs will remain good when they have been put away properly.

Eggs may be preserved in lime water provided they are kept in tall vessels; either stone crocks or butter tubs can be used. The liquid for covering the eggs is made in the proportion of 3 gal. of water to 1 lb. of salt and 1 qt. of finely slaked lime, the lime and salt to be mixed in the water. This is to be stirred frequently for a period of 1 to 2 da. Following this, the liquid should be permitted to settle. The crock or tub is then almost filled with eggs, placed, as far as possible, with the small end down. The clear liquid solution of lime and salt is poured over them until the surface of the water is fully an inch above the top of the eggs. The vessel should be kept in an out-of-the-way place, where the temperature will not exceed 50° F. A thin covering of lime will form on top of the liquid. If undisturbed, this covering will protect the contents from outer influences.

A solution made of 1 gal. of sodium silicate, or water glass, and 9 gal. of water is an efficient preservative for eggs. The water glass must be diluted with warm water and be stirred until thoroughly mixed with the water.

When cool, this solution should be poured over eggs placed in vessels as described in the foregoing paragraph. Eggs will keep fairly fresh in this solution for 5 or 6 mo., and they have been kept in edible condition for a year. This can be accomplished, however, only when they are kept in cool places and in a temperature not above 45° F. Experiments have shown that under some conditions a solution of 5% of water glass and 95% of water will answer for the keeping of eggs; and they have kept fairly well in a 3% solution of the same material. The quantity used depends on the strength of the water glass, which is a chemical preparation that may be of several strengths. When the water glass used is of the highest grade, less is required than of the lower grades.

It is of advantage to know the size of the receptacle needed for the eggs and the quantity of liquid needed to submerge them. A 5-gal. jar will hold about 16 doz. eggs. The best results in keeping eggs in water glass will be realized by placing them in a solution made of 1 part water glass and 9 parts water. This solution will evaporate more or less. For this reason water should be added to keep the solution properly balanced for preserving the eggs. If waste by evaporation is permitted, the solution will become thick and heavy. When this occurs, the eggs in the solution will not continue to be so good as they will be if the solution is kept of the proper consistency.

Mr. Olsen, of the Washington Experiment Station, suggests the following as sufficient solution to cover the number of eggs indicated:

Capacity of Container	Number of Eggs	Water-Glass Solution
1 gallon	40	3¾ pints
2 gallons	80	7¼ pints
3 gallons	120	10¾ pints
4 gallons	160	14½ pints
5 gallons	200	18 pints
10 gallons	400	36 pints

When the eggs are removed from the solution they should be rinsed so as to be entirely free from the lime water or the solution of water glass. To do this, the eggs can be placed either in a sieve or a colander, and a running stream of fresh water permitted to pass over them, or buckets of fresh water may be poured over them. After being thoroughly rinsed, and before they are packed for shipment, they should be laid out on a dry cloth or on boards until they have become thoroughly dry.

A sodium-silicate powder is now used to some extent for preserving eggs in place of liquid water glass. It has the same property and it is called water-glass powder. One pound of this powder mixed with 9 pints of warm water will make a solution that is fully equal to the solution made of the liquid water glass and warm water. Eggs will keep quite as well in this as in the liquid water-glass mixture. The powder form is more cleanly and less difficult to handle. It is used in the same way as the liquid water glass. When purchasing the powder be sure to get the true water-glass powder.

Another substitute which is called a lime-water preparation is known as Garantol.

JUDGING EGGS

The largest displays of dressed poultry and market eggs have been made in Boston. Efforts have been made with more or less success toward the holding of egg displays in other parts of the country. The colleges at Lafayette, Ind., Mountain Grove, Mo., Ithaca, N. Y., and State College, Pa., have all held such displays. The score-card method of judging such displays has been used to a greater or less extent. The first score card of which we have any knowledge was compiled by George Fletcher and used by him in judging egg displays in Boston.

In the use of a score card an entry of eggs consists of one dozen, an exhibit consists of three dozen, and a display of six dozen.

Official Score Card for Eggs

(Copyright 1915 By The American Poultry Association)

....
(Name of Show or Association)

....
(Date, Month, Days and Year of Show)

EXHIBITOR...

Address...

Class...Entry No................................

Color..Weight..............Oz.................

SCORE CARD FOR EXHIBITION AND FOR COMMERCIAL EGGS

When judging an exhibit of eggs, the scores of the eggs forming each individual entry are to be added together; the total then being divided by the number of eggs comprising the entry; and the average so obtained shall be the score of the entry.

DISQUALIFICATIONS

Exhibition Egg: Cracked shell; extremely dirty or stained shell; foreign shell-color; pronounced irregularity of shape; sign of incubation or germ-growth; decay, rot, mould, or mustiness; blood rings; foreign odor; or any condition that renders it unfit for food.

Commercial Egg: Sign of incubation or germ growth; decay, rot, mould, or mustiness; blood ring; or any condition that renders it unfit for food.

Divisions and Score of a Perfect Egg		Score of This Entry	Remarks
Size or Weight (including uniformity)	15	....	....
Cleanliness	15	....	....
Shape (including uniformity)	5	....	....
Shell Color (including uniformity)	5	....	....
Shell Texture	5	....	....
Fullness (as indicated by air cell)	15	....	....
Quality and Firmness of Yolk	20	....	....
Quality and Firmness of White	20	....	....
Total Value	100		

JUDGE ....

SECRETARY ....

Several of the poultry departments of colleges located in the eastern part of the United States have compiled score cards. One of the best of these was compiled by the committee of the American Poultry Association for use in the "American Poultry and Egg Standard," which had not been published up to 1919. This score card (shown on page 139) has been copyrighted by the American Poultry Association and can be obtained from the secretary of the association for general use.

The color of the shell of all the eggs in any entry should be alike, that is, 1 doz. of white eggs should be all pure white, 1 doz. of brown eggs should be, all of them, one even shade of brown and all alike.

A perfect egg should be oval in shape, about one and a half times as long as thick, and should taper evenly. Uniformity of shape should be demanded and color should have almost equal consideration with shape. All eggs must be perfectly clean and free from stains, and the surface of the shell must be firm, smooth, and free from uneven places.

The size of the air cell is likely to be the best external test of age. An egg that is perfectly fresh should not show an air cell that is larger than a 10-cent piece. The albumen, or white, of the egg should be firm, and the shell should be almost entirely filled, leaving only the very small air cell visible to a strong light. All eggs should be candled, especially in keen competition.

EGG PRICES

The prices of eggs throughout the world are governed largely by the prices paid in the densely populated centers. These prices for the United States are governed by the prices paid in Boston, Chicago, and New York. Toronto is the market center of Canada; London and Manchester make the prices for Europe. Eggs are quoted in the United States and Canada by the dozen, or by the crate, which contains 30 doz. In London the quota-

tion is by the long hundred (120). Eggs are designated
in the London market according to the locality from
which they are sent, and as this is, to a certain extent,
an indication of their freshness and quality, it has an
influence on the quotations. The highest quotations are
for the best English eggs, and they are usually fully
equal to the prices asked in America for fancy hennery
eggs. French, Danish, and Italian eggs will grade with
what we call near-by eggs and eggs for storage in
America. The best of the eggs that are sent from Ireland over to London are sold for English eggs. Eggs
from more distant countries are graded about the same
as our second or third qualities in America.

Prior to 1914, eggs like those sold in the New York
market as fancy hennery for 25c. a dozen sold in London
at about 22c. a dozen. During 1917 and 1918, eggs that
sold in New York as fancy hennery at 70c. sold in
London for $1.20. During the winter of 1918-1919 the best
grade of fancy hennery eggs sold in New York for 90c.
to $1.00 a dozen, while the same grade of eggs sold in
England for $1.78 a dozen. Eggs have sold in New York
prior to 1914 from as low as 17c. a. dozen in April to as
high as 52c. in winter. The average price on the New
York market during 1917 was 52c.

Prior to 1912 there was published in this book a
comparison of egg prices in the New York and London
markets, a part of which we repeat. The following comparison is made from the quotations given in the New
York and London markets for the month of May, 1909.
As an English shilling was then equivalent to 24⅓c. in
American money, and an English penny was equivalent
to 2c., the London quotations of 8/4 to 9/2 for 120 eggs
is about equivalent to 20c. to 22c. a dozen. The quotations given cannot be accepted as a guide for the selling
price of eggs, but they furnish an approximate indication
of the relative selling prices in New York and London.
Eggs sold in New York at that same date at from 23c.
to 25c. a dozen. The prices fluctuate considerably in
both markets at different seasons of the year. During

the years 1917 and 1918 eggs sold in the London market at about 20c. to 25c. a dozen more than they were sold for in the New York market.

The indications are that eggs will continue to be very high in price throughout the world for several years.

The prices paid for eggs in America during the winter and spring of 1918 and 1919 are some indication of what they are likely to sell for in the future. The grading of eggs is likely to be changed throughout the world, thus to standardize, if possible, all grades of eggs in all countries. There will be an effort to do the same as to price grading of market poultry.

SELECTING HENS FOR EGG PRO-DUCTION

RULES FOR JUDGING

The poultry departments of agricultural colleges and of experiment stations have worked continually for several years to devise a plan or method which might be followed in the selecting of the best laying hens in flocks of poultry.

The pelvic-bone system which is a part of the Hogan system has been used to a considerable extent. This system describes the best layers as having pelvic bones that are thin and so placed that four fingers may be held between the point of the breast bone and the end of the pelvic bone. This can be done only when the hen is a prolific layer and in full lay. Another test is that the points of the pelvic bone of a good layer stand wide apart. The disadvantage of this system is that if the best layers are examined when in full lay and examined again when not laying at all there will be a marked difference in the distances between both of these measurements. This is caused by a shrinkage in the abdomen when the hen is not laying.

Poultrymen of New York, New Jersey, and parts of Connecticut and Pennsylvania are partial to White Leghorns. The experts at the head of the poultry departments of these states have devised a plan for judging the past record of laying hens; in other words, they have devised a set of rules which may best be applied to laying hens during the fall to make certain which of them have produced the most eggs during the past year. The work done along this line in these several states was presented to a large gathering of poultry experts, poultry judges, and college professors at Cornell University early in July of 1918. All who had done work along this line presented the results obtained by them, and after considerable consultation a set of rules was adopted for judging fowls for good production. These rules are as follows:

A METHOD OF JUDGING FOWLS FOR EGG PRODUCTION

(Formulated at the Judging School held at Cornell University, Ithaca, N. Y., July 1-6, 1918, and approved by the American Association of Instructors and Investigators in Poultry Husbandry.)

In order to lay well a fowl must have a sound body. As a first consideration it must be vigorous and healthy if it is to be able to lay well. Vigor and health are shown by a bright, clear eye, a well-set body, a comparatively active disposition, and a good circulation. Further, the fowl must be free from physical defects such as crooked beak, long toe nails, eyelids that overhang so that it cannot see well, scaly leg, or anything that would keep it from seeing or getting an abundance of food.

In the illustration on the following page the parts of a fowl that receive particular attention in judging fowls for egg production are numbered, and the names of the numbered parts are given.

Loss of Fat Due to Laying.—A laying fowl uses up the surplus fat in the body, especially that just under the skin. In yellow-skinned breeds this loss of fat can

readily be seen by the loss of the yellow color. The different parts of the body tend to become white, according to the quantity of the fat stored in the body and the amount of circulation of blood through that part. The changes occur in the following order:

The vent changes very quickly with egg production so that white or pink vent on a yellow-skinned fowl gener-

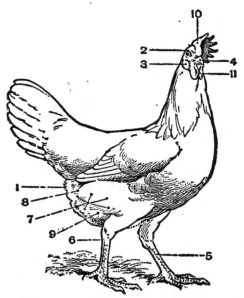

NAMES OF NUMBERED PARTS

1. Vent
2. Eye ring
3. Ear lobes
4. Beak
5. Shank
6. Heel of shank
7. Abdomen
8. Pelvic arches
9. Sternal processes
10. Comb
11. Wattles

ally indicates that it is laying; a yellow vent means the opposite. It should be recognized that all yellow color changes are dependent on the feed, coarseness of skin, and size of the fowl. A heavy fowl fed on an abundance of green feed or other material that will color the fat deep yellow will not bleach out nearly so quickly as one of a pale yellow color.

The eye ring, that is, the inner edges of the eyelids, bleach out a trifle more slowly than the vent. The ear lobes on Leghorns and Anconas bleach out a little more slowly than the eye ring, so that a bleached ear lobe means a little longer or greater production than a bleached vent or eyelid.

- The color goes out of the beak beginning at the base, and gradually disappears until it finally leaves the front part of the upper beak. The lower beak bleaches faster than the upper but may be used where the upper is obscured by horn or black. On the average-colored, yellow-skinned bird, a bleached beak means heavy production for at least 4 to 6 wk.

The *shanks* are the slowest to bleach out and hence indicate a much longer period of production than the other parts. The yellow goes out from the scales on the front of the shanks first and finally from the scales on the rear. The scales on the heel or rear of the hock joint of the shank are the last to bleach out and may generally be used as an index as to the natural depth of yellow color of the fowl. A bleached-out shank usually indicates fairly heavy production for at least 15 to 20 wk.

The yellow color comes back into the vent, eye ring, ear lobes, beak, and shanks in the same order that it went out, only the color returns much more quickly than it goes out. A vacation or rest period can sometimes be determined by the end of the beak being bleached and the base being yellow.

Body Changes Due to Laying.—A laying hen has a large, moist *vent* showing a dilated condition and looseness as compared with the hard, puckered vent of a non-laying hen.

The whole *abdomen* is dilated as well as the vent, so that the pelvic arches are widespread and the keel is forced down, away from the pelvic arches so as to give large capacity. The more eggs a fowl is going to lay the following week the greater will be the size of the abdomen. The actual size of the abdomen is, of course,

influenced by the size of eggs laid and by the size of the fowl.

Heavy production is shown by the quality of the *skin* and the thickness and stiffness of the *pelvic arches*. Fat goes out from the skin and body with production, so that the heavy producers have a soft, velvety skin that is not underlaid by layers of hard fat. The abdomen in particular is soft and pliable.

The *sternal processes* are very prominent and are generally bent outward. The thicker and blunter the pelvic arches and the greater the amount of hard fat in the abdomen the less the production or the longer time since production.

One of the finer indications, but yet one of the most valuable in picking a good layer is the fineness of the *head* and the closeness and dryness of *feathering*. The head of a high layer is fine. The wattles and ear lobes fit close to the beak and are not loose and flabby. The face is clean cut. The eye is full, round, and prominent, especially when seen from the front. The high layer is trimmer, that is, the feathers lie closer to the body, and after heavy production the oil does not keep the plumage relatively sleek and glossy but the plumage becomes worn and threadbare.

Changes in Secondary Sexual Characters.—The *comb*, *wattles*, and *ear lobes* enlarge or contract, depending on the ovary. If the comb, wattles, and ear lobes are large, full, and smooth, or hard and waxy, the bird is laying heavily. If the comb is limp, the bird is only laying slightly, and is not laying at all when the comb is dried down, especially at molting time. If the comb is warm, it is an indication that the fowl is coming back into production.

Molting.—When a fowl stops laying in the summer she usually begins to molt. The later a hen lays in the summer or the longer the period during which she lays, the greater will be her production, so that the high producer is the late layer and hence the late molter. The length of time that a hen has been molting or has

stopped laying can be determined by the molting of the primary feathers. It takes about 6 wk. to renew completely the primary feathers next to the axial feathers and an additional 2 wk. for each additional primary to be renewed.

Temperament and Activity.—A good layer is more active and nervous and yet more easily handled than a poor layer. A high layer shows more friendliness and yet elusiveness than a poor bird. A low producer is shy and stays on the edge of the flock and will squawk when caught.

While the characters discussed have dealt specifically with the one year's production, it should be borne in mind that a high producer one year is, generally speaking, a high producer in all other years.

SCORE CARD

The table on page 148 is a sample score of 15 White Leghorns that was made at Cornell University in July, 1918. The numbers 1, 2, 3, etc. refer to the grade in which the fowl is classed, 1 being the highest. The terms used are the same as those used in the preceding rules, as, for instance, vent, eye ring, etc. Abdomen and capacity are used quite like the ruling in the Hogan system. By studying carefully the rules for judging and this table you will have all the information relative to this work that has been evolved up to the time of the printing of this book. The number of eggs estimated and the number of actual eggs are shown in comparison. The estimate was made by the expert who examined the 15 White Leghorns and made this record card. The actual number of eggs laid, as shown in the last column, was obtained through the use of trap nests. In the table, x indicates a blank and the term **capacity** relates to capacity as an egg layer.

SCORE CARD TO CONFORM WITH THE CORNELL TEST

Band No.	Vent	Eye Ring	Ear Lobe	Beak	Shank	Comb	Molt	Abdomen	Capacity	Laying Now?	Estimate	Actual
1	1	1	1	1	1	1	x	2	2	Yes	52	51
2	1	1	2	x	1	3	x	4	4	No	15	34
3	1	1	x	1	1	1	x	3	2	Yes	95	100
4	1	1	x	1	1	1	x	2	2	Yes	110	74
5	2	2	x	2	2	1	x	3	2	Yes	47	72
6	1	1	x	1	1	1	x	1	3	Yes	125	109
7	1	1	x	1	1	1	x	1	1	Yes	147	101
8	2	1	x	1	1	1	x	3	2	Yes	135	45
9	1	2	x	2	3	2	x	1	2	No	65	44
10	1	1	x	1	1	1	x	1	2	No	138	103
11	2	1	x	1	3	1	x	1	1	Yes	141	142
12	1	2	2	3	4	1	x	1	2	No	52	15
13	1	2	1	3	1	1	x	1	2	No	90	97
14	1	1	1	2	1	1	x	1	2	Yes	136	124
15	2	1	1	2	1	1	x	2	2	Yes	115	114

BARRON METHOD OF SELECTING LAYERS

Thomas Barron, of England, was the first to make a careful study of the breeding of hens for egg production. He was very successful in this. His efforts aroused poultrymen throughout the world, and today in every land where poultry is kept there is an unusual effort being made to breed for better egg production. The results of these efforts have shown themselves very plainly in the increased number of eggs per hen laid throughout the civilized world.

Mr. Barron was the first to present a model in writing describing the physical characteristics of layers. This is his description:

Physical Characteristics of Layers

Size.—Medium for the breed, tending toward neither extreme.

Plumage.—Rather tight in feather.

Head.—Skull rather narrow, with full, bright eye. Rather short, stout bill. Comb fine in texture. Size not as important as texture.

Neck.—Rather long, not too thick.

Body.—Breast prominent and rather long. Back long and wide across the hips. Good cushion. In short, a square-built bird with body held at such an angle as to throw the stern much lower than the breast.

Legs.—Medium in length and set well apart.

Tail.—Carried rather high.

The whole appearance of the bird should be trim and active.

I also pay some attention to the pelvic bones, the pointed bones, which may be felt just above the vent. These should be well separated.

The above, in brief, outlines my method of breeding and selecting heavy layers. It is given to the poultrymen of America in the hope that it may be of benefit to them.

THOMAS BARRON

ARTIFICIAL LIGHT TO INCREASE EGG PRODUCTION

By the use of artificial light in the laying houses, it has been found possible to make hens lay more eggs during the months when the daylight is shortest and the price of eggs is highest.

Writing in February, 1919, Professor James E. Rice, of Cornell University, says: "One of the most sensational developments of modern poultry husbandry is the discovery that by the use of artificial light as an aid to feeding and activity the distribution of egg production throughout the year can be radically changed. So great is the change and so certain the results when artificial light is properly applied to the right kind of stock, in conjunction with proper methods of feeding, that it is destined to revolutionize egg production and the market egg receipts.

"It will have the double effect of (1) materially increasing the production and hence the market receipts of the autumn and early winter eggs, and (2) proportionately decreasing the production and receipts during the spring and early summer months.

"The place where the most marked results from the use of artificial light are seen is in the more rapid development of late-maturing pullets and hens which under normal conditions would not have laid until toward spring. Here the difference due to the use of artificial light is truly surprising. Here also is where the largest profits are to be made by aiding the hens to lay the eggs in the autumn and winter months when they are normally highest in price, instead of boarding the hens until spring and then getting the same eggs when they are cheap. Then, however, nearly as many eggs are produced in the spring as if the hens had not laid during the autumn and winter. Those which have ceased to lay in the spring after a winter of heavy production can

be sold on a higher priced market than was available for the same fowls in the previous autumn."

Probably thirty to forty commercial egg farms in New Jersey tested, in 1918-1919, the use of artificial illumination for increasing egg production during the short-day period from September 1 to March 1. Fourteen of these plants reported monthly to the Poultry Department of the State Agricultural College, New Brunswick, N. J., where the records were inspected by Harry R. Lewis, Professor of Poultry Husbandry, and placed in charge of his assistant for compilation. It is expected that a Bulletin telling of the results of these experiments will be published by the State Agricultural College, New Brunswick, N. J. A complete thesis on the subject can be obtained from the *Reliable Poultry Journal,* Quincy, Ill.

The theory advanced is that the use of artificial light in the poultry houses allows the hens more hours for eating, thus giving them as much time for feeding as they would ordinarily have in the spring and the additional food eaten results in increased number of eggs.

Electric lights are used where they can be had at a reasonable price. Lanterns are made especially for this purpose and some use tubular lanterns. The houses are lighted from 4:30 P. M. until 8 or 10 P. M., and from 5 A. M. till daylight.

MARKET POULTRY .

Digestibility of Poultry and Other Foods.—In poultry and other meats and fish, about 70% of the protein, 95% of the fat, and 98% of the carbohydrates are digestible. The food principles in vegetable foods are not as fully digestible, for in such foods only about 84% of the protein, 90% of the fat, and 97% of the carbohydrates are digestible.

In the table giving ,the comparison of poultry and certain other foods is shown the composition of some foodstuffs, and it will be seen from this that poultry meat compares very favorably in food value with beef, fish, eggs, milk, and potatoes. On an average, the various kinds of poultry furnish not far from 5% more protein and a little more ash than do the other kinds of meat included in the table. On the other hand, the poultry meats

SILVER-GRAY DORKING

most used—chicken and fowl—contain relatively little fat and have a relatively small fuel value. Pound for pound, poultry contains `a trifle more of the building materials required by the body, but furnishes less of the energy-giving materials than the fat meats. As a general thing, young fowls contain less refuse than older ones, which means that the proportion of total bone weight is smaller; their flesh also contains more water, which indicates that it is not so solid and compact as in older fowls.

COMPARISON OF POULTRY AND CERTAIN OTHER FOODS

Kind of Food	Refuse Per Cent.	Indigestible Nutrients Per Cent.	Water Per Cent.	Protein Per Cent.	Fat Per Cent.	Carbohydrates Per Cent.	Ash Per Cent.	Fuel Value per Pound Calories
Chicken: As purchased..	18.8	.9	55.5	17.3	6.8		.7	749.85
Edible portion..........		1.2	68.4	21.2	8.4		.8	921.71
Fowl: As purchased.....	25.2	1.0	47.3	14.0	12.0		.5	880.89
Edible portion.........		1.7	59.5	19.8	18.2		.8	1,297.66
Turkey: As purchased..	14.3	1.9	49.2	18.4	15.4		.8	1,142.08
Edible portion........		2.2	57.4	21.5	18.0		.9	1,334.72
Duck: As purchased	15.9	1.8	51.4	14.9	15.2		.8	1,039.97
Edible portion........		2.0	61.1	17.8	18.1		1.0	1,239.91
As purchased	11.1	1.5	48.0	14.4	24.2		.8	1,406.25
Edible portion		1.8	54.0	16.1	27.3		.8	1,582.52
Miscellaneous foods: Beef, sirloin steak, as purchased.........	12.8	1.2	54.0	16.0	15.3		.7	1,073.63
Halibut, fresh steaks, as purchased........	17.7	.7	61.9	14.8	4.2		.7	573.26
Eggs, as purchased.....	11.2	2.3	65.5	11.5	8.8		.7	679.00
Milk..............		.6	87.0	3.2	3.8	4.9	.5	334.85
Wheat bread, white...;		3.4	35.6	7.9	1.1	51.1	.9	1,184.98
Potatoes, as purchased.	20.0	.9	62.6	1.5	.1	14.3	.6	303.82

Loss of Weight in Dressing Fowls.—On an average, nearly one-third of the total weight of a fowl is lost in dressing and in preparing it for cooking. In the case of fowls thin in flesh, the loss is much greater than this. The least waste occurs in fowls that have been properly fattened. Excessively fat fowls and also those that are poor in flesh show a large proportion of waste on being dressed.

The table showing the loss in dressing fowls is a summary of an investigation at the Storrs Experiment Station, Connecticut. In this experiment fowls in all conditions—well-fattened, thin, and excessively fat—were used, and their weights at different stages in the process of dressing were noted. Consequently the results given in the table may be considered as applicable to average conditions.

LOSS IN DRESSING FOWLS

Kind of Fowls	Number of Birds	Live Weight Pounds	Weight— Bled and Plucked Pounds	Loss Per Cent.	Weight— Intestines, Head, and Feet Removed Pounds	Loss Per Cent.
Cocks.....	18	127.9	117.9	7.8	97.8	23.5
Cockerels .	278	1,773.0	1,577.5	11.0	1,312.0	26.0
Hens	201	1,195.0	1,103.4	7.7	906.3	24.2
Pullets....	47	261.1	240.0	8.1	193.7	25.8
Total...	544	3,357.0	3,038.8	9.5	2,509.8	25.2

The per cent. loss in dressing fowls of different breeds is given in the following table.

Classes of Market Poultry.—There are two general classes of market poultry, the heavy-weight and the medium-weight. The heavy-weight class includes such fowls as the Brahmas, Cochins, Dorkings, and Orpingtons.

LOSS IN DRESSING FOWLS OF DIFFERENT BREEDS

Breed of Fowls	Number of Birds	Live Weight Pounds	Weight— Bled and Plucked Pounds	Loss Per Cent.	Weight— Intestines, Head, and Feet Removed Pounds	Loss Per Cent.
Barred Plymouth Rocks	187	1,199.9	1,090.8	9.1	910.4	24.1
White Plymouth Rocks	125	859.1	779.4	9.3	644.7	25.0
White Wyandottes	103	618.2	558.3	9.7	460.8	25.5
Buff Wyandottes	6	39.4	35.2	10.7	28.5	27.7
Rhode Island Reds	18	109.7	98.0	10.7	80.2	26.9
Black Langshans	32	200.5	182.7	8.9	151.4	24.5
Single-Comb White Leghorns	22	88.3	78.0	11.7	62.1	29.7
Rose-Comb Brown Leghorns	35	129.6	116.0	10.5	90.4	30.2
White Wyandotte-Light Brahma cross	16	112.3	100.4	10.6	81.3	27.6
Total	544	3,357.0	3,038.8	9.5	2,509.8	25.2

The medium-weight class includes such general-purpose fowls as the Wyandottes and Barred Plymouth Rocks. In addition to these fowls, broilers and other small market fowls are often made from Leghorns and crosses of Leghorns with some of the general-purpose fowls.

Classes of Broilers and Roasters.—Broilers are divided into three classes: squab broilers, spring broilers, and fryers or large broilers or small roasters. *Squab broilers* range in size from ¾ to 1 lb. each in weight. They are used by hotels and restaurants during the winter and early spring. *Spring broilers* are used a little later in the season. When plump they range in weight from 1 to 1½ lb. The weight demanded increases as the season advances, until the 2-lb. size is most popular. *Fryers, large broilers,* or *small roasters* range in weight from 2 to 3 lb. Roasters are generally of two kinds: plump, meaty roasters and soft roasters.

The time required to produce broilers and roasters is shown in the accompanying table. The time required for a chick to grow to marketable size depends largely on the quality of the chick and its breed. Not all breeds mature alike, and the individuals of any one breed will not develop at a uniform rate, but when bred and fed as they ought to be the average is about as indicated in the table.

TIME REQUIRED TO RAISE BROILERS AND ROASTERS

Breeds of Fowls	Growth, in Pounds, in 8 Wk.	Growth, in Pounds, in 10 Wk.	Growth, in Pounds, in 12 Wk.	Growth, in Pounds, in 21 Wk.	Growth, in Pounds, in 26 Wk.	Growth, in Pounds, in 30 Wk.
Leghorns		1	1¼			
American breeds	1	1½	2	4	6	7
English and Belgian breeds	1	1½	2	4	6	7
Brahmas	1¼	2	2¼	5	7	9

KILLING AND PLUCKING OF POULTRY.

Killing.—The most satisfactory methods of killing poultry are by dislocating the neck, and by sticking in the roof of the mouth and piercing the brain with a knife.

In *killing by dislocating the neck*, the fowl is held in front of the operator with the head hanging down; both shanks are firmly grasped with the left hand; the neck of the fowl at the base of the skull is taken between the thumb and forefinger of the right hand, with the back of the hand toward the tail of the fowl and the head held firmly in the palm of the hand; the head is then pulled downwards to extend the neck to its full length; the final step in the operation is taken by pulling with a jerk the already taut neck and at the same time twisting the head upwards. This will dislocate the head from the backbone, paralyzing the fowl, snap the arteries in the neck, and pull the head away from the neck, leaving a cavity in the neck large enough to hold the blood of the fowl. In this operation no blood will escape from the body, and it is preferred by some as the best method of killing fowls intended for immediate sale. When such fowls are prepared for cooking, if the head is severed 1 or 2 in. back of where the blood has settled, all of the blood clot will be removed.

Killing by sticking in the roof of the mouth may be done with a special killing knife or with a common pocket knife that has a sharp point and blade. Both shanks of the fowl are tied with a small piece of rope and the loose end of the rope is tied to some support so that the fowl will hang head downwards and at about the height of the operator's shoulder. The head of the fowl is grasped in the left hand, the mouth pressed open, and the blade of the knife thrust through the roof of the mouth and up into the brain almost in a line with the eye; a cross-cut is made to sever the arteries. This operation paralyzes the fowl instantly, and the cutting

of the arteries allows the fowl to bleed freely from the mouth. To avoid being splashed with blood, the mouth of the fowl should be held away from the operator. This method of killing is commonly practiced in most market poultry establishments.

Plucking.— To make the best appearance when offered for sale in the market, a fowl must be plucked carefully so that the skin will not be torn. An experienced plucker will rub the feathers down the wrong way both on the back and breast, using the flat of his hand to press down and open up the plumage. When the feathers are

HOUDAN

separated in this way they may be quickly plucked from the body by holding the shanks and the tips of the feathers in the hand. The feathers should first be pulled from the back, then from the breast and body, leaving only the long, stiff feathers. These should be plucked and placed by themselves. The best plan is to put the long feathers or those having heavy quills into a box or barrel separate from the smaller or lighter feathers. With some practice the operator will soon learn to remove all of the feathers quickly from the body of the fowl. The process should begin immediately after the fowl has been killed. By whatever method it is killed, the feathers will come away easier immediately after killing than they will after the body of the fowl has cooled and become set.

The practice of scalding before plucking is generally followed. The chief difficulty in this is that the fowls are dipped into water that is too hot and are frequently kept immersed so long that the skin is scalded and breaks and pulls from the body, leaving an ugly dark

complexion. In scalding the fowls, the water should not be boiling when they are immersed, nor should boiling hot water be poured over them. They should be immersed in water not quite boiling, and as quickly as the feathers are thoroughly soaked they should be plucked gently from the body. Great care should be taken not to tear the flesh or skin.

POULTRY PRICES

A careful inspection of poultry prices over a period of years shows plainly that market poultry of good quality will sell at the highest prices from the middle of Dec. to the end of June. This is due, to a large extent, to the scarcity of farm-grown poultry in the market during these months.

The condition in which poultry is offered for sale has an important influence on the price it will sell for. The relative selling price per pound live weight, plucked weight, and drawn weight of the same fowl is shown in the accompanying table. The plucked weight is the weight of the fowl with the feathers removed but with the head and feet left on. The drawn weight is the weight with the head, feet, and entrails removed and the fowl ready for cooking. It will be seen from this table that the selling price per pound, plucked weight, is about 33⅓% more than the live weight, and that the price per pound, drawn weight, is about 100% greater

MARKET VALUE OF FOWLS AT DIFFERENT STAGES

Live Weight Cents per Pound	Plucked Weight Cents per Pound	Drawn Weight Cents per Pound
9	12¼	18¼
10	13½	20
11	14½	22
12	16	23½

than for the live weight, and about 50% greater than for the plucked weight. This increase in the selling price is due, of course, to the removal of the waste parts and also to the labor entailed. The table furnishes a guide to decide the price to be fixed on the plucked or drawn weight of any grade of poultry.

BREEDING

The most important systems of breeding poultry for exhibition are *line breeding, inbreeding, strain breeding,* and *cross-breeding.* In any system of breeding, only the best breeding fowls obtainable should ever be used in the breeding pen. All fowls having defects should be promptly discarded, even if this leaves only two or three fowls in the breeding pen. Fully enough poor specimens come from the best matings, and so few good specimens come from matings in which either of the fowls are defective that time and money is wasted in such breeding. Only fowls having the proper size, shape, and color required for the variety can produce satisfactory offspring. The plan of mating fowls defective in one section with other fowls having excellent quality in the corresponding section usually results in the production of offspring having not more than medium quality in that section.

Line Breeding.—Line breeding is a system of breeding from a limited number of original fowls, in which the fowls mated SILVER LACED WYANDOTTE are not so closely related as in inbreeding; line breeding is really a modified form of inbreeding. Line breeding is often continued for a number of years without the introduction of new blood into the

flock, but in such cases great care is taken to breed from only the healthiest and most vigorous members of the flock. To maintain the vitality of the flock, only mature hens in their second or third year of laying are bred from. The success of any work in line breeding depends on the quality of the original fowls that are selected as breeders, and the judgment with which the later breeders are selected, both for their quality and for their vitality.

Inbreeding.—Inbreeding is a system of breeding in which the fowls mated are very closely related, being direct descendants of a very few original fowls. Inbreeding differs materially from line breeding on account of the closeness of the relationship of the fowls. The best fowls produced each year are mated with breeders of the previous season and with each other, even to the extent of pairing brother with sister. Inbreeding is carried on chiefly with a view to improving color in a flock. Shape may be improved by this system of breeding, but this is not usually the case. Loss of size and deterioration of shape are undesirable features that usually attend inbreeding, and the maintenance of vitality is also a serious problem. The undesirable consequences of inbreeding can be avoided only by the most careful attention to the details of breeding and to the selection of the breeding fowls. In most cases, the introduction of new blood into the breeding stock will be necessary.

Strain Breeding.—Strain breeding is a system of breeding consisting in breeding fowls of one variety in line for a number of generations from a few original fowls; this breeding must also be conducted by one breeder, or his successors. A strain cannot be said to be established, even after three or four generations of breeding, unless the indications are plain that the original fowls selected for the foundation of the strain have been able to transmit their characters through the series of generations, and also to cause the production of offspring of better quality than themselves.

From the preceding statements, it is evident that a valuable strain can be produced only by the most careful selection of the foundation stock, and the most skilful breeding during the succeeding generations. Chance breeding cannot be relied on to produce satisfactory results.

Cross-Breeding.—Cross-breeding is of two kinds: breeding together of fowls of different breeds; and breeding together of fowls of the same variety but which come from different localities or from different strains. Most commonly, cross-breeding is understood to be the mating together of fowls of different breeds, such, for instance, as a Plymouth Rock to a Wyandotte, or a Rhode Island Red to an Indian Game. This form of cross-breeding is often utilized in the production of broilers and roasters for market, the offspring from such crosses being useless for breeding together. The other form of cross-breeding, or of breeding for an out-cross, is usually practiced in the breeding of poultry for exhibition, and for the purpose of introducing new blood into a strain to improve vitality.

WHITE WYANDOTTE

Methods of Mating.—Mating is the act of pairing a male and a female for the purpose of producing offspring. The two general methods of mating are single mating and double mating. Single mating consists in mating together a male and a female.

When fowls are mated for the production, from the same pair, of both male and female offspring fit for exhibition, the process is called *single mating*. This is the method of mating commonly practiced in the mating of fowls of most varieties. This method of mating does not, however, produce the best results when the production of the most delicately marked fowls of the varieties most difficult to produce is desired.

The mating of one pair of fowls for the purpose of producing male offspring fit for exhibition and another pair for the production of female offspring fit for exhibition is called *double mating*. This is practiced to a great extent in the production of Barred Plymouth Rocks, Brown Leghorns, partridge-colored fowls of all breeds, and to some extent in producing fowls that have penciling or lacing in their plumage. In double mating, great care is taken to see that the male and the female blood lines are kept separate, for if blood lines are crossed, color will be injured.

ENEMIES AND DISEASES OF POULTRY

ENEMIES

GENERAL REMARKS

A *parasite* is any creature that secures the whole or part of its living from another. The parasites that attack poultry are insects.

Methods of Infestation by Parasites.—Poultry become infested with parasites in many ways, and it is advisable for the poultryman to keep a close watch to prevent such infestation. Some of the most common ways in which poultry becomes infested with parasites are: (1) by the introduction of an infested fowl into a flock; (2) by a hen infesting her chicks when they are incubated or brooded in a natural way; (3) by allowing infested fowls to roam at liberty; (4) by sparrows; (5) by the parasites crawling up on roosts that are not protected by safety appliances; (6) by the parasites dropping on the fowls from the ceilings of houses; (7) in nest boxes; (8) in dust baths.

Effects of Parasites on Poultry.—Parasites cause more disease, ill health, and death among poultry than all

other causes combined. The following are the principal specific effects resulting from parasites: (1) They reduce the vitality of poultry; (2) they lessen egg production; (3) they deduct from the table qualities of fowls intended for market poultry; (4) they interfere with the proper performance of the natural duties of incubating and brooding; (5) they cause the loss of parts of a fowl's body; (6) they infest poultry with other and additional varieties of parasites; (7) they infect poultry with fungous and bacterial diseases.

Rapidity of Reproduction of Poultry Parasites.—The exact time required for poultry parasites to produce new generations cannot be stated definitely. Under favorable conditions, however, all kinds of poultry parasites are very prolific and will increase to an alarming extent. Salmon states that the third generation from a single louse may number more than 120,000, and all of these may be produced within a period of 8 wk. Such a rapid increase being possible, the result of introducing into a flock a fowl that is thoroughly infested with parasites can readily be surmised. Such a fowl is sure to do injury.

Poultry parasites multiply particularly fast in damp, filthy, unsanitary places—surroundings that are unfavorable to poultry even when not infested with parasites. Poultry parasites, however, will also develop rapidly in clean places if the air is allowed to remain hot and moist for any length of time.

PARASITES ATTACKING DOMESTIC FOWLS

The parasites that are found occasionally on domestic poultry are: Large chicken louse (*Goniocotes abdominalis*); lesser chicken louse (*Goniocotes hologaster*). The *Goniodes dissimilis* and the *Goniocotes burnettii* are rarely found on fowls.

A louse that is sometimes found on fowls and which does considerable damage to the feathers when present in large numbers is the variable chicken louse, or feather louse (*Lipeurus variabilis*).

The parasites that frequently infest domestic poultry are: Common hen louse (*Menopon pallidum*); red mite, chicken mite, or red spider louse (*Dermanyssus gallinae*); itch, or scab, mite (*Cnemidocoptes laevis,* var. *gallinae*), scaly leg mite (*Cnemidocoptes mutans*).

The parasites infesting turkeys, peafowls, and guinea fowls, in addition to the common hen louse and the red mite are *Lipeurus polytrapezius, Goniodes' stylifer, Goniocotes rectangulatus, Goniodes falcicornis,* and similar ones.

The parasites most commonly infesting water fowls are *Trinoton luridum; Lipeurus squalidus,* which is commonly found on ducks; *Trinoton lituratum; Ornithobius cygni,* which is commonly found on geese; and *Docophorus cygni,* which is commonly found on swans.

The parasites most commonly infesting pigeons are: Common pigeon louse (*Goniocotes compar*), *Lipeurus baculus, Goniodes damicornis,* and two varieties of fleas.

INSECTICIDES

The substances that are used to kill insects are called *insecticides.* The three general classes of insecticides that are employed to kill the parasites that infest poultry are powders, liquids, and fumes. The powders have to be dusted on the bodies of the parasites so that the fine particles of the material will be drawn into the breathing tubes of the insects. These tubes are thus clogged, and the insect dies of suffocation. The liquids kill because they are corrosive or because they get into the breathing tubes of the insects and suffocate. The fumes employed kill because they suffocate.

All poultry parasites except mites can be kept under control, so far as their presence on the bodies of birds is concerned, by the use of insect powders. Insect powders, however, are not so efficient for destroying parasites about poultry buildings as liquid and fume insecticides. Insecticides containing arsenic, such as Paris green, or other deadly poisons, should never be used about poultry buildings, as they are likely to poison both poultry and attendants.

Powder Insecticides.—To be suitable for killing the parasites of poultry that can be destroyed by powders, a powder must be very fine—at least as fine as ordinary road dust—perfectly dry, and not possess any adhesive qualities. Many kinds of powders are used for destroying the parasites of poultry. They consist of substances that range from the most deadly poisons to the most harmless materials, and from ill-smelling powders to those that have no odor. No advantage is gained by using either poisonous or offensive smelling powders to kill the parasites of poultry, and they are dangerous both to the poultry and the person applying them.
Some of the many kinds of insect powders are mentioned and briefly described here because one or more of them can be found in any locality. The powders described do not include those that are specially prepared and sold in packages under a trade name. Any of the following powders may safely be used for dusting on poultry of *all kinds.*

Aniseed powder is made from the seed of the anise plant, which grows in many parts of Europe. This powder is suitable for use about young chicks, poults, ducklings, and goslings.

Pyrethrum powder is also commonly known as *Persian* or *Dalmatian* insect powder and as *Buhach.* It is usually sold by the pound in drug stores. This powder is commonly made from the dry flowers of certain species of chrysanthemums which are grown in Persia, Dalmatia, and neighboring lands, and in California. When pure, this powder is one of the very best powders that can be used for dusting into the plumage of fowls, both old and young.

Fine tobacco dust, which is a refuse from tobacco factories, is an effective insecticide. It is suitable for dusting into nests, and will destroy body lice. Tobacco dust has the disadvantage that it will stick to the skin of the fowls. It also has a disagreeable odor, which is intensified by the heat and moisture of the bodies of the birds.

Stavesacre seed powder is made from the seed of a species of larkspur that grows in Southern Europe. It is a poisonous substance, and delphinin, a poisonous drug, is made from this seed. When fine, this powder is a good insecticide.

Dry. air-slaked lime makes an effective insect powder on account of its extreme fineness.

Road dust will answer as an insecticide when used alone, provided it is very fine. It is also used as a base to mix with finely ground powders to make insecticides. To make sure that road dust is fine enough to be valuable as an insecticide, it should be passed through a very fine sieve, similar to that used by druggists for separating the coarser from the finer particles in a powder.

Compound insect powders composed as follows will be found effective:

1. Fine road dust that has been carefully sieved and mixed with an equal quantity of Pyrethrum

WHITE LEGHORNS

powder. This will be very effective provided the Pyrethrum powder is pure and the road dust very fine.

2. Equal parts of air-slaked lime, tobacco dust, and fine dust from coal ashes. If very fine and dry, this mixture will be suitable for dusting into nest boxes or on the bodies of fowls. It may, however, adhere to the bodies of the fowls and cause irritation.

Liquid Insecticides.—Liquid insecticides are more effective for application to the interior of poultry buildings than powder insecticides, for the reason that they can be sprayed into all the cracks and crevices. When thoroughly applied, a good liquid insecticide will rid

a house of practically all the parasites that are in it. Some insects such as red mites can conveniently be exterminated only by the use of liquid insecticides. When liquid insecticides of any kind are used as either a spray or a· paint, on poultry buildings, they should be allowed to soak into the wood and dry thoroughly before the fowls are permitted to go inside of the building. Liquid insecticides of some kinds may also be applied to the bodies of poultry.

Some liquid insecticides are applied by themselves without dilution or combination with any other material; in the form of an emulsion with other liquids; or with other materials in solution in them. A description of the principal liquid insecticides in use at the present time follows:

Creosote is widely used as an insecticide. It is also known in some localities as *crude carbolic acid* and as *creosote stain.* Creosote is a coal-tar product. It is not an expensive material and is usually sold in paint stores. In large quantities it can be purchased at from 40c. to 50c. per gal., and in small quantities at from 80c. to $1 per gal. Creosote is used for shingle stains and as a wood preservative for many other kinds of woodwork. If it is desired to color the inside or outside of the houses to which creosote is to be applied, dry paint can be added to it. Creosote is the best liquid insecticide for spraying on the interior of poultry houses. Two or three applications of this material will rid any building or coop of insect vermin of all kinds.

Creosote bought at different times and in different places will not always be of the same viscosity or thickness. When very thick it may need to be diluted in the proportion of 1 part of creosote to from 3 to 4 parts of kerosene oil, in order to get it in the proper condition for spraying. Thinner samples of creosote may need to be diluted with only 2 parts of kerosene oil to make it suitable for spraying. For painting roost poles and nest boxes, the thinner kind of creosote is commonly used without any dilution; the thicker kind is usually

diluted with 2 parts of kerosene oil when used for this purpose. Roost poles may also be satisfactorily painted with a wash made up of equal parts of creosote and hot water. When roost poles and nest boxes are treated with this mixture, they should be allowed to dry in the sun before being put back in the house; when the roost poles are put back in the house their ends should be painted with a coat of the undiluted thick creosote. A mixture of 2½ gal. of creosote, 2½ gal. of water, and 1 lb. of washing soda will also make an effective wash for nests, roosts, and brood coops. If this is used hot and applied in a spray, its effectiveness will be increased.

After a house has been thoroughly freed of parasites, the roost poles and the interior of the nest boxes should be coated with one of the above mixtures of creosote once a week for a month, and occasionally thereafter. This work should always be done before noon so that the creosote will have time to dry before night.

Crude petroleum is an inflammable oily liquid from which a number of other oils that are used for commercial purposes are obtained by processes of refining. It is also called *coal oil, earth oil, mineral oil, natural oil, rock oil,* and *Seneca oil.* Crude petroleum is a dark brown to greenish liquid.

Kerosene is an inflammable oil distilled from crude petroleum or any mineral hydrocarbon. Kerosene is suitable for spraying the interior of poultry houses, but is not well suited for applying to the bodies of fowls. Inflamed eyes, blisters, and sore spots on the skin will result when kerosone is applied direct. It is absolutely unfit to use on the bodies of young chicks.

Benzine is a colorless, inflammable, and volatile liquid obtained from distillation of crude petroleum. While it is often used as an insecticide, it is dangerous to handle because of its inflammability.

Gasoline is also a colorless, volatile, and inflammable liquid obtained from the distillation of crude petroleum. It is dangerous to handle for the same reason that benzine is dangerous.

Turpentine is a product of such trees as the pine and other similar trees. It is much used in the making of paints and varnishes and also in medicine. It is inflammable and will irritate the skin.

Creoline, a liquid manufactured especially for use as an insecticide, is effective in killing the insect enemies of poultry. Creoline may be used in the interior of poultry houses diluted in the proportion of 3 fluid oz. of creoline to 1 gal. of water.

Carbolic acid is largely used in the destruction of poultry parasites. A solution made of 1½ fluid oz. of carbolic acid to 1 gal. of water is strong enough for this purpose. Carbolic acid is sometimes added to whitewash so that sanitary conditions can be improved at the same time that an insecticide is applied. When used in this way, however, carbolic acid does not have as effective insecticidal properties as when it is used without whitewash.

Milk emulsion is usually first made up in a concentrated or stock solution, or cream solution as it is sometimes called, and then diluted just before it is applied. To make the stock solution, add 2 gal. of kerosene to 1 gal. of milk and churn or mix thoroughly with a force pump or other agitator. This stock solution should be diluted in the proportion of 1 gal. of the stock solution to 4 gal. of warm water. Crude petroleum, benzine, gasoline, or turpentine may be substituted for kerosene in this formula. Kerosene, however, can usually be purchased cheaper than the other liquids except crude petroleum.

Soap emulsion is also usually first made up in a stock solution and then diluted just before it is to be applied. To make a stock solution of soap emulsion, dissolve 1 lb. of hard soap in 1 gal. of hot water; when the soap has all dissolved and while the solution is hot, add 2 gal. of kerosene; mix thoroughly with a force pump or an agitator of some kind. When to be used for spraying the interior of poultry houses, this stock solution should be diluted in the proportion of 1 gal. of the stock solution

to 4 gal. of water. Crude petroleum, benzine, gasoline, or turpentine may be substituted for kerosene in this formula also.

Liquid lice killer is a name frequently applied to an insecticide made from kerosene oil and powdered naphthalene flakes or balls, in the proportion of 2 lb. of naphthalene to 1 gal. of kerosene. The can containing this solution should be covered so that the liquid will not leak out of it, and the solution should be agitated frequently by shaking. The solution should be allowed to remain in this can about a week, when it should be poured into another receptacle, so that another batch can be mixed if necessary. If 2 fluid oz. of creoline or of creosote are added to the clear solution, the effectiveness of the solution will be improved. The cans containing this solution should be kept in a temperature that never goes below 40° F. or the naphthalene will go out of solution and appear in flakes. The solution should be kept for about 24 hr. in a warm place before it is used, so that it will be at about 70° to 80° F. when it is applied. This solution should never be kept close to a fire, nor should any attempt be made to heat it over or near a fire, as it is inflammable. This liquid lice killer may be used for either painting or spraying the interior of poultry houses and brood coops.

Compound liquid insecticides made up according to the following formulas may be used with safety on the bodies of young chicks: 1 oz. of oil of sassafras to 2 or 3 oz. of sweet oil; 1 oz. of oil of aniseed to 3 oz. of sweet oil.

Lard can also be rubbed on the heads and throats of young chicks for use as an insecticide.

Whitewash is not effective as an insecticide unless it is mixed with carbolic acid in the proportion of 1½ fluid oz. of carbolic acid to 1 gal. of whitewash. Even when containing carbolic acid, however, it cannot be depended on to kill mites. If applied hot, the effectiveness of this mixture will be increased. Whitewash applied by itself will not kill insects unless it happens

to so completely cover them that the creatures will drown in it. Whitewash can be recommended to help maintain sanitary conditions about a poultry house, but unfortunately when it is used it often gives the poultryman a false sense of security against parasites and frequently causes him to neglect the proper measures to exterminate the insect enemies of his poultry.

Fume Insecticides.—Fume insecticides are produced by burning various substances. Fumes that are extremely poisonous should not be used for killing poultry parasites, as there is no necessity for their use, and persons, animals, and the poultry may be accidentally exposed to them. The following can be recommended as effective on parasites, and not necessarily fatal to other creatures if inhaled in small quantities, though they will prove fatal to any person, animal, or bird if inhaled in sufficient quantities:

Sulphur fumes can be produced by burning sulphur. Either lump sulphur, which is frequently called brimstone, sulphur candles, or powdered sulphur can be used for this purpose. The powdered sulphur will produce fumes more rapidly than the lump sulphur. The sulphur should be placed in an iron pot or pan to avoid fire and should be moistened with some inflammable liquid to make it burn more freely.

Tobacco fumes may be produced by burning any kind of tobacco. Such fumes are usually produced by burning the waste leaves or stems of the tobacco plant, as these can be purchased cheaply. The tobacco stems or leaves should be placed in an iron receptacle of some kind to avoid the danger from fire and should also be moistened with some inflammable liquid to make them burn quickly.

Creosote fumes or *liquid lice-killer fumes* are sometimes used for killing the parasites on a few fowls confined in a small space. This treatment is difficult to perform and dangerous to use.

INSTRUMENTS FOR APPLYING INSECTICIDES

Powder Guns.—Insect powders can be applied by hand, but they are more effectively applied by the use of powder guns. A small powder gun is shown in Fig. 1. This will answer when only a few fowls are to be dusted, but where there are a large number of fowls to dust, a larger powder gun will be required. A bellows powder gun is shown in Fig. 2. With this it will be

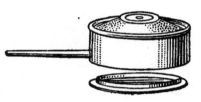

FIG. 1

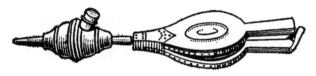

FIG. 2

possible to dust a large number of fowls in a short time. This can be used at night by going about among the fowls and quietly inserting the point of the gun among the feathers of the fowls while on the roost, and in this way dust them thoroughly.

Sprayers.—Liquid insecticides can be most effectively and economically applied in spray form. Where there is only a small surface to go over, a small hand-spraying outfit similar to that shown in Fig. 3 will answer. Where a large amount of surface has to be covered, a spraying outfit like that shown in Fig. 4 will be found more convenient. There are many makes of these com-

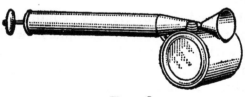

FIG. 3

pressed-air sprayers on the market. Those with galvanized-iron receptacles for the liquid will answer for

spraying insecticides but will not prove satisfactory for spraying Bordeaux mixture on plants. By using spray pumps to apply insecticides, a large quantity of liquid is saved as compared with applying them by means of a brush, and the insecticide is also applied more effectively. When applied in a fine spray, it penetrates into the cracks and crevices in the building and forms an even covering over the flat surfaces.

FIG. 4

KILLING OF PARASITES

A constant watch must be kept for parasites, because from the moment chicks come from the shell they are menaced by insect vermin. The most practical way of meeting the problem is continually to practice preventive measures.

If poultry parasites are allowed to become numerous they will sap the vitality of the fowls, and although the parasites themselves may be gotten rid of, it will be impossible to restore the physical condition of the fowls. For application to poultry houses, liquid and fume insecticides are most effective, but usually liquid insecticides are the more convenient to apply. Powder insecticides are ordinarily effective on the bodies of fowls, but it must be borne in mind that they will not kill all classes of parasites.

Houses that are maintained in a cleanly condition, well lighted with sunlight, and free from dampness will never be badly infested with parasites, if they are given regular sprayings with some good liquid insecticide. Nothing can take the place of sanitary conditions as a preventive measure, but sanitary conditions combined with regular spraying is most effective.

Prevention of Infestation by Fowls From Other Flocks. To avoid the chance of carrying parasites into a house

or to a flock that is free from parasites, all fowls brought in from other flocks should be kept in a sort of quarantine by themselves and specially treated for a number of days. The place of quarantine should be a small coop or cage that is free from parasites. For a period of about 10 da. some effective powder insecticide should be frequently dusted into the feathers of such fowls. To do this, the fowl should be held in one hand by the shanks, with the head hanging down, and the insect powder should be worked into the feathers of every part of the body and down on to the skin with the fingers of the other hand. In especially bad cases, a thorough washing should follow this dusting.

Method of Ridding a Poultry House of Parasites.—The thorough cleaning of a poultry house that has become badly infested with parasites is a difficult problem and drastic measures are required. If the building is a cheap affair, like a small coop, it is often best to burn it, but burning would be too expensive in the case of a large poultry house. Before attempting to clean a poultry house, all the fowls should be removed to other quarters, dusted with insect powder and kept by themselves until the house cleaning is completed. To get a badly infested poultry house in good sanitary condition and free from parasites will require several days. The following treatment will be found effective, but in exceptionally bad cases a repetition of the treatment may be necessary.

1. The house should be thoroughly fumigated. After removing the poultry, stop up every crack and crevice, so that the fumes will not escape. A number of substances can be used for fumigation, but sulphur and tobacco are the ones that can be recommended. If either of these are used they should be burned in some metallic receptacle such as an iron pot or kettle, to avoid fire. If these substances are moistened with some inflammable material they will burn more freely. Whatever material is burned to produce the fumes, enough of it should be used so that the interior of the

building will be filled with enough fumes to darken it. The building should be kept tightly closed for 24 hr.

2. The interior of the house should be dusted with dry air-slaked lime. To do this a person should take a bucket, bag, or pailful of the fine lime and start at the end of the house farthest from the door, and walk slowly backwards toward the door, scattering the lime with the right hand in the same way that seed is sown. The lime should be thrown against the ceiling, side walls, nest boxes, roosting places, etc. The air should be filled with a cloud of lime dust. This dust will settle gradually into every crack and crevice of the house. While the lime dust is being scattered, the house should be closed as tightly as possible. About a half bushel of lime dust will answer for a poultry house 20 ft. wide and 40 to 50 ft. long. A thin cloth that the operator can see through should be tied over the eyes, nose, and mouth to prevent the lime dust from getting into them. Any parasites that may have escaped the fumes of the sulphur or tobacco will more than likely be killed by the lime dust. The house should be closed again for 24 hr. to allow the lime dust to settle thoroughly.

3. The house should then be brushed or swept clean. The ceiling, walls, floor, and every appliance and fixture inside the house should be carefully brushed. No dust or dirt should be left. The straw from the nest boxes, and the straw and dirt from the floor should be taken outside, saturated with kerosene, and burned. After all that will burn has been burned, the rest should be buried deep in the ground.

4. The house should be thoroughly sprayed both inside and out with one of the liquid insecticides described. Creosote and liquid lice killer are to be preferred, in the order named. The liquid insecticide applied at this time should be allowed to dry thoroughly.

5. A second application of the liquid insecticide should be made to the interior of the house, the nest boxes, and roosting poles before the fowls are allowed

to return. This application should be made on the morning of the day the fowls are to be returned to the house; after the liquid has dried sufficiently, fresh straw should be placed in the nest boxes.

6. The fowls should be thoroughly dusted with insect powder immediately before they are allowed to return to the house. They should be returned to the house at dusk with the powder in their feathers so that they can roost the first night without shaking out the powder.

7. Sanitary conditions must be maintained continually in the house and a strict watch must be kept for the appearance of parasites, both on the fowls and about the house. If this is not done the house is likely to be reinfested with parasites. If parasites appear the house should be thoroughly cleaned and sprayed again. To maintain cleanliness the interior of the buildings, the side walls, ceilings, roosting places, nest boxes, etc. should be brushed frequently with a stiff broom, and all filth should be systematically removed from the floor before it has a chance to accumulate in any quantity.

ANIMALS DESTRUCTIVE TO POULTRY

Nearly all flesh-eating animals attack poultry when the occasion offers. The animals that do the most harm to the average poultry flock are wildcats, raccoons, opossums, skunks, weasels, minks, rats, dogs, and cats. It is said that the tiger of India and the smaller members of the feline family hunt the peafowl and the pheasant. Where foxes are found in the neighborhood they will also attack poultry. The great proportion of animals destructive to poultry hunt by night, and hence if all openings in the poultry houses are closed with wire netting, practically all of the animals most likely to attack would be excluded.

For the capture or destruction of animals destructive to poultry the usual spring and box traps are used.

BIRDS DESTRUCTIVE TO POULTRY

It is difficult to determine just which birds are destructive to poultry, because many birds that live on rodents, such as field mice, rats, etc., will attack poultry when short of other food. As a general rule, however, birds are not very destructive to poultry, because even the birds that attack domestic fowls the most frequently come far from being the worst enemies of poultry. One rat, for instance, will often destroy more chicks in a single night than a pair of hawks will carry off in a month, and the insect enemies of poultry do more damage than all other agencies combined.

Falcons, hawks, and owls are the principal birds of prey that attack poultry and may be separated into four classes, grading from the least destructive to the most destructive as follows:

The hawks and owls least destructive to poultry are:

1. The large rough-legged hawk, the squirrel hawk, and the white-tailed, Mississippi, swallow-tailed, and English kites. These birds will not disturb or hunt for poultry so long as they can find a satisfactory supply of other food to supply their wants. They are generally considered as being entirely beneficial to mankind.

2. According to Dr. A. K. Fisher the majority of hawks and owls are usually beneficial to mankind, but will often kill poultry when the occasion offers. He names the following as belonging to this class: Marsh hawk, Harris's hawk, red-tailed hawk, short-tailed hawk, white-tailed hawk, red-shouldered hawk. Swainson's hawk, short-winged hawk, broad-winged hawk, Mexican black hawk, Mexican goshawk, sparrow hawk, barn owl, long-eared and short-eared owls, great gray owl, western owl, Richardson's owl, screech owl, snowy owl, hawk owl, and other smaller species.

3. Fisher also classes the following birds as doing about as much good by destroying other creatures as they do harm by destroying poultry: Golden eagle, bald eagle, pigeon hawk, Richardson's hawk, falcons, and the great horned owl.

4. Birds that are very destructive to poultry and **not** of much benefit through destroying other creatures are: Gray falcon, duck hawk, **sharp-shinned** hawk, Cooper's hawk, **and** goshawk.

The birds that are classed as least destructive to poultry subsist almost entirely on rodents that destroy field crops and trees, but notwithstanding the fact that they prefer this kind of food they cannot be trusted where young chicks are being raised. Under starving conditions all of these birds will kill the young of chickens, turkeys, and water fowls. The sparrow hawk, the smallest and most beautiful of all the above birds, lives almost entirely on insects and field mice, but will, if tempted by their presence, kill young chicks.

In addition to the above birds, ravens, blackbirds, and crows will destroy young poultry.

WHITE MINORCA

It is not unusual for the raven and the crow to fly away with chicks that are 2 or 3 wk. old. This, however, will occur only where the poultry have the range of the farm near the nesting places of these birds.

Well-built houses are a good protection against birds of prey. Scarecrows and hawk traps are also sometimes effective. The presence of a few guinea fowls and a well-trained dog will often keep a fair-sized farm free from birds of prey. Neither guinea fowls nor dogs will do any harm to birds of prey, but the guinea fowls will make a loud outcry whenever birds of prey appear, and

the **dog** that is trained for the purpose will bark at the noise and will chase the birds of prey away.

DISEASES

GENERAL REMARKS

A *disease* is any derangement of a living organism, but the term *ailment* is usually· applied to slight disorders. Though there are many diseases of poultry, and some serious ones, comparatively few fowls are diseased, when the large numbers of fowls in the country are considered, and poultry that is kept in sanitary quarters and has proper food is the least likely to become diseased. Hence, the importance of preventive measures.

Poultry in poor health will exhibit a dull, sluggish, and listless appearance, which is the strongest evidence of a lack of vitality, and will go to roost early and remain there in the morning until long after the other fowls are out looking for food. When they do leave the roosts they will walk about as if they were not strong enough to drag their legs and feet after them. Fowls in poor health will have a bloodless appearance, will have an absence of healthy brightness in their eyes, faces, combs, and wattles, and will show a general lack of condition, which is always accompanied by a lack of appetite and a failure to assimilate properly the food they eat. Hens in poor health will lay but few eggs. Whenever fowls have had their vitality reduced so that they exhibit the symptoms described they will be susceptible to the attacks of all kinds of diseases.

There are few symptoms that are of practical value in the diagnosis of the diseases of poultry, for the reason that many symptoms are common to several different diseases. A few general symptoms are, however, of value. Fowls that are diseased become listless; they are inclined to stay apart from other fowls, and will stand in out-of-the-way places or beside a fence sunning themselves, their heads hanging and their feathers·

ruffled. It is natural for fowls to sun themselves, but there is a marked difference between the healthy fowl basking in the sun for recreation and the sick fowl standing there in the hope of warming its body. Disease in poultry is always accompanied by a loss of appetite and generally by frequent voidance of the bowels.

The temperature of normal fowls ranges from 106° to 107.5° F., but the temperature of fowls is rarely taken, chilliness being usually accepted as an indication of fever. The heart beat of fowls is quite rapid, varying from 110 to 140 per minute. The rapidity, however, is not of so much importance as the regularity. The normal breathing rate of fowls is from 50 to 60 respirations per minute. When the respiratory organs are diseased, the respirations are quickened. The regularity or irregularity of the heart beat or of respiration will be plainly heard if the ear is placed against the backbone or the ribs.

Preventive measures are the best treatment for poultry troubles. The fowls should be handled in such a way that they will contract as few diseases as possible, and the slightest ailment should be treated before it has a chance to gain headway. This requires constant attention, but this is the only way to success.

None but very simple treatment is ordinarily necessary for poultry, and any ailment that will not yield readily to simple treatment is usually so serious that even if a fowl is enabled to recover from it, the results will not be satisfactory, for the vitality of the fowl will be seriously impaired. Hence, the practical poultryman, except in the case of particularly valuable fowls, usually kills any ailing fowls that do not recover quickly from simple treatment.

Medicine is most satisfactorily administered to a flock of fowls by being fed mixed in a warm or slightly warm mash. Pills are usually the most convenient form in which to administer medicine to individual fowls. When liquids are poured down a fowl's throat care should be taken to avoid strangulation.

FUNDAMENTAL PRINCIPLES OF TREATMENT

There are a few fundamental principles of treatment that it would be well for every poultryman to have continually in his mind. Morse's maxims cover this ground so well that they are given here:

"Clean out by means of Epsom salts, administered in an evening mash, estimating one-third of a teaspoonful to each adult bird. When disease is raging this may be practiced with the sick two or three times a week until there is an abatement of the outbreak. Even the well birds should receive one such dose at the beginning of an outbreak of disease. After disease has swept through a flock, until one is certain that it has been entirely eradicated, it is well to give the flock at least one dose monthly during the cooler weather and twice a month during the heated term.

"Clean up the poultry houses by sprinkling powdered, air-slaked lime over the runs, dropping-boards, and floors. This should be practiced at the time of giving the salts, as the lime will destroy the parasites that are deposited in the droppings.

"Clean the water supply by adding to the drinking water enough permanganate of potash to turn the water a claret red; that would ordinarily be as much as you can spread on a silver 10c. piece to the gallon of water. Instead of this, iron sulphate may be added in the proportion of 10 gr. to 1 gal. of water. Or, instead of either, 1 teaspoonful of strong carbolic acid (not crude) may be added to 1 gal. of water. This should be practiced constantly during the prevalence of disease. Healthy fowls not threatened with disease do not need it.

"Clean eggs by dipping them in 90% alcohol, just before placing them in the incubator. Instead of the alcohol, a 3% solution of some good coal-tar disinfectant may be used, with this exception, that instead of dipping, as in the use of alcohol, they should be wiped with the coal-tar disinfectant. The purpose of this rule is to remove from the shell of the egg the various

contaminating microbes that are deposited on the shell in its passage through the cloaca.

"By all means furnish your poultry with nothing but clean food. Moldy food is certain to produce disease and death. However, circumstances sometimes arise in which it appears impossible to avoid the use of food that has been exposed to the conditions favorable to the production of mold. In such circumstances, destroy the mold by the application of strong heat. Do not think that this suggestion is a happy thought to permit you to lessen your expenses by buying seconds, thirds, etc. in the feed line. If you practice it, it will be to your certain loss. An emergency suggestion is never a rule to be regularly carried out.

"Clean incubators and brooders by thoroughly scrubbing them with hot water and common soap. This practice, alone, has helped to cut down the cases of white diarrhea and brooder pneumonia. Having once used the incubators and brooders, remember that danger, disease, and death lurk in them until they are disinfected.

"Breed from the youngest females consistent with the needs of good breeding. Investigators have recently shown that there are fewer cases of egg infection by bacteria in the eggs that come from virgin pullets. A study of the anatomy of fowls and the physiology of fertilization makes plain at once how all kinds of bacteria may be introduced into the egg tube by the male bird in the act of copulation. Once in the egg tube it is not difficult for the bacteria to eventually reach the ovary and thus we may have infection of eggs in the ovary and in the upper part of the egg tube."

SIMPLE REMEDIES FOR POULTRY

Every poultryman should have at hand a few simple remedies that may be safely used in the treatment of poultry diseases and ailments. Many of the common remedies kept in the home for use with children will be valuable for poultry. The following materials are all convenient for the poultryman to have on hand:

Epsom salts, called also *bitter salt,* is a white, hydrated, crystalline salt known chemically as *magnesium sulphate.* It is used as a purgative in doses of ⅓ teaspoonful to each fowl.

Castor oil is a thick yellowish-white oil expressed from the castor bean. It is used as a purgative.

Olive oil, called also *sweet oil,* is an oil expressed from the ripe fruit of the olive. It serves the purpose of butter in some countries, but in most parts of the civilized world is used chiefly in salad dressings. Olive oil is the most nearly perfect laxative for use with poultry, as it is both healing and nutritious, thus possessing an advantage over castor oil. A tablespoonful of olive oil can be safely administered.

Camphor is a gumlike, translucent, crystalline compound with a penetrating, fragrant odor; it is distilled from the wood and bark of the camphor tree. It may be used as a medicine for poultry to allay irritation, as in colds and in cases of slight diarrhea.

Copper sulphate, called also *bluestone,* is a blue crystalline substance that is used as an astringent and stimulant, but not more than from ⅛ to ¼ gr. should be administered more than once a day to any fowl.

Iron sulphate, called also *copperas,* is a green, crystalline substance that is used for the same purpose as copper sulphate and can be administered in doses of ¼ to ½ gr.

Douglas mixture is used as a tonic for both poultry and pigeons, and is made by mixing ½ lb. of iron sulphate with 1 oz. of sulphuric acid dissolved in 2 gal. of water. This may be used in the drinking water—2 tablespoonfuls of the mixture to each pint of water.

Table salt is sparingly used to season mash foods for poultry. A large quantity of salt will kill poultry, and it is better to give them none than too much. Less salt should be used to season food for poultry than is needed for human beings.

Rhinitis tablets, half strength, are an excellent remedy for a cold in its early stages. They are given to

.poultry that have slight colds—two tablets two or three times a day for from 1 to 3 da.

Homeopathic remedies are used by many poultrymen for their poultry with satisfactory results. Such remedies should be given to poultry in quantities about as recommended for children.

Healing powders for applying to sores of any kind are useful to have on a poultry establishment. Equal parts of burnt alum and zinc oxide; or zinc oxide, powdered magnesia, and Venetian red are effective for this purpose. Burnt alum and the mixture of burnt alum and zinc oxide are excellent for use on any kind of sores. The zinc oxide and the powdered magnesia are very healing and painless. The Venetian red is slightly caustic and may be used where a light cauterization is needed.

Hydrogen peroxide, a clear solution that looks like water, is useful for cleansing and disinfecting ulcers or other sores on poultry.

Paraffin oil is a mineral oil derived from petroleum. It may be used for relief in cases of scaly leg and bumblefoot and may be applied to injuries of the shank, but should not be applied to the skin of the body or to the feathers.

Ointments are sometimes needed for irritations of the skin. Fresh zinc-oxide ointment is useful for this purpose, but when it becomes rancid it is unfit for use. An ointment made of equal parts of glycerine and rose water mixed in a mortar with zinc oxide until the whole assumes a thick mass, may also be used.

Iodine, turpentine, creoline, zenoleum, and *tincture of iron* are effective for destroying warts on poultry.

Tonics for preventing illness should never be given to poultry. Fowls in good health do much better without them. A tonic for young or half-grown chicks that have been weakened from any cause may be given in pill form according to the following formula: 2 dr. of iron citrate and 30 gr. of quinine sulphate, mixed into a mass with sirup of gum arabic so as to make

enough for 60 pills. One of these pills may be given night and morning for 3 da.

AILMENTS AND TREATMENT

Colds, Canker, Catarrh, and Roup.—The most common ailments of fowls are colds, canker, catarrh, and roup. All of these troubles are likely to come from exposure to damp or cold at seasons of the year when the temperature rises and falls quickly. Fowls are just as likely to take a cold in July and Aug. as in midwinter; they are especially likely to take cold on rainy days in the summer when they go to roost with wet plumage.

As a matter of fact, colds, canker, catarrh, and roup are often merely stages of the same disease. A cold may begin by a slight discharge from the nostrils, accompanied, perhaps, by watering of the eyes. Canker and catarrh, which are inflammations of the mucous membrane, are mild forms of diphtheria in which patches may grow on the inside of the throat and on the tongue or at the opening of the windpipe. These conditions follow one another quickly, unless prompt attention is given to the first symptoms of cold. The earlier forms of the disease do not seem to be contagious, but roup is contagious.

So many remedies are used in the treatment of these diseases that it is difficult to choose between them. The best remedy of all, perhaps, is permanganate of potash administered in the drinking water. The bathing of the head, face, throat, and nostrils with warm water in which some antiseptic solution is mixed, and the maintenance of perfect cleanliness in their surroundings is also advisable. The giving of internal remedies is very unsatisfactory, and any attempt to cure fowls afflicted with roup by any such means is almost useless. Fowls badly affected with roup should be promptly killed, their bodies buried, and the premises cleaned and disinfected with creosote or some other similar material. Permanganate of potash should be given to

the rest of the flock in their drinking water. A saturated solution may be made by placing 1 oz. of the crystals of permanganate of potash in a 2-oz. bottle of water. One teaspoonful of this saturated solution will be sufficient for 1 gal. of drinking water. A warm mash with a little ginger and red pepper added as a tonic may also be given with advantage.

Gapes.—Gapes is a disease caused by parasites or gape worms growing and adhering to the inner lining of the windpipe. This causes the chicks to gasp for breath; they open their mouths wide and sneeze or cough in an effort to throw the parasite out of the windpipe.

Among the remedies used for this is the feeding of asafetida, garlic, or onion tops in soft food. A teaspoonful of powdered asafetida to a pint of food will be plenty of this. Garlic and onion tops as much as they will eat will not injure them. Another means of relief is to introduce a feather down the throat and into the windpipe, the point of the feather being dipped in sweet oil before being introduced to the windpipe.

Bronchitis.—Bronchitis is a disease of the lining of the air tubes. Fowls that take cold are apt to have irritation of the bronchial tubes. When this becomes aggravated a rattling in the throat is apparent. Treatment is difficult. One drop of tincture of aconite may be given every hour until four or five doses have been administered. The fowl should be fed on warm bread and milk or a warm mash. When the rattling in the throat becomes aggravated there is but little chance for relief. The use of pills made of iron, quinine, and strychnine of the same strength that would be given to a 10-yr.-old child may be administered one each morning and evening.

Diseases of the Intestines.—Diseases of the intestines are caused by improper feeding, poorly kept or unsanitary houses, yards, and buildings, or long-continued exposure to damp and cold. These intestinal irritations cause diarrhea, dysentery, and like ailments, which may bring about what is known as *going light*. The

only safety against such ailments is perfect cleanliness, protection from cold and damp, and proper feeding.

. Fowls that are attacked with looseness of the bowels or diarrhea may be treated by separating them from the rest of the flock, cutting off their supply of green food, and giving them water to drink in which a tea-spoonful of tincture of iron has been mixed in each quart of water, feeding them warm mash composed of either stale bread, ground oats, and wheat bran equal parts, or of ground oats, wheat middlings, and wheat bran equal parts, either to be moistened with hot milk or hot water and seasoned with a teaspoonful of red pepper to each quart of mash.

Of recent years the scourge of white diarrhea has spread throughout the world. Some persons claim that nearly one-half of all the little chicks hatched are lost through this ailment. Whether or not so large a per-centage of all chicks hatched die from this disease, it is a fact that entirely too many die in this way and that nearly all of the little chicks that die of looseness of the bowels have white diarrhea. The symptoms of white diarrhea are unmistakable. It usually attacks little chicks within the first week after they come from the shell. They shiver, hang down their wings, close their eyes, and stand about and peep in a most painful manner, and the discharges from their bowels is like a mixture of milk and lime. Other kinds of diarrhea and looseness of the bowels may be caused by cold, exposure to damp, or eating food that ferments in the bowels. Diarrhea from these causes does not make little chicks nearly so sick as does white diarrhea.

The cure for all these troubles is care and manage-ment. If little chicks are exposed to too much heat under the brooder or are chilled at night under the brooder, if they run out in the damp and wet and take cold, or if any of them eat bad food they are almost certain to be afflicted with looseness of the bowels. This can be cured or prevented by avoiding the troubles that cause the ailment and by a system of perfect sanitation

and cleanliness and the feeding of proper kinds of food. Looseness of the bowels of this kind can usually be cured by feeding equal parts of bread crumbs and rice boiled in milk. If there is sufficient moisture in the rice to moisten the bread, no more moisture is needed. If a little more moisture is needed use hot milk. This treatment can be safely given to all little chicks troubled with looseness of the bowels. It will not hurt the chicks with white diarrhea. There is, however, no known cure for little chicks that are afflicted with white diarrhea.

Diseases of the Legs and Feet.—*Leg weakness, rheumatism,* and *gout* are troubles that cause lameness in fowls. Lameness may also come from corns or bumblefoot. Rheumatism and gout are often called leg weakness, although the leg weakness may be due to any one of a number of causes, as for instance too high a temperature in the brooder, to the chicks being kept too long on board floors, to insufficient nutrition, or to a lack of bone-forming material in the food. In most cases dietetic and hygienic treatment will prove sufficient.

Rheumatism and gout are kindred diseases caused by the fowls being exposed to dampness and by being shut up in badly ventilated houses. In fact, nine-tenths of all poultry troubles come from damp and unsanitary houses; if the houses were kept perfectly clean, dry, and free from insects, fowls would have but few ailments. There is no cure for rheumatism and gout, and scarcely any relief.

Scaly leg is a disease of the shanks caused by little mites that come from damp and filthy conditions. The mites get under the scales on the shanks and toes and cause swellings on these parts. Scaly leg may be quickly cured if treated at the beginning, but it is hard to eradicate at an advanced stage. It may be treated by rubbing the shanks thoroughly each day with an application of lard and kerosene until the growths are cleaned off. The most effective way of dealing with the trouble is to sell off the afflicted fowls for market

poultry and put the houses and surroundings in a sanitary condition.

Bumblefoot is an ulcer on the bottom of the foot of a fowl and is usually caused by a bruise. It may be treated by applying some kind of ointment or healing salve or by cauterizing with strong iodine or a saturated solution of permanganate of potash.

Chicken Pox.—Chicken pox is an ailment that comes usually in the fall of the year. The first appearance is noticed from the little black specks growing on the face and eyes, usually of young fowls. These continue to grow until they close the eyes completely and the fowls die of starvation, because they cannot see to eat. This ailment is the most prevalent in warm or tropical climates, where it is called sorehead. Frequently the entire head becomes raw, and when in this condition the fowl is so afflicted with flies, bugs, and mosquitoes that it is almost eaten up. The only treatment to be relied on is cleanliness and the bathing of the afflicted parts with a 5% or a 10% solution of creoline in water.

Bad Habits.—Egg eating and picking of sore places on the bodies of one another are bad habits acquired by fowls kept in confinement with nothing to do. There does not seem to be any remedy for these bad habits when they are once acquired. In some instances they may be checked by transferring the fowls from place to place or by giving them perfect freedom.

POULTRY JUDGING

METHODS OF JUDGING

In America there are three methods of judging: (1) By the *official score card* of the American Poultry Association; (2) by the *decimal score card;* and (3) by *comparison.*

The practice of judging by score card was begun and has continued in the United States and Canada ever since the compilation of the first Standard by the American Poultry Association. A few shows that are held during Nov. and a large number that are held between Dec. and April are judged by the score-card method. The shows that are held from April to Nov. are judged by comparison. The score-card method of judging has been recognized by the American Poultry Association since its origin.

The decimal score card was introduced by the late I. K. Felch in 1890, and since that time both the official and the decimal score cards have been used. Although the decimal score card has never been recognized by the American Poultry Association, its use continues to some extent, although its advocates are decreasing in number.

Although comparison judging has been used for so long in the placing of awards, in fact, much longer than the score-card method, it did not have the sanction of the American Poultry Association until 1904. Judging by comparison is practiced each year at all shows held prior to Nov. 1 throughout the United States and Canada. Nearly all the larger exhibitions are judged under the comparison system.

The advantages of each method of judging depend on the ability of the judges accurately to determine how nearly the fowls under consideration approach the re-

OFFICIAL SCORE CARD OF THE

Fancier's Poultry Association

DATE_____VARIETY_____

OWNER_____ SEX_____

ADDRESS_____ BAND NO _____

ENTRY NO _____WEIGHT_____

	Shape	Color	Remarks
Symmetry_____			
Weight or Size____			
Condition_____			
Head and Beak____			
Eyes____			
Comb____			
Wattles & Ear Lobes____			
Neck____			
Wings____			
Back____			
Tail____			
Breast____			
Body and Fluff____			
Legs and Toes____			
*Hardness of Feather			
†Crest and Beard____			

Total Cuts_____Score_____

*Applies to Games and Game Bantams
†Applies to Crested Breeds

_____Judge

_____ Secretary

Fig. 1

quirements of the standard. The use of the score card is considered of the greatest advantage to the amateur, who gains knowledge by a careful study of his own fowls in comparing them with the decisions of the judge, which are shown in detail on the cards, which go to the exhibitors. Comparison judging, however, is equally beneficial, provided the exhibitor is present and can understand the reasons for the various awards and rejections. Comparison judging becomes of more general use in neighborhoods where poultry shows have been held annually for a considerable length of time. Score-card judging is in more common use in localities where the practice of holding poultry shows is in its infancy. More shows are judged by score cards throughout the United States and Canada than are judged by comparison. Comparison judging is really an advanced system of judging that can be employed by those who are familiar with the distinctions considered of the greatest importance.

SCORE CARDS

A copy of the official score card of the American Poultry Association is shown in Fig. 1. The only change needed to make this score card local is to print at the top in place of "Fancier's Poultry Association," the name of the local association using it. This card gives a list of the parts of a fowl in respect to which it is to be scored, and a space is provided for noting the score for each part. A definite number of points is assigned to each part, the total number of points indicating perfection in all parts being 100. The figures scored after each part indicate the degree to which it approaches perfection according to standard requirements, and the total score shows how closely a fowl approaches perfection in all respects, which is 100 points. This method is a mathematical analysis of the defects found in a fowl, and enables a judge to make a discount for each.

THE DECIMAL SCORE CARD

Date_____

Breed_____

Sex_____ Entry No._____

Coop No.____ Ring No.____ Weight____

Owner or Exhibitor, Copyright by I K Felch	**Each Section 10 Points**	CONDITION WEIGHT or SIZE			**DIRECTIONS FOR USING THIS CARD.**—To cut for weight, comb, head, legs, check (X) the features defective and cut in the column. For shape, make cut above the dotted line. For color, below the line. Shape being more defective than color, cut in space for shape, but low enough to include the dotted lines. Color being the greater evil, commence the figure just above the dotted line and carry deep down into color space. This secures despatch in use for exhibitions.
		COMB, or CREST AND COMB			
		HEAD AND ADJUNCTS	BEAK EYE EAR LOBE WATTLES		
		NECK	Shape Color	--------	
		BACK	Shape Color	--------	
		BREAST	Shape Color	--------	
		BODY and FLUFF	Shape Color	--------	
		WINGS	Shape Color	--------	
		TAIL	Shape Color	--------	
		LEGS and TOES	Shape Plum'g Color		

Total Defects	Score

_____Judge

_____President

_____Secretary

FIG. 2

194

The score card was designed for judging poultry at exhibitions. The object was not only to decide the awards, giving the highest scores and the best prizes to the fowls least defective, but to give every fowl exhibited a rating in terms of the standard requirements and in comparison with competing fowls of the same sex and variety. This system can be used also by fanciers and breeders as a guide in computing values in sale fowls, and in selecting breeding and exhibition fowls.

A copy of the decimal score card is shown in Fig. 2. This card provides ten divisions for the features in respect to which a fowl is to be scored, and the perfect score for each feature is 10 points. Provision is made where necessary for scoring features separately in respect to shape and color. The decimal score card differs materially from the official score card, which provides for scoring more features, and these are valued differently for different breeds.

The arguments for or the objections against the decimal system that have arisen have been directed to the fact that no two breeds can be valued the same. Those who favor the decimal system claim that a perfect back in a Plymouth Rock is of equal value to the back of a Partridge Cochin or a Game Bantam, and that neither should have the advantage over the other in the general division of points; that backs for Plymouth Rocks, Cochins, or Bantams can be valued at 10 points as well as to have the back of each fowl estimated at a different percentage. There is evidence of value in the decimal method of calculation from the fact that the monetary system of several countries and the metric system are based on the decimal system. When matters of such vast importance can be conducted best under a decimal system, there should be no hesitation in conceding that the same system will apply equally well in poultry judging. The adoption of the official score card of the American Poultry Association seems to have been based more on the preference of the members of that organization than on a consideration of its relative convenience.

COMPARISON CARD

Variety_____ Judge_____

Sex and Age_____ At Exhibition held at_____

Date_____

Entry or Coop Number	Symmetry, Shape, or Station	Color of Plumage	Comb, Wattles, and Ear Lobes or Dubbing	Size, Condition Legs and Toes, or Toe-Feathering	Rank or Award	Remarks

Fig. 3

196

A convenient comparison-judging score card is shown in **Fig. 3.** Any number of lines needed to complete an entry may be added to this card. The comparison method of judging consists in a careful examination of every section of the fowl, and a determination of the quality by this means, the final placing of awards being decided without numerical estimates. In fact, to judge by comparison is to select the best, by applying, by means of sight estimates, the criteria of perfection established by the Standard.

Comparison judging gives due credit to superior value in individual fowls. No other system gives consideration to unusual quality so equitably as does the comparison system.

When properly applied, comparison judging can be made more equitable in placing awards than any other system; for selecting the best fowls in the classes, no system is superior to it. The main objection, and, in fact, the only real objection that can be made against it, is that no record is made, nor is there any reason apparent to the absent exhibitor for the award of prizes. A record by scores and the results published conveys a numerical value for individual fowls to the mind of the absentee. In the score card he has comparative numerical values of the fowls that were outside the list of awards.

JUDGING OF FARM FLOCKS AT FAIRS AND SHOWS

When at Pennsylvania State College, Mr. Kilpatrick, then of the Bureau of Animal Industry, displayed a remarkable interest in having farmers show their poultry at county fairs. He suggested that the flocks to be exhibited should consist of 6 females and 1 male, that each lot be placed in a coop or runway, where they could be readily viewed, and he suggested that the accompanying score cards should be used to judge them. One score card is for judging the general-purpose type of fowls, the other for judging the egg-laying type.

Since then several systems for selecting poultry by outward appearance have been evolved. One, and perhaps the best of these, is the Cornell System, given under Selecting Hens for Egg Production. Another system that has attracted attention the world over is that of selecting the physical characteristics of layers, as suggested by Mr. Barron.

SCORE CARD FOR FARM FLOCK
GENERAL-PURPOSE TYPE

	PERFECT SCORE	JUDGE'S SCORE
Head: Small, with small combs and wattles; beak, short, stiff, and strong; bright, full eye; face, comb and wattles bright in color and of fine texture	5	————
Neck: Rather short, neat, tapering to head	2	————
Wings: Small and neat	2	————
Back: Of good length, rather broad	6	————
Breast: Large, full, rounding, well developed	6	————
Body: Very deep, broad, and compact, well fleshed; keel straight and long, well rounded out with flesh; should resemble a parallelogram in shape	30	————
Skin: Smooth and of fine texture; yellow skin preferred	4	————
Flesh: Firm, evenly distributed; deep, especially in regions of desirable cuts; should give indication of tendency to fatten easily	10	————
Shanks: Short, stiff, and clean	3	————
Plumage: Abundant, bright, and well kept; free from dark pin feathers	2	————
Disposition: Docile; quiet but active	2	————
Vitality: Strong; fowls should give evidence of perfect health, freedom from vermin, etc., and must be neat and clean in appearance	10	————
Size: Females shall weigh not less than 5 lb. each, males not less than 7 lb.	8	————
Uniformity: Flock to consist of 6 females and 1 male; females as uniform as possible in type, size, color of plumage, etc.; male, same color as females	10	————

	PERFECT SCORE	JUDGE'S SCORE

Disqualifications: Any evidence of disease, low vitality, scaly leg destroying the natural color of the shank, roach back, crooked toe, or wry tail. Fowls badly infested with lice shall also be disqualified.

EGG TYPE	PERFECT SCORE	JUDGE'S SCORE
Head: Bright in color, of moderate size, short, broad, and neat; beak, short, stiff, and strong; eye, bright, fully filling the socket, giving an impression of alertness and brightness; comb well developed, medium to large in size, full of blood, and of fine texture	8	——
Neck: Of medium length, neat and trim	3	——
Back: Long and reasonably broad........	8	——
Body: Compact, broad, and deep, especially in abdomen and fluff, giving plenty of room for vital organs; well rounded out with flesh; plump, yet not fat; good width between pelvic bones, 1½ in. or better, with good distance between rear joint of keel bone and pelvic arch; wings of medium size	20	——
Breast: Shallower than rear, presenting a wedge shape when viewed from above. Should be rounded, of medium size, giving good lung capacity	8	——
Shanks and toes: Shanks, stocky, not rangy; of medium length. The fowl should stand up stiff and straight, with body well supported on the tops of the legs, the fowl standing firmly on the toes. Shanks to have full, highly colored skin, loose around the shanks; should carry some flesh. Toenails, short and straight...............	5	——
Tail: Full and flowing, not pinched or stinted; a tendency to be carried high	2	——
Plumage: Glossy, flowing, abundant, bright, and well kept...................	2	——
Disposition: Always busy, singing constantly, docile, elusive. The male should be courteous to the hens and exhibit great courage	2	——

	Perfect Score	Judge's Score
Flesh: Hard, firm, muscular, showing little tendency to lay on fat............	5	———
Vitality: Strong, as evidenced by general appearance and condition of the fowl, giving evidence of perfect health, freedom from lice, etc.; must be neat and clean in appearance................	12	———
Size: Of medium size, female ranging from 3½ to 6 lb.; male, from 4½ to 7 lb.	5	———
Eggs: Eggs to be of good size, weighing not less than 26 oz. per doz.; must be uniform in shape, size, and color; white eggs to have the preference over brown or tinted eggs, other things being equal; eggs not to be considered unless all flocks are laying during the competition	10	———
Uniformity: Flock is to consist of 6 females and 1 male; females should be as nearly alike as possible in type, size, plumage, etc.; male should be of same color as females................	10	———

Disqualifications: Any evidence disease or low vitality, scaly leg destroying the natural color of the shank, roach back, or wry tail. Fowls badly infested with lice shall also be disqualified.

UTILITY SCORE CARD

Another score card for judging layers at utility poultry shows is shown in Fig. 4. It was compiled by Irving C. Lewis, of Ulysses, Pa., and is copyrighted. The card can be purchased from Mr. Lewis.

UTILITY SCORE CARD
All Varieties
For Use in Utility Poultry Shows

Type..Date...............

Coop No......................Band No..................

Breed.............................Sex.................

	Cuts
Weight..	....
Condition..	....
Color Comb......................................	....
Capacity...	....
Prepotency......................................	....
Pelv. { Left....................................	....
Right...................................	....
Average.................................	....
Shape..................................	....
Egg Type..	....
Total Cuts..............................	....
Score..................................	....

Judge..

Show...

Secretary..

Copyright, 1914, by Irving C. Lewis, Ulysses, Pa

FIG. 4

POULTRY SHOWS AND ASSO-CIATIONS

BEGINNING OF POULTRY SHOWS

The first poultry exhibition is thought to have been the one held in the Zoological Gardens of London, England, in 1846; the first poultry show held in Birmingham, England, was in 1849. The first poultry exhibition held in America is credited to Boston in 1849. The first American poultry show to attract world-wide attention was held in the American Museum, New York City, in February, 1854, under the management of P. T. Barnum. The second show was held a year later at the same place. This show was really the beginning of live interest in the breeding of fowls for exhibition in America.

From 1860 to 1865 but little interest was taken in poultry exhibitions in America. From then to the present time they have increased so fast as to surprise the world. During the show season of 1911 and 1912 more than 700 poultry exhibitions were held in the United States and Canada, and more than 200 in England. The number of shows held in the United States and Canada during the years 1917 and 1918 were considerably less than prior to these dates. The same conditions prevailed in England.

The great shows of England were the Dairy, the Birmingham, and the Crystal Palace shows. These were discontinued to some extent from 1914 to 1919. These shows were formerly held between the fifteenth of October and the first of December. The Crystal Palace show of London, England, was for many years the largest and most highly considered of all poultry shows, but within the last few years the New York, Boston, and Chicago shows have ranked very high. The New York and Boston shows have come to be considered of equal importance with the Crystal Palace exhibition.

AMERICAN POULTRY ASSOCIATION

The American Poultry Association, a national organization of breeders of standard-bred poultry is the authoritative body of the United States and Canada. This organization owns the copyrights of the Standard of Perfection, issues show rules and regulates the handling of shows, and lends its best efforts to the general upbuilding of poultry culture.

AMERICAN POULTRY ASSOCIATION SHOW RULES

Poultry associations or societies, Associate Members of the American Poultry Association, giving poultry shows or exhibitions, governed by and subject to the Association's Rules and Regulations, must print in the premium lists or on their entry sheets in bold-faced type:

"The (full name of the association) being a member of the American Poultry Association, their——— Annual Show (dates here), will .be governed by and run under the latest revised Official Poultry Show Rules of the American Poultry Association. All prizes will· be awarded strictly in accordance with the American Standard of Perfection."

Section 1. Under normal conditions entries shall close the day advertised (entries bearing postmark of that date being eligible) and entry fees must be paid on or before that time, except when telegraphed, and in such cases remittance must follow by first mail.

Sec. 2. Any person under disqualification by the American Poultry Association is ineligible to enter, to compete, or to act as judge or in any capacity.

Sec. 3. All entries must be the bona-fide property of the exhibitor. Otherwise he forfeits all entry fees, all prize money, and all other premiums, as well as the right to have his birds remain in the show room. In cases of disqualifications under this rule other exhibits shall, if qualified, be moved up in the list of winners, subject·to the disqualified exhibitor's right of appeal.

Sec. 4. In cases where it shall come to the knowledge of the management that disqualified parties have, unknown to them, succeeded in making an entry or entries, the right is reserved to cancel such entries, and such party shall forfeit his entry fee, prize money, and other premiums.

The show management reserves the right to refuse entries from exhibitors whose conduct, in their opinion, makes it desirable for the welfare of the show that their birds be debarred from competition.

Sec. 5. Each specimen regularly entered as provided by the rules of the local association will be judged in its order unless removed from its coop by written order of the secretary or marked "Not for competition" when the entry is made. Exhibitors will not be allowed to handle or interfere with any of the exhibits in any class after the judging of any variety has commenced.

In cases where entries are made at shows where catalogs are issued and exhibits are not sent, entry fees will not be returned. *Associations that do not issue catalogs may use their discretion in this matter.

Sec. 6. Exhibitors attempting to interfere with or influence the judge or judges shall be dealt with as provided in Section 3.

Sec. 7. Judges shall be required to sign the judge's book or card provided by the show association. An official record of these awards shall be preserved by the secretary for 3 yr. for reference.

Sec. 8. No specimen shall be removed from the show until after its close except upon the written consent of the show secretary or superintendent.

Sec. 9. All entries are entered and shown at the risk of owners, and while associations are expected to exercise all reasonable care in the handling and protection of the exhibits, such associations will in no case be liable except as provided in Rule 10.

Sec. 10. Birds must be returned promptly at the close of the show, and any lost in the reshipping through proved carelessness or negligence on the part of the

show association, are to be paid for by such association at a value not to exceed $10 per bird, as agreed liquidated damages, it being understood that in subscribing to this rule the exhibitor does not waive any rights he may have at law.

Sec. 11. Any exhibitor disqualified for fraudulent practices shall have the right of appeal to the Executive Board of the American Poultry Association within 1 yr. from the date of his disqualification.

Sec. 12. Notices of a disqualification with a detailed statement shall be mailed, by the show association, within 10 da., to the secretary of the American Poultry Association and by registered mail to the disqualified party.

Sec. 13. Protests are to be entertained by local associations only in cases of apparent dishonesty, ignorance, or carelessness on the part of the judge. In scoring the specimens in dispute, the judge, together with the president and secretary of the local association (or representatives appointed by the management of the local association), shall constitute a committee of three, and the majority decision of this committee shall be final. Score cards made out by the judge in deciding protested awards are to be retained by the local association.

When protests are entertained, where judging has been done by score card, the specimens under dispute shall be rescored by the judge, he to act as a member of the committee of three, as provided, the rescoring to be done in the presence of the other two members of the committee on protests.

Protests are not to be entertained except when made in writing, and the person making same shall deposit with the secretary of the local association the sum of five dollars, this money to be returned to the person making the protest if his protest be sustained; if protest be not sustained, the deposit becomes the property of the local association.

See. 14. Notice of protests that are sustained shall be mailed within 10 da. to the Secretary of the American

Poultry Association, to be brought by him before the Executive Board, before whom an appeal may be taken by the judge within 1 yr.

Sec. 15. No judge shall exhibit in any class which he is judging and he shall refuse to consider any bird that he may recognize as having been owned by him 6 mo. previous to the show, and no exhibitor or any one interested in any exhibit that may be in the class shall act as assistant to the judge.

Sec. 16. Associations shall have the right to reassign judges for cause or to add to the list of judges as occasion may require.

Sec. 17. The placing of names, leg bands, or marks of any sort, not provided by the show, on birds or on or in the coops shall be left to the rules of the show associations.

Sec. 18. Show managements shall have the right to refuse entry to the show room, or to remove from the same all diseased or unsightly birds, and are expected to avail themselves of this right. Entry fees on such birds shall be forfeited.

Sec. 19. All specimens must be exhibited in their natural condition with the exception of Games and Game Bantams. Any violation of this rule shall exclude such specimens from competition and cause the withholding of all premiums awarded.

Sec. 20. Any matter not provided for in the foregoing rules and regulations will be referred to the executive committee of the local show for decision.

Sec. 21. Where Standard varieties of poultry that require the double-mating system are exhibited, local associations are permitted to offer special prizes only for both single entries and pens containing specimens bred in accordance with the system of double mating practiced in such varieties. These specials must be plainly designated "Special Prizes" so as to be distinguished from the regular premiums offered for the Standard awards.

Sec. 22. Every exhibitor hereby agrees to submit to the jurisdiction of the American Poultry Association and

to abide by these rules whether he is a member of the Association or not.

Sec. 23. Any show association may make additional rules or regulations provided they are not inconsistent with or in conflict with these rules.

Sec. 24. All poultry associations that are members of the American Poultry Association shall be permitted to designate their exhibitions as official poultry shows, and to use the official entry books, entry blanks, judges' cards, ribbons, and other supplies furnished by the American Poultry Association.

Sec. 25. These Show Rules are official and are copyrighted and can be used only by poultry associations or societies that are associate members of the American Poultry Association.

Sec. 26. Local associations must offer premiums on all varieties of Standard-Bred fowls.

Sec. 27. Special for best display any one variety shall be made on the points, first prize to count 6; second, 4; third, 3; fourth, 2; fifth, 1; pens to count double.

If more than five awards are placed in any class, all places below 5, shall receive one point for each such award in the single classes and two points for pens.

Sec. 28. Premium ribbons shall be displayed only at the show, time, and place where the ribbons were awarded, and no other ribbons or special prizes shall be placed on exhibition at any other than the show at which they were awarded.

Sec. 29. Exhibitors making charges of dishonest practices or statements of a defamatory nature against any exhibitor or exhibitors, judge or judges, at any show that is an associate member of the American Poultry Association, shall be required to appear before the board of directors or show committee of that show and prove that the charges so made are true, and if the said charges are not substantially true the exhibitor making the said charge shall forfeit back to the association all ribbons, medals, and awards of any and all kinds and nature, and the exhibit of the said exhibitor shall either be

treated as a display exhibit or removed from the show, at discretion of the management of the show.

A report of the committee, together with a charge of conduct unbecoming a member of the American Poultry Association, must be made in regular form by the president or secretary of the associate member. In case such charges are not made as above provided, the member or members considering themselves defamed may make such charges direct to the President or Secretary of the American Poultry Association.

MEMBERSHIP IN AMERICAN POULTRY ASSOCIATION

The rules governing membership in the American Poultry Association will be found in their publications. Those desirous of becoming members should send to the secretary of the association for the latest revised rules of organization and application for membership.

The American Poultry Association has issued a book of rules for the holding of shows, and non-members may obtain a copy of the rules by application to the secretary of the association.

THE AMERICAN STANDARD OF PERFECTION

The American Standard of Perfection, the only guide for judging poultry in America, is issued by the American Poultry Association. This book has been revised about every 5 yr., and the next revision will occur in 1923. Changes are made in the Standard of Perfection only after due consideration of written notices specifying word for word the proposed change or changes, and the written copy must be filed with the secretary of the Association fully 3 mo. before the annual meeting.

Admission of New Breeds and Varieties to American Standard of Perfection.—New breeds and varieties are

admitted to the American Standard of Perfection under the regulations given in the constitution and by-laws of the American Poultry Association, a copy of which can always be procured from the secretary of that Association. Any one who contemplates making application for such admission should study these rules very carefully, for there is no other way to obtain recognition except through a full and complete compliance with these rules.

STANDARD AND NON-STANDARD. VARIETIES OF POULTRY

Show-room classifications are not the same in all countries or even in all parts of the same country. In America they are usually made to conform to the breeds and their varieties as listed in the American Standard of Perfection. But in addition to such varieties, some show-room classifications will include a few of the non-standard varieties, and the greater number of them will permit classes for any of the non-standard varieties, either of a particular breed or of many breeds.

The list of breeds and varieties of poultry in the tables on pages 210 to 220 includes only those that are known to reproduce their kind of a settled type of form and color. In the column headed Standard Varieties are listed the varieties of fowls included in the American Standard of Perfection; in the column headed Non-Standard Varieties are listed the varieties not included in that publication, but which are bred in the United States and other countries, many of them being standard varieties in other countries. In this list, for convenience, the Antwerp Brahma is classed as an Asiatic fowl. This is not strictly correct, as it is not a true Brahma and might be classed as a Belgian fowl.

BREEDS AND STANDARD AND NON-STANDARD VARIETIES OF POULTRY

Classes and Breeds	Standard Varieties	Non-Standard Varieties	Color of Eggshell
American fowls:			
Plymouth Rock.........	Barred	Black	Brown or tinted
	Buff	Buff Barred	Brown or tinted
	Columbian	Pea-Comb	Brown or tinted
	Partridge	Rose-Comb	Brown or tinted
	Silver Penciled		Brown or tinted
	White		Brown or tinted
Wyandotte... ...	Black	Buff Columbian	Brown or tinted
	Buff	Cuckoo	Brown or tinted
	Columbian	Pyle Colored	Brown or tinted
	Golden Laced	Violet	Brown or tinted
	Partridge	White-Laced Buff	Brown or tinted
	Silver Laced		Brown or tinted
	Silver Penciled		Brown or tinted
	White		Brown or tinted
Rhode Island Red.......	Rose-Comb	Pea-Comb	Brown or tinted
	Single-Comb	White	Brown or tinted
Dominique..............	Rose-Comb		Brown or tinted
Java...................	Black		Brown or tinted
	Mottled		Brown or tinted
Jersey Blue............		Blue	Brown or tinted
Buckeye...............	Pea-Comb		Brown or tinted
Asiatic fowls:			
Brahma...............	Light	Antwerp	Brown or tinted
	Dark	Buff	Brown or tinted

Breed	Variety	Variety	Egg color
Cochin	Black		Brown or tinted
	Buff		Brown or tinted
	Partridge		Brown or tinted
	White		Brown or tinted
Langshan	Black		Brown or tinted
	White		Brown or tinted
Belgian fowls:			
Antwerp Brahma		Cuckoo	Brown
Ardenne		Blue	White
		Buff	White
Brabant		Ermine—White	White
		Black-Red	White
		Black	White
		Mottled	White
Braekel		Black	White
		Black-Headed	White
		Blue	White
		Chamois	White
		Golden	White
		Silver	White
		White	White
		Black	White
Bruges	Golden		
Campine	Silver		
Flemish		Silver-Gray	Pale yellow
		Blue	White
Herve		Cuckoo	Tinted
		Ermine	Tinted
Huttegem		Golden	Tinted
Malines		Black	Brown or tinted
		Cuckoo	Brown or tinted

BREEDS AND STANDARD AND NON-STANDARD VARIETIES OF POULTRY
(*Continued*)

Classes and Breeds	Standard Varieties	Non-Standard Varieties	Color of Eggshell
Belgian fowls—(*Continued*)			
Malines		Silvered Black Turkey-Headed White	Brown or tinted Brown or tinted Brown or tinted
Dutch fowls:			
Breda..........		Black Blue Cuckoo White	White White White White
Drente......		Numerous varieties	White White White White White White
Hamburg...	Black Golden Penciled Golden Spangled Silver Penciled Silver Spangled White		White White White White White White
Owl-Bearded Dutch.....		Numerous varieties	White
Red Cap.........	Rose-Comb		White
English fowls:			
Dorking.......	Colored Silver-Gray White	Cuckoo Rose-Comb Silver-Gray Red	White White White
Orpington......	Single-Comb Black Single-Comb Blue Single-Comb Buff Single-Comb White	Columbian Cuckoo	Tinted Tinted Tinted Tinted

Breed	Variety	Sub-variety	Color of egg
		Jubilee Rose-Comb	Tinted
		Jubilee Single-Comb	Tinted
		Rose-Comb Black	Tinted
		Rose-Comb Buff	Tinted
		Rose-Comb White	Tinted
		Spangled Rose-Comb	Tinted
		Spangled Single-Comb	Tinted
Scotch Dumpy		Numerous colors	Tinted
Scotch Gray		Barred or Cuckoo	White
Sussex	Light		Tinted
	Red		Tinted
	Speckled	Brown	Tinted
French fowls:			
Creveceur	Black	Black	White
Houdan	Mottled	Blue	White
	White	Gray	White
La Flèche	Black	White	White
La Bresse	Black	Parti-colored	White
		Parti-colored black and white	White
Bourbourg			White
Faverolle	Salmon	Black	Tinted
		Light	Tinted
		White	Tinted

BREEDS AND STANDARD AND NON-STANDARD VARIETIES OF POULTRY
(Continued)

Classes and Breeds	Standard Varieties	Non-Standard Varieties	Color of Eggshell
Game fowls:			
Exhibition Game......	Birchen		Tinted
	Black		Tinted
	Black-Breasted Red		Tinted
	Brown-Red		Tinted
	Golden Duckwing		Tinted
	Red Pyle		Tinted
	Silver Duckwing		Tinted
	White		Tinted
		Wheaten	Tinted
Cornish, or Indian, Game......	Dark		Tinted
	White		Tinted
	White-Laced Red		Brown
Malay......	Black-Breasted Red		White
Sumatra......	Black		Tinted
Aseel......		Black-Red	Tinted
		Brown-Red	Tinted
		Duckwing	Tinted
		Pyle	Tinted
		White	Tinted
Old-English......		Black	Tinted
		Black-Red	Tinted
		Brown-Red	Tinted
		Duckwing	Tinted
		Pyle	Tinted
		Spangled	Tinted
		White	Tinted

		Parti-colored	White
German fowls:			
Lakenfelder........			White
Mediterranean fowls:			
Ancona........	Mottled Single-Comb	Mottled Rose-Comb	White
Andalusian........	Blue		White
Leghorn........	Single-Comb Black	Blue	White
	Single-Comb Brown	Dominique	White
	Rose-Comb Brown	Mottled	White
	Single-Comb Buff	Partridge	White
	Rose-Comb Buff	Pyle	White
	Silver	Rose-Comb Black	White
	Single-Comb White		White
	Rose-Comb White		White
Minorca....	Single-Comb Black		White
	Rose-Comb Black	Barred	White
	Single-Comb White	Blue	White
	Single-Comb Buff	Rose-Comb White	White
Spanish.....	White-Faced Black	White-Faced White	White
Polish fowls:	White-Crested Black		White
	Buff Laced		White
	Bearded Golden		White
	Non-Bearded Golden		White
	Bearded Silver		White
	Non-Bearded Silver		White
	Bearded White		White
	Non-Bearded White		White

BREEDS AND STANDARD AND NON-STANDARD VARIETIES OF POULTRY
(Continued)

Classes and Breeds	Standard Varieties	Non-Standard Varieties	Color of Eggshell
Miscellaneous fowls:			
Frizzle............	Bay		Tinted
	Black		Tinted
	Red		Tinted
	White		Tinted
Naked Neck........		Numerous colors	Tinted
Rumpless..........		Numerous colors	Tinted
Silky.............	White	Numerous varieties	Tinted
Sultan............	White		Tinted
Yokohama, Tosa, or Phoenix.....		Numerous varieties	Tinted
Bantam fowls:			
Booted............	White	Black and other varieties	Tinted
Brahma............	Dark		Tinted
	Light		Tinted
Cochin............	Black	Cuckoo	Tinted
	Buff		Tinted
	Partridge		Tinted
	White		Tinted
Exhibition Game Bantam	Birchen	Old-English	White or slightly tinted
	Black	Wheaten	White or slightly tinted
	Black-Breasted Red		Slightly tinted

Breed	Variety		Eggs
Japanese...	Brown-Red		White or slightly tinted
	Golden Duckwing		White or slightly tinted
	Red Pyle		White or slightly tinted
	Silver Duckwing		White or slightly tinted
	White		White or slightly tinted
	Black	Buff	White or slightly tinted
	Black-Tailed	Duckwing	White or slightly tinted
	White	Splashed	White or slightly tinted
Polish...	Bearded White	White-Crested Black	White or slightly tinted
	Buff Laced	Golden	White or slightly tinted
	Non-Bearded	Silver	White or slightly tinted
Rose-Comb...	Black		White or slightly tinted
	White		White or slightly tinted
Sebright...	Golden		White or slightly tinted
	Silver		White or slightly tinted

BREEDS AND STANDARD AND NON-STANDARD VARIETIES OF POULTRY
(Continued)

Classes and Breeds	Standard Varieties	Non-Standard Varieties	Color of Eggshell
Miscellaneous bantams:			
Andalusian........		Blue	White or slightly tinted
Aseel.............		Black-Red	Tinted
Frizzle...........		Numerous varieties	Tinted
German...........		Numerous varieties	Tinted
Langshan.........		Black	Tinted
Leghorn..........		Numerous varieties	Tinted
Malay............	Black-Red	Numerous varieties	Tinted
Minorca..........		Black	Tinted
Nankin...........		Buff	Tinted
Rumpless.........		Numerous colors	Tinted
Scotch Gray......		Cuckoo	Tinted
Silky.............	White		Tinted
Spanish..........		Black	Tinted
Sultan...........		White	Tinted
Yokohama........		Numerous varieties	Tinted
Ducks:			
Aylesbury........	White		White or tinted with green
Call.............	Gray / White		Tinted / Tinted
Cayuga..........	Black		Green
Crested..........	White		Tinted
East India.......	Black		Green

Breed	Variety	Variety	Egg color
Huttegem	Fawn-White	Broken colors, Blue-white	Tinted
Indian Runner		White	White
Khaki	Colored	Buff (female is penciled)	Tinted
Muscovy	White		White
Orpington	White	Buff	White
Partridge	Colored	Partridge colored	Tinted
Pekin			Tinted
Rouen			White
Swedish	Blue		Greenish tint
			Blue tinted
Geese:			
African	Gray		White
Buff		Buff colored	White
Chinese	Brown		White
	White		White
Egyptian	Colored		Tinted
Embden	White		White
Toulouse	Gray		White
Wild, or Canadian	Gray, marked with black		Tinted
Guinea fowls:			
		Gray	Speckled
		Pearl	Speckled
		Vulturine	Speckled
		White	Speckled
Peafowls:			
		Black-Winged	Speckled
		Common	Speckled
		Javan	Speckled
		White	Speckled

BREEDS AND STANDARD AND NON-STANDARD VARIETIES OF POULTRY
(Continued)

Classes and Breeds	Standard Varieties	Non-Standard Varieties	Color of Eggshell
Turkeys:	Black Bourbon Red Bronze Buff Narragansett Slate White	Cambridge Bronze Ronquieres Fawn Gray	Speckled Speckled Speckled Speckled Speckled Speckled Speckled

Note.—Bantam fowls of the same breed are apt to lay either white or tinted eggs. Ducks of the same breed may lay either white or tinted eggs; some have a greenish and others a bluish tint. The eggs of geese may be white, grayish white, or cream colored.

STANDARD WEIGHTS OF POULTRY

The table on pages 222 to 225 gives the standard weights of all poultry having standard weights, the average weights of those standard fowls that do not have standard weights, and the average weights of non-standard poultry. The following list contains the notes corresponding to the references in the table and includes the disqualifying weights of bantam fowls:

NOTES ON STANDARD WEIGHTS OF POULTRY

*Non-standard breed.

[1]Cock and cockerel.

[2]Hen and pullet.

[3]No standard weights.

[4]At 10 mo.

[5]Penciled Hamburgs. In other Hamburg varieties the fowls are somewhat heavier.

[6]Colored Dorking cocks often weigh from 12 to 14 lb.; hens and cockerels, from 9 to 10 lb.; and pullets, from 7 to 8 lb.

[7]It is not unusual for Houdans to exceed these weights.

[8]Standard height, cock, 26 in.; hen, 18 in.; cockerel, 18 in.; pullet, 15 in.

[9]Disqualifying weights for Booted Bantams: cocks, 28 oz.; hens, 24 oz.; cockerels, 24 oz.; pullets, 22 oz.

[10]Disqualifying weights for Brahma Bantams: cocks, 34 oz.; hens, 30 oz.; cockerels, 30 oz.; pullets, 28 oz.

[11]Disqualifying weights for Cochin Bantams: cocks, 34 oz.; hens, 30 oz.; cockerels, 30 oz.; pullets, 28 oz.

[12]Disqualifying weights for Black-Tailed Japanese Bantams: cocks, 30 oz.; hens, 26 oz.; cockerels, 26 oz.; pullets, 24 oz. Disqualifying weights for White Japanese Bantams: cocks, 30 oz.; hens, 26 oz.; cockerels, 26 oz.; pullets, 24 oz. Disqualifying weights for Black Japanese Bantams: cocks, 30 oz.; hens, 26 oz.; cockerels, 26 oz.; pullets, 24 oz.

[13]Disqualifying weights for Polish Bantams: cocks, 30 oz.; hens, 26 oz.; cockerels, 26 oz.; pullets, 24 oz.

[14]Disqualifying weights for Rose-Comb Bantams: cocks, 28 oz.; hens, 24 oz.; cockerels, 24 oz.; pullets, 22 oz.

[15]Disqualifying weights for Sebright Bantams: cocks, 30 oz.; hens, 26 oz.; cockerels, 26 oz.; pullets, 24 oz.

[16]English standard weights for Malay Bantams: cocks, $3\frac{1}{2}$ lb.; cockerels and hens, 3 lb.; pullets, 2 lb.

[17]Weight of adult Bronze turkey cock; yearling cock weighs 33 lb.

[18]Weight of adult Narragansett turkey cock; yearling cock weighs 25 lb.

STANDARD WEIGHTS OF POULTRY

Fowls

Classes and Breeds	Cock Pounds	Hen Pounds	Cockerel Pounds	Pullet Pounds
American fowls:				
Plymouth Rock.	9½	7½	8	6
Wyandotte	8½	6½	7½	5½
Rhode Island Red	8½	6½	7½	5
Dominique	7	5	6	4
Java	9½	7½	8	6½
*Jersey Blue	10	8	7	5
Buckeye	9	6	8	5
Asiatic fowls:				
Light Brahma	12	9½	10	8
Dark Brahma	11	8½	9	7
Cochin	11	9½	9	7
Langshan	9½	7½	8	6½
Belgian fowls:				
*Antwerp Brahma	12	9½	10	8
*Ardenne	[1]5 to 6½	[2]4 to 5		
*Brabant	8	6	7	5
*Braekel	[1]6 to 8	[2]4 to 6		
*Bruges	[1]8 to 10	[2]7 to 9		
*Campine	[1]4½ to 5	[2,3]3½ to 4		
*Flemish	[1]6½ to 9	[2]4½ to 6		
*Herve	[1]3 to 4	[2]2 to 3		
*Huttegem	[1]9 to 11	[2]7 to 9		
*Malines	[1]9 to 11½	[2]8 to 10	[4]10	[4]8
Dutch fowls:				
*Breda	[1]6 to 9	[2]5 to 6½		
*Drente	[1]5 to 5½	[2]4 to 4½		
[3]Hamburg	[5]5	[5]4		
*Owl-Bearded Dutch	7½	5½	6½	4½
Red Cap	7½	6	6	5
English fowls:				
[6]Colored Dorking	9	7	8	6
Silver-Gray Dorking	8	6½	7	5½
White Dorking	7½	6	6½	5
Orpington	10	8	8½	7
*Scotch Dumpy	[1]8	[2]5 to 6		
*Scotch Gray	[1]9 to 11	[2]7 to 9		

TABLE—(Continued)

Classes and Breeds	Cock Pounds	Hen Pounds	Cockerel Pounds	Pullet Pounds
English fowls—(Continued):				
Sussex..........	10½ to 11½	8½ to 9½	9 to 10	7 to 8
French fowls:				
Crevecœur......	8	7	7	6
[7]Houdan........	7½	6½	6½	5½
La Flèche.......	8½	7½	7½	6½
*La Bresse.......	[1]5 to 6½	[2]4½ to 5½		
*Bourbourg......	[1]6¾ to 9	[2]6 to 7		
*Faverolle.......	7 to 8½	6 to 7	6 to 7	5 to 6
Game fowls:				
[3]Exhibition Game	[1]7 to 9	[2]5 to 7		
Cornish, or In-dian, Game...	9	7	8	6
White-Laced Red Cornish..	8	6	7	5
[8]Malay..........	9	7	7	5
[3]Sumatra........	[1]5 to 6	[2]4 to 5·		
*Aseel...........	[1]6	[2]5		
*Old-English.....	[1]4½ to 7	[2]4 to 5		
German fowls:				
Lakenfelder.....	[1]5 to 6	[2]3½ to 4½		
Mediterranean fowls:				
Ancona........	5½	4½	4½	3½
Andalusian.....	6	5	5	4
Leghorn........	5½	4	4½	3½
Single-Comb Mi-norca........	9	7½	7½	6½
S.-C. White, and Buff, and Rose-Comb Black Minorca......	8	6½	6½	5½
Spanish........	8	6½	6½	5½
[3]*Polish fowls:*......	[1]5½ to 6½	[2]4 to 5		
Miscellaneous fowls:				
[3]Frizzle.........	9½	7½	8	6
*Naked Neck....	9½	7½	8	6
*Rumpless.......	7	5	6	4
[3]Silky..........	6	4	5	3
[3]Sultan..........	[1]5	[2]4		
*Yokohama, Tosa, or Phoenix....	[1]4½ to 6	[2]2½ to 4		

TABLE—(*Continued*)
BANTAM FOWLS

Classes and Breeds	Cock Ounces	Hen Ounces	Cockerel Ounces	Pullet Ounces
Standard bantam fowls:				
[9]Booted.........	26	22	22	20
[10]Brahma........	30	26	26	24
[11]Cochin.........	30	26	26	24
Exhibition Game Bantam......	22	20	20	18
[12]Japanese.......	26	22	22	20
[13]Polish..........	26	22	22	20
[14]Rose-Comb.....	26	22	22	20
[15]Sebright........	26	22	22	20
Miscellaneous bantams:				
*Andalusian.....	26	22	22	20
*Aseel...........	26	24	24	22
*Frizzle.........	30	26	26	24
*German........	30	26	26	24
*Langshan.......	30	26	26	24
*Leghorn........	26	22	22	20
[16]Malay..........	26	24	24	22
*Minorca.......	30	26	26	24
*Nankin........	30	26	26	24
*Rumpless.......	30	26	26	24
*Scotch Gray....	30	26	26	24
[3]Silky..........	30	26	26	24
*Spanish........	26	22	22	20
*Sultan.........	30	26	26	24
*Yokohama......	30	26	26	24

DUCKS

Classes and Breeds	Adult Drake Pounds	Adult Duck Pounds	Young Drake Pounds	Young Duck Pounds
Aylesbury.......	9	8	8	7
[3]Call.............	[12]2½ to 3	[22]2 to 2½		
Cayuga.........	8	7	7	6
Crested.........	7	6	6	5
East India.......	7	6	6	5
*Huttegem.......	7	6	6	5
Indian Runner...	4½	4	[3]4	[3]3½

TABLE—(*Continued*)

Classes and Breeds	Adult Drake Pounds	Adult Duck Pounds	Young Drake Pounds	Young Duck Pounds
*Khaki...........	7	6	6	5
Muscovy.........	10	7	8	6
*Orpington.......	7	6	6	5
*Partridge........	7	6	6	5
Pekin...........	9	8	8	7
Rouen...........	9	8	8	7
Swedish.........	8	7	6½	5½

GEESE

Classes and Breeds	Adult Gander Pounds	Adult Goose Pounds	Young Gander Pounds	Young Goose Pounds
African.........	20	18	16	14
*Buff.............				
Chinese.........	12	10	10	8
Egyptian........	10	8	8	6
Embden.........	20	18	18	16
Toulouse........	25	20	20	16
Wild, or Canadian	12	10	10	8

TURKEYS, GUINEA FOWLS, AND PEAFOWLS

Classes and Breeds	Cock Pounds	Hen Pounds	Cockerel Pounds	Pullet Pounds
Turkeys:				
Black..........	27	18	18	12
Bourbon Red...	30	18	22	14
Bronze.........	[1]736	20	25	16
Buff...........	27	18	18	12
*Cambridge Bronze.......	[1]18 to 24	[2]12 to 16		
*Fawn..........	[1]18 to 20	[2]12 to 16		
*Gray..........	28	16	18	10
Narragansett ...	[1][8]30	18	20	12
*Ronquieres.....	30	18	20	12
Slate..........	27	18	18	12
White..........	28	18	20	14
Guinea fowls:				
All varieties	[1]4 to 6	[2]3 to 5		
Peafowls:				
All varieties	[1]12 to 18	[2]7 to 12		

MARKING OF POULTRY FOR IDEN-TIFICATION

MARKING OF FOWLS

To attain the greatest success in breeding poultry, whether for egg production, market purposes, or fancy stock, a poultryman must know the pedigree of the fowls mated, and in order to be able to identify each fowl, some system of marking chicks must be adopted.

A *system of toe markings* that can be used for a limited number of fowls is shown in Fig. 1. As shown in the illustration, fifteen different combinations can be made by punching holes in the toes of chicks. A number of forms of punches are made for this purpose; several of these are shown in Fig. 2 (*a*), (*b*), (*c*), (*d*), and (*e*). Care must be exercised to entirely remove the severed portion of the web to prevent it from growing together again. The wound will heal in a few days.

In building up a strain of good layers, the beginning is usually made by marking chicks from the most prolific layers. The same principle is applied in the establishment of a good strain of market poultry. These markings are used on the progeny of selected stock only and serve as a guide for the selection of the pullets that should be saved for winter layers. Those that have toe markings should be kept, no matter what their appearance may be, for in this way only can a good start be made.

FIG. 1   Records can be kept quite as readily with chicks artifically hatched as with hen-hatched chicks. The partitioned incubator egg tray can be used for holding the eggs from selected hens. The eggs are marked

with numbers before they are placed in the incubator for hatching. On the eighteenth day of incubation, the numbered eggs are transferred from the regular egg tray into the special tray. When hatched in this tray, the chicks cannot get out of it. After they have been marked, the chicks may be placed in a brooder with other chicks with no danger of their identity becoming lost. Separated trays can be used in any incubator. Partitions can be made of tin or wood, and they can be placed in the egg trays to separate the eggs as well as the chicks when they are hatched. When they are used, the unmarked chicks must not be allowed to drop into the nursery; if this is permitted, their identity will be lost.

To keep a correct record of chicks hatched by hens, each hen should have eggs from only one hen given her for hatching.

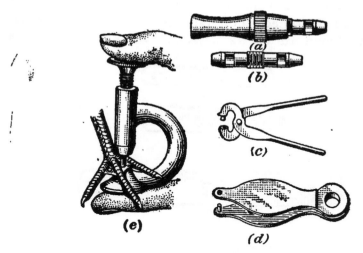

FIG. 2

The toe-marking system is satisfactory for a small number of selected fowls, but when the breeding operations are on an extensive scale some other system of marking must be adopted. Bands of some kind for attaching to the shanks, as shown in Fig. 3, are satisfactory for marking fowls and permit of sufficient

variations. Several forms of aluminum bands are shown
in Fig. 4. The small band shown in (*a*) is suitable

F<small>IG</small>. 3

for placing around the shank of a chick, and later, when
the shank grows too large for this band, it may be
removed and fastened thorough the web of the wing.
The band shown in (*b*) is used for chicks also, but is

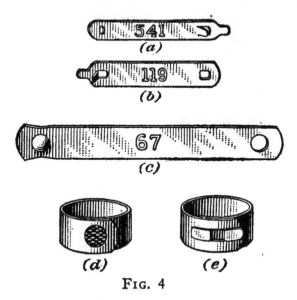

(a)

(b)

(c)

(d)   *(e)*

F<small>IG</small>. 4

rather too wide to insert in the web of the wing. **After**
a fowl reaches its full growth, a band like that shown **in**

(c), which may be sealed, may be fastened about the shank. This band, fastened with a rivet, is shown in (d). The fastening is done very easily with a pair of pincers, as shown in Fig. 5. After being well fastened

FIG. 5

or sealed, such a band will last the lifetime of a fowl, unless removed by cutting. All of these bands may be stamped with any number or other characters desired. A type of aluminum band known as an interlocking band is shown in Fig. 4 (e).

Colored celluloid bands are used for marking fowls kept in large flocks. They are most useful when used in connection with the metal bands and serve as a means of quick identification for various large groups

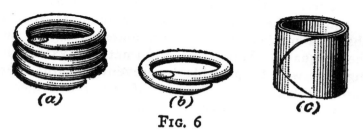

(a)   (b)   (c)

FIG. 6

of fowls when they are kept in big flocks; that is, all the chicks hatched in one year may have a blue band; those hatched the next year, a red band; the next, a yellow band; and so on. In this way the age of fowls

may be told at a glance. The bands may be used also to identify strains or families of fowls. Though they have their usefulness in this way, they are not an absolutely accurate means of identifying fowls; in addition they are liable to be lost from the shank; in such cases, if no other band were used, the identity of a fowl would be lost. Three celluloid markers are shown in Fig. 6. The ring shown in (*a*) encircles the shank a number of times. One end of this is hooked about the shank and then the rest is wound around much in the same manner that a key is worked on a key ring. The ring shown in (*b*) is a small one of the same type as that shown in (*a*). In (*c*) is shown a flat celluloid band. Poultry supply houses sell celluloid rings and bands in as many as eight different colors.

MARKING OF PIGEONS

To build up the productiveness of a flock of pigeons and to maintain the quality of the squabs, it is necessary to mark breeding pigeons in such a way that their identity can be easily determined. This is usually done by fastening a suitably marked band of some kind about the shank of each bird. A careful record of each breeding pigeon should be kept in a record book. This record should include the ancestors of each bird, their egg production, the time it takes for them to hatch their squabs, the time it takes for them to rear their squabs to a marketable size, and notes as to the quality of their squabs. With this information systematically arranged it will be possible to prevent harmful inbreeding and to mate the offspring of different pigeons in such a way as to improve the productiveness and quality of the flock.

Bands suitable for marking breeding pigeons can be obtained in several styles from dealers in poultry supplies. Some of these bands are made so that they indicate only the year in which the breeders were first mated. This is usually done in one of two ways, either by having

different-colored bands for each year, samples of which are shown in **Fig. 7**, or by stamping the year on the band,

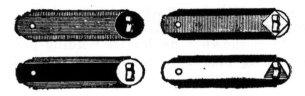

FIG. 7

as shown in **Fig. 8**. The colored bands are usually more easily distinguished at a little distance than those stamped with figures. Other shank bands, in addition to indicating the year in which the breeders were first mated, have a numeral or some other mark that indicates

FIG. 8

the ancestors of the birds. Such bands, however, are used principally in the breeding of exhibition pigeons, the system being too complicated for the producer of commercial squabs.

In marking breeding pigeons, it is customary to place the band on the right shank of male birds and on the left shank of female birds. Squabs that are to be kept for breeders should have a band placed on them as soon as they are ready to leave the nest. At this time it is impossible to determine the sex, but

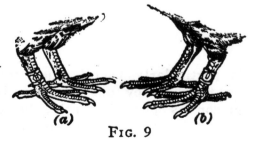

FIG. 9

the band can be placed on either shank to preserve the identity of the squabs, and can be shifted, if necessary,

when the sex can be determined. Two shank bands attached to birds are shown in Fig. 9; the one shown in (*a*) is attached to the right shank of a male pigeon, and that shown in (*b*) is attached to the left shank of a female pigeon.

In Fig. 10 is shown a device for holding pigeons while bands are being placed on their shanks. Such a device

Fig. 10

is particularly useful when the band must be placed on the bird by one person. In using this device the pigeon is pushed gently, head down, into the cone, where it is held without injury. The band is then fastened about the shank and the pigeon released from the cone.

CALENDAR FOR THE POULTRYMAN'S YEAR

OCTOBER

October is usually the beginning of the poultryman's year. Ring out the old and ring in the new is usually practiced at this time. All of the old fowls that are useless should be marketed; the flock should be separated and the old hens and young pullets placed in different apartments.

As the weather grows colder, more precaution must be taken to prevent ailment from creeping into the flock. All specimens, old or young, which lack size, strength, or vitality should be culled out from the flock; nothing but strong, healthy specimens should remain.

The poultry buildings should be of such a character that no drafts of air can blow through them. All air and ventilation should come in from the front of the building.

NOVEMBER

The spring-hatched pullets should be laying at this time, and the best of egg-producing rations should be fed to them and to the old hens as well.

The growing green food having disappeared, a plentiful supply of sprouted oats, alfalfa hay, and other green foods should be provided to take its place. The floor of the poultry house should be well covered with dry litter and the green food should be thrown on it. This will encourage the fowls to work for all the food they get, and in this way they will be made active and more healthy. Fowls that are too weak to work for a living are usually poor layers and might as well be sold to market.

An additional culling of the flock should be made at this time. No male over 2 yr. old should be kept. The earliest and best cockerels of the year are best for breeding purposes.

No hen or pullet that does not show the proper indication for egg production should be kept after this period.

November and December are the early winter months during which time all hens and pullets should begin to lay. If they have been carefully fed they will do so.

Hens and pullets should have a good egg-producing diet at this time. One of the necessities of poultry during winter months is that they shall be protected from the elements, have plenty of exercise of some kind, and be fed on a liberal grain ration composed of the grains best suited to egg production. A liberal supply of green food, also, should be fed during the winter months.

December

This month is the most severe on poultry and the most trying on poultrymen of all months of the year. The houses should be kept warm and dry and free from drafts; all cracks and openings should be carefully covered or stopped up to prevent drafts through the houses.

Hens will lay but few eggs at this time, when the price is high and the eggs most desirable. For this reason every effort possible should be made to make the hens lay. The only way to secure a good supply of eggs for market at this time is to have a thorough knowledge of the possibilities of egg production through scientific management and feeding. No one not fully informed on these matters can hope to have a full egg supply from hens or pullets during midwinter months.

Plenty of green food, well-selected grains, the proper quantity of nourishing food, and fresh water are necessities at this time.

January

Poultry work requires constant attention during this month.

Cull out the less perfect fowls and sell all those not intended for producing market eggs or for breeding.

During the last part of January look over the fowls and become acquainted with those suitable for breeding, so that no time will be lost when the season for mating arrives.

Fowls will need more fattening food, such as corn and barley. A good plan to follow during the winter is to feed a grain ration composed half of corn and the other half of equal parts of wheat, oats, and barley.

Twice a week or every other day feed green cut bone.

Dry mash is one of the most popular kinds of food for poultry during the winter months. One-third of a winter dry-mash mixture should consist of corn meal and the rest of wheat bran and wheat middlings and some ground oats. The same ration should be fed during Jan., Feb., and March, especially in parts of the world where these months are cold and stormy.

Supply fowls with plenty of green foods, such as turnips, rutabagas, cabbage, lettuce, cut clover hay, cut alfalfa, etc.

FEBRUARY

Winter is coming to a close, and spring-like diseases will prevail in some localities. Farthest north, cold weather will continue for some time.

Houses should be protected from spring rains, snow and sleet; either glass windows or curtain fronts make good protection.

It is now time to mate fowls for the production of eggs for hatching; select the best of all and keep them separate for special breeding. No sick fowls nor fowls that have deformities or that lack superior quality should ever be used in the breeding pen. The best of all the fowls on any farm will produce many culls; this is reason enough for using only the selected specimens for breeding.

A liberal supply of green food is always beneficial at this time, because such food increases the density of the albumen of an egg, and the heavier or more dense the albumen of the egg the greater strength it will have for nourishing a chick in the embryo state.

MARCH

March is the most uncertain month of the year. Weather conditions cannot be depended on. March winds are the most piercing of the year, and the fowls must be protected from the elements.

Little chicks should be kept under hovers that are inside of a building that is tight enough to protect them from the elements. March chicks make Nov. layers.

Incubators should now be in action. Nests made for sitting hens should be deep so as to provide a comfortable nest for the hen. Always dust the body of a sitting hen with insect powder. Persian insect powder is the best. Dust it down well into the feathers and close to the skin of the fowl. This dusting should be renewed every 3 or 4 da. for 1 wk. or 10 da.

A soap box 18 in. or 2 ft. square with some sand or earth in the bottom and dry hay or straw packed well down on top of this, provides an excellent nest for a sitting hen.

The nest for a sitting hen should always be placed where she will have plenty of room, light, and shelter from the elements, yet be confined where she cannot run away from the eggs. She should be watched and put back on the eggs if she seems to neglect them.

APRIL

April is usually the most favorable month of the year for hatching chicks; at this time the grass and all vegetables are sending up new growth, and there is plenty of natural food for the little chicks.

April is the month when all incubators should be filled with eggs for hatching, and all broody hens should have a clutch of eggs.

See to it that the brooding hens are well fed while doing their family duty. Laying hens should have more green food at this time than before. Corn bread is good food for the mother hen and little chicks. To make such corn bread mix 1 teaspoonful of baking powder into a mixture composed of 1 pt. of corn meal, ½ pt. of wheat bran, 4 oz. of good meat scrap, and a little

bone meal, and add a pinch of salt. Stir the mass up, moistening it well with milk or water, milk preferred, and bake in the oven. When well baked and cool, **it** can be crumbled and fed to the little chicks.

April, May, and June are the spring months **in** northern latitudes. Less fattening grain should be fed during this period; some wheat and less corn should be fed to the poultry, and they should have an increased supply of green food; if bugs and worms are not plentiful on the range, they should have animal food of some kind.

Young chicks and growing stock should be fed liberally during this period; they cannot have too much wholesome grain. Some dry mash is helpful; if it is desirable to grow them quickly for market purposes, wet mash may be used.

MAY

Both old fowls and young chicks should have greater freedom during the month of May than during the preceding months.

All parts of the poultry houses, the nest boxes, and

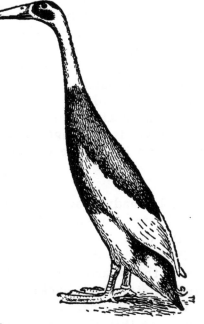

INDIAN RUNNER DRAKE

the runways should be thoroughly cleaned. Brush the ground thoroughly with a stiff broom; after the top cover has been swept away, dig up the soil and turn it under.

Chicks of the Asiatic, American, and English breeds should be hatched prior to the middle of May; those of the Mediterranean breeds should be hatched before the end of May. Chicks of all kinds will do well if hatched after June 1, but they are seldom of much value to the poultryman except for table purposes.

JUNE

In some localities the weather will be very warm during the month of June. Shade is an important consideration at this time, and where it does not exist naturally it must be supplied artificially.

During this month less fattening foods than given in preceding months will answer, and less corn and more wheat and oats should be fed. Dry mash that contains but little corn meal should be used.

The warmer the weather the more green food and pure fresh water will be needed for the fowls. No fat meat, but some lean meat should be fed to the laying hens during this month.

June is apt to be the last month of the year in which chicks are hatched and the eggs from which they are hatched should be strong and full of vitality to infuse abundant health and vigor into the chicks. If the fowls can have free range through the fields and woods at this time it will be of benefit to them.

JULY

Cool, shady places and freedom from the irritation of overheated houses and insect vermin should be the order of the day.

Poultry must have shade at this time to protect them from the glaring rays of the sun, which will scorch and blister their backs and make life a burden to them.

On the farms, all the male fowls should be taken away at this time and sold. They are of no further use after the hatching season is over.

Thousands of eggs shipped to market during the heated term are destroyed because the eggs begin to hatch. This will occur in the egg boxes traveling on trains when the temperature is above 100° F. If no males are kept with the hens, especially on farms in the southern climates, there will be fewer spoiled eggs in transit.

If all the hens can be turned into a wood or on land from which grain has been harvested it will be beneficial to them.

Plenty of fresh, cool water for drinking and a clean place for roosting must be provided during the heated term.

Insect vermin, including lice and mites, will throng the poultry in the poultry houses during the heated term, unless prevented through cleanliness and care.

July and August are the hardest months of the year in the latitude where heat is intense during that period. During the hot period fowls should have principally wheat and oats—ground oats, wheat bran, and wheat middlings as a dry mash.

Fowls intended for market during fall months should be fed liberally during this period with fattening food and be sold to market as soon as they are well fattened.

Shade is an absolute necessity during the heated period. If natural shade does not exist artificial shade of some kind must be provided.

Fowls should be in full molt at this time. Hens that are overly fat do not molt quickly; hens that are very thin in flesh are slow to molt. Fowls in good condition usually molt the best; those that are too fat should, have less to eat; those that are thin in flesh should be fed liberally; those that molt well should be protected from cold drafts and have a good, nourishing ration. Fowls that have free range will need only proper grain diet.

August

During the heated term of dog days, old and young fowls of all kinds, including turkeys and water fowls, suffer intensely from heat, and plenty of green food, grit, and fresh water should be provided.

At this time all old fowls, male and female, past 2 yr. old should be sold. The hens would lay but few eggs from now until winter, and as market poultry they will probably bring more than at any other time for the next 3 mo.

Continued cleanliness in and about the poultry houses, freedom from insect vermin, and free range are the necessities at this time.

September

September is the turning point in the life of both young and old fowls. The old fowls are in molt and the young fowls finish their coat of feathers at this time, and they must be well cared for and fed. They must be built up for the coming winter, and for this reason should have more nourishing, more strengthening, and more fattening foods than they have had during the summer.

Cold rains, changeable weather, and cool winds may be injurious to poultry at this time. Colds, catarrh, and

INDIAN RUNNER DUCK EGGS

roup may injure the fowls. A change from outdoor life or from closed coops into unclean poultry buildings may do great injury to them.

All of the buildings should be swept out perfectly clean, and all cracks and crevices should be brushed and freed absolutely from dust, dirt, and lurking vermin. The floors, doors, and windows should be put in good repair and the inside of the buildings sprayed with some material that is both healthy and a perfect insect destroyer and disinfector. Plenty of green food

and an increased quantity of animal food should be fed at this time.

September is the beginning of the fall, and at this time hens lay but little. Early-hatched pullets should begin to lay; these should have special care and feeding. All poultry should be fed at this time with reference to the winter egg production.

MISCELLANEOUS INFORMATION

How to Ascertain the Age of Fowls.—It is difficult for an amateur to decide the age of fowls. Experienced poultrymen are at times unable to decide from outward appearance. But few rules are safe to follow; some of them, however, may be depended on.

The surface of the skin under the wing of a pullet will be interspersed or marked with rose-colored veins; these are totally absent in hens that are more than 12 mo. old. The skin of pullets will be fairly well covered with long, silky hair; this disappears directly after the first molt.

In an adult hen the skin will be white and free from either veins or hairs. If these are absent it can be seen at a glance that the fowl, if a hen, must be more than 1 yr. old.

The points of the pelvic bones grow much closer together in a pullet than in a hen, yet this cannot always be depended on, as the cause of the spreading of the pelvic bone is prolific egg production. Hens that never lay may have the points of the pelvic bones close together, even though very old. Usually, however, this test can be depended on.

The scales and skin on the shanks and feet of young fowls are usually smooth and tender, and the toenails are longer and more pointed than the toenails of older fowls. The scales and skin on the shanks and feet of older fowls become rough and turn a whitish gray with age. Scaly legs and roughness of any kind on the

shanks and feet indicate an age of more than a year, in all kinds of poultry, including turkeys, ducks, and geese.

The faces of poultry more than 1 yr. old lose their smooth finished appearance and become wrinkled and drawn. The eyes and eyelids of fowls more than 1 yr. old do not have the fresh appearance of young poultry.

One of the best indications of the age of fowls is the appearance of the secondaries. At the conclusion of the first complete molt, which occurs when the fowl is about 12 mo. old, the secondaries alter in shape and

Fig. 1 ,

show evidence of the dividing line between the young and the old fowl. This change of the secondaries cannot be readily described. The wings of pullets and of old hens must be held alongside of one another and compared and studied in order to appreciate the marked change that occurs in the shape or form of these feathers.

Proper Way to Hold a Fowl.—When a fowl is carried about or held in the hands it should be held in a position that is comfortable for it and cleanly for the person holding it. When a fowl is held by the shanks and feet with the head hanging down, it suffers considerable pain, and if the crop contains water, the water will

run out through the gullet and partly strangle the bird.

One of the most cleanly ways to carry a fowl is shown in Fig. 1. The thighs are held in the hand with one finger in between them to avoid too much pressure on the bones, and the breast of the fowl rests on the forearm of the person holding it. The fowl suffers no inconvenience, and there is little danger of the clothing of the holder being soiled by voidings from the bird.

When the fowl is held as shown in Fig. 2, the feet of the fowl are free to rub against the clothing of the holder, and any filth from it will be liable to drop on

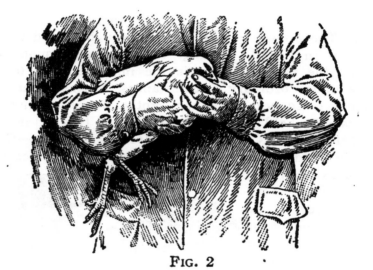

FIG. 2

and smear the clothing of the person holding the bird.

The rule to observe in carrying a fowl is to carry it with the head toward and the tail away from the holder.

Proper Way to Hold a Squab.—Great care should be exercised in picking up squabs, as it is very easy to injure them. Squabs should be picked up by gently passing the fingers of the right hand under the crop and breast, placing the left hand on the back, and sliding the bird into the palm of the right hand without gripping it with the fingers. Care should be taken to see that the crop of the bird is not injured. When the

crop of a squab is full it is heavy and apt to be injured if held tightly. It is not necessary to close the fingers

FIG. 3

about the squab unless it becomes restless and tries to get away. When a squab tries to escape from the hand, the fingers s h o u l d be closed gently about the body in such a way as to prevent the wings from being flapped about. The proper way in which a squab should be held is shown in Fig. 3. In Fig. 4 is shown a squab being held by the fingers. This is the improper way to hold squabs under ordinary circumstances, because there is a tendency to squeeze them too tightly, but it is sometimes necessary to hold very lively squabs in this manner.

Proper Way of Catching and Holding Pigeons.—Catching and holding pigeons should be done with care, or

FIG. 4

the birds may be injured. P i g e o n s should never be roughly handled or held by the feet or by the wings alone. The proper method of holding a pigeon is shown in Fig. 5. As shown, the hand is placed around the rear portion of the body, the wings and tail are held gently but firmly by the hand, and the shanks are held between two fingers to prevent them from moving. When pigeons are held in this way they will be comfortable and will not struggle to free themselves, hence the wing and tail feathers of the birds will not become broken, and females will not be

injured during their egg-laying period. If female pigeons are chased in a pigeon house and roughly grabbed with the hands or caught in a dip net, they are very likely to be injured, especially if this is done during their egg-laying period. In pigeon houses that are so built that the birds are able to roost high overhead, no attempt should be made to catch them except at night, and then a box or a step ladder should always be used to stand on.

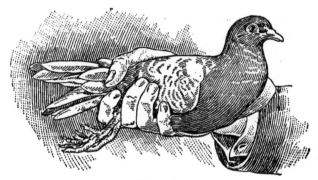

FIG. 5

LEGAL WEIGHTS PER BUSHEL

Following are the legal weights per bushel for various commodities. Those listed in tabular form, shown on pages 246 to 253, have been widely adopted, the others have been adopted only in the states mentioned.

Alsike (or Swedish) seed, 60 lb. (Md. and Okla.).

Beggar weed seed, 62 lb. (Fla.).

Bermuda grass seed, 40 lb. (Okla.).

Blackberries, 30 lb. (Ia.); 48 lb. (Tenn.); dried, 28 lb. (Tenn.).

Blueberries, 42 lb. (Minn.).

Bromus inermus, 14 lb. (N. Dak.).

Bur clover, in hulls, 8 lb. (N. C.).

Cabbage, 50 lb. (Tenn.).

Canary seed, 60 lb. (Tenn.); 50 lb. (Iowa).

Cantaloup melon, 50 lb. (Tenn.).

Castor seed, 50 lb. (Md.).

(Continued on page 255)

LEGAL WEIGHTS PER BUSHEL OF VARIOUS COMMODITIES FOR WHICH BUSHEL WEIGHTS HAVE BEEN WIDELY ADOPTED

	Alfalfa Seed	Apples[1]	Dried Apples	Apple Seeds	Barley	Beans[1]	Castor Beans (Shelled)	Beets	Blue-Grass Seed	Bran[1]	Broom-Corn Seed	Buckwheat	Carrots	Charcoal	Chestnuts	Clover Seed	Coal[1]	Anthracite Coal	Bituminous Coal	Cannel Coal	Mineral Coal	Stone Coal
U.S.					48		50					42							80			
Ala.			24		47							52				60						
Ariz.					45				14	20	48	40				60						
Ark.			24		48							52				60						
Cal.		[3]50			50	60						48										
Colo.			25		48	[2]55																
Conn.		48	24		48	[2]60			14	20												
Del.																						
D.C.			24			60		[4]60														
Fla.		[3]48			48	60	48		14	20		52	50	20		60	80	80			80	80
Ga.					47	[5]60	46			[7]20				20			80					
Hawaii					48	[6]60	46															
Ill.			24		48	[6]60	46	56	14	20	50	52	50			60						80
Ind.			25		48	60	46	56	14	20		50	50			60						
Iowa.	60	48	24		48	[8]60	46		14	20		52		20		60				76	80	80
Kans.	60	[3]48	24		48	60	[1]45		[9]14	20		50				60				76		
Ky.			24		47	[6]60			14			56					76	76	76	76	76	76

State																			
La.	60	44									·							20		80
Me.			28		48	60	60	60	14	20			50	20			60			80
Md.		48	25		48	[10]50	[11]60	60	14	20		48	50	20	80		60			
Mass.		48	22		48	46	60	50	14			48	50		80	20	60			80
Mich.		[3]50	28		48	[12]46	60	50	14	20	57	50	45				60	[14]50	80	
Minn.			26		48	46	60		14	20		48	50				60			
Miss.		48	24		48	46	[6]60	56	14	20		52	50			20	60			80
Mo.		45	24		48	46	[12]60	[9]14	14	20		52	50				64		80 / 76	80
Mont.		[3]48			48		[6]60	60	[9]14	20	46	52					60			
Neb.		[3]48	24		48	[6]60	60			20	30	50					60			
Nev.		48	24		48	60	60			20		48	50				60		70	
N.H.	60	50	25		48		2,11		14			50	50	[15,16]18		[15,16]18	60			
N.J.	60	48	25		48	[13]60	60				30	48	50	20		20	60		80	80
N.Y.		48		40	48	60	60		14	20		50					60			
N.C.	60	50			48	60	60	50				52					60		76	80
N.Dak.					48	60					42	42					64			
Ohio.	60	50	24		48	60	60	60	14	20		48	50				60			
Okla.	60	48	24	40	48	60				20	30	48	50		80		60	50	80	
Ore.		45	28		46	62		60			42	52					60			
Pa.					47	[6]60						42	50		[17]75		60	57	76	
R.I.		48	25	40	48	60	[6]60	50	14	20	30	48	50		80	22	60			80
S.C.			24		48	[12,18]60	60			20	42	42				22	[19]60			80
S.Dak.		[3]50	28	40	48	[6]60						50					60			80
Tenn.		45			48	62	60		14			42	50				60			80
Tex.		46			48	[6]60						48					60			
Vt.			28		48			60				52	50				60			
Va.		[3]45	28		46	60	60			20		42					60			
Wash.			25		48	60						52					60			
W.Va.			25		48							50	50				60		80	
Wis.		50	25		48			50		20							60			80

LEGAL WEIGHTS PER BUSHEL OF VARIOUS COMMODITIES FOR WHICH BUSHEL WEIGHTS HAVE BEEN WIDELY ADOPTED—(Continued)

	Coke	Corn[1-34]	Corn in Ear, Husked	Corn in Ear, Unhusked	Shelled Corn	Corn Meal[1]	Corn Meal, Bolted	Corn Meal, Unbolted	Cotton Seed[1]	Sea Island Cotton Seed	Upland Cotton Seed	Cranberries	Cucumbers	Flaxseed (Linseed)	Gooseberries	Hair (Plastering)	Hemp Seed	Herd's Grass[69]	Hickory Nuts	Hungarian Grass Seed	Indian Corn or Maize
U.S.		56	70	75	56	48			32					56							52
Ala.		54	70	74	56	48			33½					56							56
Ariz.			70		56	50								55							56
Ark.			70			50															56
Cal.							44	48		44	30							45			
Colo.				70	56	48			32	46				56			44				
Conn.					56	48			30							8	44				56
Del.					56	48								56		8	44				
D.C.					56	50								56			44				
Fla.					56	50						33		56		8	44				
Ga.				70	56	50								56	40	24	44		50	50	56
Hawaii													48			8				50	
Ill.					56	50										8	44		50	50	
Ind.	38	²¹50	70²⁰	75																	
Iowa		²⁵70	²²70																		
Kans.			²²70																		
Ky.																					

State	Values (reading column, top → bottom)
La.	56, 56
Me.	2270
Md.	2856, 50, 45, 44, 8, 56, 2650, 56, 2270, 2370, 2750
Mass.	50, 48, 50, 55, 32, 40, 36, 44, 70, 2270, 70, 50
Mich.	48, 40, 24, 56, 48, 48, 44, 50, 56, 70, 56
Minn.	50, 45, 50, 56, 32, 48, 50, 56, 72, 70, 68
Miss.	48, 44, 8, 56, 44, 50, 56, 70
Mo.	50, 44, 56, 55, 50, 56
Mont.	50, 44, 55, 48, 56
Neb.	50, 48, 55, 50, 56
Nev.	56, 56
N. H.	56, 2950, 45, 44, 8, 56, 48, 32, 30, 44, 30, 48, 50, 56, 56
N. J.	56, 45, 56, 44, 56
N. Y.	56, 50, 56, 44, 32, 48, 50, 56, 72, 68, 70
N. C.	56, 55, 56
N. Dak.	56
Ohio	56, 50, 48, 56, 48, 30, 44, 32, 50, 50, 56, 70
Okla.	56, 50, 56, 48, 48, 50, 56, 70, 58
Ore.	40
Pa.	56, 50, 44, 8, 56, 48, 30, 44, 3130, 48, 48, 50, 3048, 56, 70, 3274, 70, 40
R. I.	50, 45, 44, 56, 28, 56, 56, 72, 70, 40
S. C.	48, 44, 56, 32, 56, 70
S. Dak.	48, 12, 44, 44, 56, 3350, 32, 56, 70
Tenn.	45, 44, 8, 3350, 32, 50, 56, 70, 56
Tex.	48, 44, 8, 56, 56
Vt.	56, 45, 12, 44, 8, 56
Va.	48, 44, 30, 44, 70
Wash.	56
W. Va.	56
Wis.	48, 44, 8, 56, 50, 56

LEGAL WEIGHTS PER BUSHEL OF VARIOUS COMMODITIES FOR WHICH BUSHEL WEIGHTS HAVE BEEN WIDELY ADOPTED—(Continued)

	Pop Corn[8]	Peas[1]	Green Peas, Unshelled	Pears[1]	Peanuts (or "Ground Peas,*")	Dried Peaches, Unpeeled	Dried Peaches, Peeled	Peaches[1]	Parsnips	Osage Orange Seed	Orchard-Grass Seed	Onion Sets	Onions[1]	Oats	Millet	Malt	Unslaked Lime	Lime[1]	Kafir Corn
U.S.		60				33	38							32		34			
Ala.		60				33	33							32					
Ariz.		60				33	33				14		57	32	50			80	
Ark.							33						57	32				70	
Cal.													52	32					
Colo.														32					
Conn.		60				33	33		45					32			80		
Del.																			
D.C.																			
Fla.				60	22	33	33	[35]54					56	32	50				
Ga.		60	50		*25	33	38						57	32			80		
Hawaii						33							57	32	50	38			
Ill.						33						[38]30	48	32	50	[37]35			
Ind.					20	33			55	33	14		57	32	50				
Iowa	56							48	42	32	14		57	32	50				56
Kans.	[49]70	[40]60						48	52				57	32	50	32	80	80	56
Ky.	[61]56	60			*24		39				14	[42]36		[41]32	50		35		

State	1	2	3	4	5	6	7	8	9	10	11	12	13	14	15	16	17	18	19
La.		80		[87]34	[49]50	32	52				45							60	
Me.		70				[44]32	57				45	[45]40						[46]60	
Md.		70			50	32	52				42	48			[47]20			60	
Mass.		80			48	32	54		14	33	44		33		22	58		60	
Mich.	56			38	50	32	52		14	36	50		28		*24			60	
Minn.				38	50	32	57		14	32		48	[48]28					60	
Miss.		70	80	30	50	32	57	[49]28	14		50	48	33			48	56	[50]60	
Mo.				30	50	32	57	25			45	48	33			45		60	
Mont.				32	50	32	57					50	33					60	
Neb.						32	57						33	[48]33	[47]20	58		[40]60	[61]56
Nev.						32	52							[48]33				60	
N. H.		70	80			30	57		14				33	33	22			60	
N. J.	50		80			32	57						33					60	
N. Y.						32	57											60	
N. C.		80				32	52											60	
N. Dak.		70				32	55											60	
Ohio		80				32	57											60	
Okla.	56					32												60	
Ore.																			[51]42
Pa.		70	80	34	50	32	50	28	14	36	44	48	33	33	22	48	56	60	
R. I.				38			50					48	26			45		[38]60	
S. C.			80		50	32	52	[55]28	14	33	50	48	28					60	
S. Dak.		80			[53]50	32	[54]56				50		28					60	
Tenn.				38	50	32	57	28	14	34		[55]50		32	23	[57]56	30		70
Tex.					50	30	52			34		50							
Vt.						32	57						40					[58]60	
Va.						32							28					60	
Wash.			80												22	[46]45		80	
W. Va.													33					80	
Wis.		70	80	[69]34		32	57				44		33					60	

LEGAL WEIGHTS PER BUSHEL OF VARIOUS COMMODITIES FOR WHICH BUSHEL WEIGHTS HAVE BEEN WIDELY ADOPTED—(Continued)

	Potatoes[1]	Sweet Potatoes	White Potatoes	Quinces	Rape Seed	Red Top	Rough Rice	Rutabagas	Rye Meal	Rye	Salt[1]	Fine Salt	Coarse Salt	Shorts[1]	Sorghum Seed	Spelt or Spiltz	Timothy Seed	Tomatoes	Turnips[1]	Common English Turnips	Walnuts	Wheat
U. S.	60	55	60							56												60
Ala.		50								56	50								55			60
Ariz.	60					14				56	80				50		60		57			60
Ark.	60	54								56							45					60
Cal.	60									54												60
Colo.	60	60								56												60
Conn.	60	55	60				45	60	50	56	60	50	70	20								60
Del.			60																			
D. C.																				50		
Fla.				48			43								56		45		54			
Ga.		50	60							56	50						45		55			60
Hawaii		55								56	80	55					45		55			60
Ill.						14		50		56	80		50				45		55			60
Ind.	60	46		48	50					56	50					35			55			60
Iowa	60	50								56					[62]50		45	50			50	60
Kans.	60									56					50			56				60
Ky.	[66]60	55								56	50	55					45		60			60

La.										56												60
Me.	60							60	50	50		60	70							50		60
Md.	60	60			50	[63]14				56		56	70		50		45	60	60			60
Mass.	60	54		48			45		50	56		50	70	20			45	56	55			60
Mich.		56	60			[64]14				56	56						45		58			60
Minn.		55	60		50	[64]14		52		56					57		45					60
Miss.		60	60							56	50				42		45		55			60
Mo.		56	60			[64]14		50		56	50				42		45	45		42		60
Mont.	60									56	50						45		50			60
Neb.		50	60							56	50				50		45		55			60
Nev.	60	50								56	80				50		45	56	56			60
N. H.	[65]60	54		48					50	56		50	70	20			45	56	55			60
N. J.		54	60							56							45					60
N. Y.		54	60				45		50	56		56	70	20			45					60
N. C.	[65]56	56	60		50	[64]14	44			56					50		45		50		[66]50	60
N. Dak.		46	60							56	80					40	45		60			60
Ohio.	[65]60	50								56							45	56	60			60
Okla.		55	60		50	[64]14		50		56	80				50		45	45	60	42		60
Ore.	60									56												60
Pa.	56									56		[67]62	85									60
R. I.		54	60						50	56		50	70	20			45	56	50			60
S. C.																						
S. Dak.		46	60							56	80					45	42		60			60
Tenn.		50	60	48		[64]14				56	50				50		45	56	50		50	60
Tex.		55	60							56	50						45	55	55			60
Vt.	60									56	70						45		60			[68]60
Va.		56	56			12				56	50						45		55			60
Wash.	60									56												60
W. Va.	60									56							45					60
Wis.	60	54			50		45	56	50	56		50	70	20			45		42			60

Notes Relating to Preceding Table

[1]Not defined.
[2]Small white beans, 60 lb.
[3]Green apples.   [wurzels.
[4]Sugar beets and mangel
[5]Shelled beans, 60 lb.; velvet beans, 78 lb.
[6]White beans.
[7]Wheat bran.
[8]Green unshelled beans, 56 lb.
[9]English blue-grass seed, 22 lb.; native blue-grass seed, 14 lb.
[10]Also castor seed.
[11]Soybeans, 58 lb.   [30 lb.
[12]Green unshelled beans,
[13]Soybeans.
[14]Free from hulls.
[15]Commercially dry, for all hard woods.
[16]Fifteen lb. commercially dry, for all soft woods.
[17]Standard weight in borough of Greensburg.
[18]Dried beans.
[19]Red and white.
[20]Corn in ear, 70 lb. until Dec. 1 next after grown; 68 lb. thereafter.
[21]Sweet corn.
[22]On the cob.
[23]Indian corn in ear.
[24]Unwashed plastering hair, 8 lb.; washed plastering hair, 4 lb.
[25]Corn in ear, from Nov. 1 to May 1 following, 70 lb.; 68 lb. from May 1 to Nov. 1.
[26]Indian-corn meal.
[27]Cracked corn.
[28]Shelled.
[29]Free from hulls.
[30]Standard weight bu. corn meal, bolted or unbolted, 48 lb.
[31]Except the seed of long staple cotton, of which the weight shall be 42 lb.
[32]Green unshelled corn, 100 lb.
[33]Green cucumbers.
[34]See also "Pop corn," "Indian corn," and "Kafir corn."
[35]Green peaches.
[36]Green pears.
[37]Malt rye.
[38]Top sets; bottom sets, 32 lb.
[39]Shelled, 56 lb.
[40]Shelled, dry.
[41]Strike measure.
[42]Bottom onion sets.
[43]German and American.
[44]Shelled.
[45]Peaches (peeled); unpeeled, 32 lb.
[46]Cowpeas.
[47]Roasted; green, 22 lb.
[48]Not stated whether peeled or unpeeled.
[49]Top onion sets.
[50]Including split peas.
[51]In the ear.
[52]Slaked lime, 40 lb.
[53]German, Missouri, and Tennessee millet seeds.
[54]Matured onions.
[55]Bottom onion sets, 32 lb.
[56]Matured.
[57]Matured pears, 56 lb.; dried pears, 26 lb.
[58]Black-eyed peas.
[59]Barley malt.
[60]Includes Rice corn.
[61]Rice corn.
[62]Sorghum saccharatum seed.
[63]Red top grass seed (chaff); fancy, 32 lb.
[64]Seed.
[65]Irish potatoes.
[66]Free from hulls.
[67]Ground salt, 70 lb.
[68]India wheat, 46 lb.
[69]In some states herd's grass is a synonym for timothy; in other states for red top.

The states of Idaho, New Mexico, Utah, and Wyoming have no standard for bushel weights.

LEGAL WEIGHTS PER BUSHEL

(Continued from page 245)

Cherries, 40 lb. (Iowa); with stems, 56 lb. (Tenn.); without stems, 64 lb. (Tenn.).

Chufa, 54 lb. (Fla.).

Cotton seed, staple, 42 lb. (S. C.).

Currants, 40 lb. (Iowa and Minn.).

Feed, 50 lb. (Mass.).

Fescue, seed of all the, except the Tall and Meadow fescue, 14 lb. (N. C.).

Fescue seed, Tall and Meadow, 24 lb. (N. C.).

Grapes, 40 lb. (Iowa); with stems, 48 lb. (Tenn.); without stems, 60 lb. (Tenn.).

Guavas, 54 lb. (Fla.).

Hominy, 60 lb. (Ohio); 62 lb. (Tenn.).

Horseradish, 50 lb. (Tenn.).

Italian rye-grass seed, 20 lb. (Tenn.).

Japan clover in hulls, 25 lb. (N. C.).

Johnson grass, 28 lb. (Ark.); 25 lb. (N. C.).

Kale, 30 lb. (Tenn.).

Land plaster, 100 lb. (Tenn.).

Lentils, 60 lb. (N. C.).

Lucerne, 60 lb. (N. C.).

Lupines, 60 lb. (N. C.).

Meadow seed, tall, 14 lb. (N. C.).

Meal (?), 46 lb. (Ala.); unbolted, 48 lb. (Ala.).

Middlings, fine, 40 lb. (Ind.); coarse middlings, 30 lb. (Ind.).

Millet, Japanese barnyard, 35 lb. (Mass. and N. H.).

Mustard, 30 lb. (Tenn.).

Mustard seed, 58 lb. (N. C.).

Oat grass seed, 14 lb. (N. C.).

Plums, 40 lb. (Fla.); 64 lb. (Tenn.); dried, 28 lb. (Mich.).

Prunes, dried, 28 lb. (Idaho); green, 45 lb. (Idaho).

Radish seed, 50 lb. (Iowa).

Raspberries, 32 lb. (Iowa and Kan.); 48 lb. (Tenn.).

Rhubarb, 50 lb. (Tenn.).

Sage, 4 lb. (Tenn.).
Salads, 30 lb. (Tenn.).
Sand, 130 lb. (Iowa).
Seed of brome grasses, 14 lh. (N. C.).
Spinach, 30 lb. (Tenn.).
Strawberries, 32 lb. (Iowa); 48 lb. (Tenn.).
Sugar cane seed (amber), 57 lb. (N. J.).
Sunflower seed, 24 lb. (N. C.).
Teosinte, 59 lb. (N. C.).
Velvet grass seed, 7 lb. (Tenn.).
Vetches, 60 lb. (N. C.).

GLOSSARY OF TECHNICAL TERMS USED BY POULTRYMEN

A clear understanding of the meaning of the technical terms used in the poultry world is necessary before any person can judge fowls according to Standard requirements or select them for breeding purposes or the show pen or even converse intelligently on the subject of poultry.

In order to impart a clear understanding of the terms applied to the different parts of a fowl, a profile view of one is shown in Fig. 1, with the different parts numbered. Following this will be found a list of the names of the numbered parts. Farther on is a list of technical terms and expressions used by poultrymen. Some of the terms are peculiar to England and some to certain parts of the United States, but the meaning of each is fully explained and many are made clear by illustrations.

Abdomen.—The part of the body of a fowl that contains the viscera. See *32*, Fig. 1.

Albino.—A fowl that is pure white in all parts except the eyes, due to the absence of coloring pigment; a sport from black or colored fowls.

FIG. 1

NAMES OF NUMBERED PARTS

1, Crest
2, Comb
3, Eye
4, Feathers covering the ear
5, Ear lobe
6, Muff
7, Wattles
8, Beard
9, Beak
10, Face
11, Hackle
12, Neck
13, Breast
14, Breastbone, or keel
15, Thigh
16, Vulture hock
17, Hock joint
18, Shank
19, Third toe
20, Middle toe

21, Fourth toe
22, Fifth toe
23, Spur
24, Foot
25, Shank and toe feathering
26, Back
27, Saddle
28, Sickles
29, Lesser sickles
30, Tail coverts
31, Main tail
32, Abdomen
33, Wing bow
34, Shoulder
35, Wing bar
36, Wing bay, or secondary feathers
37, Primary, or flight, feathers
38, Primary coverts

257

Amateur.—A person not well informed about the art of poultry raising; a beginner; a novice.

Antler Comb.—A comb composed of two small prongs somewhat resembling antlers; a **V**-shaped comb; common in Polish, La Flèche, and some strains of Houdans. Fig. 2.

FIG. 2

A. O. C.—Any other color.

A. O. V.—Any other variety.

Atavism.—Recurrence to an ancestral type or to a deformity or disease after its disappearance for several generations; reversion.

Band.—(1) A stripe or marking of any kind at the end of or across a feather. (2) A band of metal or other material, usually stamped with numbers or letters, or colored, for attaching to the shank of a fowl so that it can be identified.

Bantam.—A dwarf, or pigmy, fowl, usually about one-fifth the size of a large fowl of the variety to which it corresponds in every particular except size.

Barb.—One of the side branches of a feather, which collectively make up the web and fluff. See feather.

Barring.—Bands of alternate colors that extend across a feather. Fig. 3.

Barred to the Skin.—An expression applied to fowls whose feathers are barred from the tip to the end of the fluff, as in Barred Plymouth Rocks.

Bay.—A reddish-brown color, approaching chestnut; also used to designate eyes in fowls that have an approach to blood-red color.

FIG. 3

Beak.—As used by poultrymen, the beak is the bony formation extending from the front of the head of chickens and turkeys; it consists of the upper and lower mandibles. See 9, Fig. 1. The corresponding part of water fowls is called the bill.

Bean.—A growth, resembling a thumbnail, on the point of the upper mandible of the bill of a duck, as shown at *a,* Fig. 4. A like growth of a smaller size is found on the bill of a goose.

FIG. 4

Beard.—(1) A tuft of feathers under the beak and about the throat of such fowls as Polish, Houdans, etc. See *8,* Fig. 1. (2) A tuft of hair growing on the breast of turkeys.

Beefy.—A term applied to coarse, overgrown combs; such combs are more commonly found on Mediterranean fowls than on those of other varieties.

Beetle Brows.—See brows.

Bib.—The English name for beard.

Bill.—The mandibles of water fowls, which correspond to the beak in other domestic fowls.

Bird.—Fowl was the term formerly applied to all winged creatures; modern usage restricts the name fowl to the larger domesticated fowls and designates the smaller wild fowls as birds. However, the term bird is frequently indiscriminatingly used instead of the term fowl.

Blade.—The rear part of a single comb, generally called the heel. See *b,* Fig. 25.

Blocky.—A term applied to a fowl that is of heavy and square build; said of a fowl that is broad, or wide, between the thighs. Compare with cobby, an English term that expresses the same meaning.

Bloom.—The gloss, sheen, or finish on the plumage of fowls.

Body.—Fanciers usually apply the term body to the trunk of a fowl only.

Booted.—Fowls that are feathered on the shanks and toes are said to be booted.

Bouquet Crest.—A crest that stands up from the head and to some extent resembles a bouquet of flowers; found on crested ducks. At one time, a bad defect in Polish fowls.

Brassiness.—A term applied to a yellow or yellowish tint commonly found in the feathers of white fowls and sometimes in the feathers of dark-plumaged fowls.

Breast.—(1) A term applied to that part of the front of the body of live fowls that extends from the throat to the point of the breastbone. See *13*, Fig. 1. ·(2) The term is applied also to the meat on both sides of the breast-bone of fowls prepared for the table.

Breed.—A family of fowls all of which are of the same distinctive shape. A breed may include a number of varieties, the fowls of all the varieties having the same shape but being distinguished by different plumage colors and markings.

Breeding Down.—A term applied to the process of producing small, or bantam, fowls from larger fowls by selecting and breeding the smallest fowls obtainable—a process usually involving breeding through a number of generations.

Brick Color.—A reddish-brown color occasionally found on fowls of black-red varieties.

Broken Colored.—See mottled and spangled.

Brood.—A number of chicks that are mothered by one hen or kept in one brooder.

Broody.—When a hen shows a desire to sit, that is, to hatch eggs, she is said to be broody.

Brows.—The projection of the skull over the eyes of a fowl, as in Asiatic and Malay fowls; termed beetle brows in England. Fig. 5.

Cap.—The upper part of a fowl's skull or comb; a term used in England.

Cape.—The feathers between the shoulders and about the neck underneath the hackle.

FIG. 5

Capon.—A castrated cock or cockerel; that is, a male from which the reproductive organs have been removed; a female from which the reproductive organs have been removed is called a poulard.

. *Carriage.*—The general appearance, pose, or bearing of a fowl; the way in which a fowl carries itself when walking.

Caruncles.—Irregular growths of flesh such as occur on the head and neck of turkeys and Muscovy ducks. Fig. 6.

Carunculated.—Covered with caruncles.

Castrate.—To remove the testicles, the organs of reproduction, from a male fowl.

Cavernous.—Said of nostrils that are prominent and deeply hollowed. Such nostrils are found on crested fowls. Fig. 7.

Chain Armor.—Faulty lacing on the claret-colored breast of a Rouen drake.

Fig. 6

Chick.—One of the newly hatched young of fowls or birds.

Chicken.—Specifically, a fowl less than 1 yr. old; commonly, a fowl of any age.

Cinnamon Color.—A dark reddish buff, formerly admissible on one variety of Cochins.

Claret Color.—Descriptive of the breast color of a Rouen drake.

Clean Legged.—A term used in describing a fowl that has no feathers on its shanks or toes.

Fig. 7

Close Feathered.—See tight feathered.

Cloudy.—A term applied to plumage that has irregular markings. See mossiness.

Clutch.—The number of eggs a domestic fowl incubates, or sits on, at one time, usually from 11 to 15. See sitting.

Coat.—The plumage of a fowl taken as a whole.

Cob.—A male swan.

Cobby.—A term applied in England to a fowl that is thick set, heavily built, and round in form. See blocky.

Cock.—A male fowl more than 1 yr. old; the term is commonly applied to pit game cocks of any age.

Cockerel.—A male fowl less than 1 yr. old. The practice in the show room is to allow males to be shown as

cockerels during the entire show season that follows their hatching. Compare with pullet.

Cockerel Bred.—Bred in line from a mating made expressly for producing cockerels for exhibition. Both males and females from such matings are said to be cockerel bred. Compare with pullet bred.

Collar.—A white ring around the neck, as in Rouen ducks and in pheasants.

Color.—A term applied to any one of the many hues that may be found on the feathers or on any other part of the body of a fowl. This term is used also in describing the coloring of the entire plumage. A fowl is said to have good color when each of its colors is of the proper tint and is found in its proper place, and to have bad color when the reverse is true.

FIG. 8

Comb.—The fleshy growth on the top of the head of a fowl. See *2*, Fig. 1, and Figs. 2, 5, 16, 20, 22, 25, and 30.

Comb Over.—An expression for lopped comb; used in England. Figs. 8 and 24.

Comparison Judging — Judging fowls by comparing them with one another, and without applying a score card.

Concave Sweep.—The continuous curve of the back from the shoulder to the tail; required in some breeds.

Condition.—The state of the health and plumage of a fowl; sometimes applied only to the finish, or appearance, of the plumage.

Conditioning.—The process of preparing a fowl for the show room.

Coverts.—Feathers that grow about the tail; also the secondary quill feathers. See *30* and *38*, Fig. 1, and wing and tail coverts and hangers.

Cradle Comb.—A term formerly applied to the Wyandotte comb; at present little used. Same as rocker comb.

Creaminess.—A term descriptive of white feathers that are tinged with a slight yellow or cream color.

Crest.—A tuft of feathers on top of the head. **Figs. 9 and 16.**

Crop.—An enlarged part of the gullet, or pouch, in which food is stored and softened prior to passing into the gizzard.

Crop Bound.—A term applied to an unnatural condition of the crop, in which that organ is stopped up and food is prevented from passing through it.

Fig. 9

Cross.—A mating of fowls of different breeds.

Cross-Bred.—The offspring from two fowls of different breeds; as from mating a Plymouth Rock and a Rhode Island Red.

Curl Feather.—One of the set of curled feathers near the base of the back of a male duck.

Curve.—Any arched or concave line on the body of a fowl, such as the curve of the back, the curve formed by the flowing tail feathers, or the arched shape of the neck in water fowls.

Cushion.—A raised mass of plumage due to an excessive development of soft feathers about the tail of Cochins and some other fowls.

Cushion Comb.—The name applied in England to the comb of the Silky; a circular cushion of flesh with a number of small protuberances on it. Same as strawberry comb.

Cut.—A deduction made from the score of a fowl; as a cut of 2 points.

Cygnet.—A young swan.

Daw Eyed.—A term used at one time to describe game fowls that had peculiar eyes resembling those of a jackdaw, which were of a pearl color; pigeons with eyes of the same kind are said to be pearl eyed.

Deaf-Ear.—The ear lobe.

Debarred.—Barred from competition.

Deep Bodied.—Said of fowls that have a good depth of body from the top of the back to the lower side of the breastbone.

Defect.—Any blemish, imperfection, fault, or lack of some feature or quality.

Dewlap.—A growth of loose skin below the beak or bill, as in Brahmas and water fowls. Fig. 5.

Diamond.—An expression formerly used in place of wing bay.· See *36,* Fig. 1.

Dished.—When hollows or depressions appear in the bill of a water fowl, it is said to be dished. See *b,* Fig. 4.

Disqualification.—A defect that will debar a fowl from competition.

Disqualified.—Condemned; unfit for exhibition.

Double Comb.—A term formerly applied to all combs except the single comb.

Double Lacing.—A double ring or penciling about the outer edge of a feather. Fig. 10. See supplementary lacing.

Double Mating.—A system of mating in which males fit for exhibition are produced from one pair of breeding fowls, and females fit for exhibition are produced from another pair.

Down.—(1) The first downy covering of young chicks. (2) The soft cottonlike part of a feather below the web. See *b,* Fig. 12. (3) A mosslike growth between the toes.

Fig. 10

Drake.—A male duck.

Dubbing.—The cutting off of the comb, wattles, and ear lobes of game fowls.

Duck.—A species of water fowl, including both sexes; also, a female of the species, as distinguished from the male.

Duckling.—A young duck.

Duck Foot.—See web foot.

Duck Footed.—A fowl is said to be duck footed when the back toe is carried close to the other toes, instead of being well spread out behind. Fig. 11.

Ear Lobe.—The fleshy growth below the ear; this may be red, white, or other color, according to the variety. Same as deaf-ear. See *5,* Fig. 1.

Eggs for Hatching.—Eggs that are suitable for incubation.

Exhibition Fowls.—A fowl suitable for exhibition in a show room.

Face.—On a fowl, the part of the head about the eyes that is bare of feathers.

Fig. 11

Faking.—A term equivalent in meaning to deceiving; it is in frequent use by poultrymen. Faking consists in removing or dyeing objectionable feathers, in coloring shanks and feet, in removing side sprigs, or in the use of other unfair means to win a prize in a show room.

Fancier.—A breeder of poultry, pigeons, or pet stock.

Fancy.—A lax term for fanciers collectively.

Feather.—One of the appendages peculiar to and growing out of the skin of a fowl or a bird, collectively forming the p l u m a g e. Fig. 12. A feather is commonly composed of the following principal parts: *web a,* in which the barbs are stuck together, forming a thin, smooth sheet; the *fluff,* or *down b,* in which the barbs are not united; the *shaft,* quill, or barrel, which is composed of a lower hollow and tubular part *c,* and an upper part *d,* which is filled with pith.

Fig. 12

Feather Cell.—The cell in the body from which a feather grows.

Feather Legged.—Said of fowls that have feathers growing on the sides of the shanks and toes; booted. See *25,* Fig. 1.

Fillers.—The small feathers that grow between the main tail feathers.

Finish.—Gloss on plumage.

First-Cross Fowls.—Fowls resulting from the first crossing of standard-bred males and females of different breeds.

Flat Shin.—A flat part on the shank of a game fowl.

Flight Coverts.—Short feathers that grow at the base of the flight feathers and partly cover them. See *38*, Fig. 1.

Flights, or Flight Feathers.—The primary feathers on the wing of a fowl. See *37*, Fig. 1.

Flow.—Said of feathers that hang loosely or sweepingly.

Fluff.—(1) The downy or lower part of a feather; see *b*, Fig. 12. (2) The profuse soft feathering about the thighs and abdomen. See *32*, Fig. 1.

Fluffing.—The act of bending or breaking the shafts and quills of the feathers in the fluff, cushion, and tail feathering of Asiatic Bantam and other Asiatic fowls, to build them out into unnatural size. This constitutes faking.

Folded Comb.—A comb that falls over to one side and folds back, forming a loop.

Foreign Color.—Any color found on a fowl that is not characteristic of or standard for the variety to which the fowl belongs.

Form.—As applied to fowls in the show room, form refers to their condition and finish.

Foul Feathers.—Feathers that are marked with foreign color.

Fowl.—A domestic cock, hen, cockerel, or pullet.

Foxy.—See rusty.

Frizzle Feathers.—Feathers that are crinkled or curled.

Frosting.—Irregular markings or lacing of a light color. Similar markings of a dark color give the appearance of mossiness.

Furnished.—A fowl is said to be furnished when it has a complete growth of tail, hackle, and saddle plumage, and a well-developed comb and other head points.

Furnishings.—Same as hangers.

Gaff.—A steel spur.

Gamy.—Like a game fowl; full of fight.

Gay.—A fowl is said to be gay when it has spangled, splashed, or colored plumage with an excessive amount of white on it.

Gills.—An improper name for the wattles.

Gloss.—The luster on the surface of feathers.

Gobbler.—A male turkey.

Gray.—A color produced by a mixture of black and white; it is of different shades, according to the proportions of black and white, as in the plumage of Dark Brahmas and Silver-Gray Dorkings.

Ground Color.—In fowls, the main, or principal, color in the plumage; for example, in a Buff Laced Polish fowl, the buff is the ground color.

Gullet.—The opening through which food passes.

Gypsy Color.—Purple color, as found on the face of some game fowls; also called mulberry color.

Hackle Feathers.—The long, flowing feathers that grow on the neck of a fowl; more plentiful in males than in females. See *11*, Fig. 1. See hackle.

Hangers.—An improper name for saddle feathers.

Hatch.—(1) To produce young from, that is, to cause young to develop in and come forth from an egg by either natural or artificial incubation. (2) A brood hatched at one sitting or one incubation.

Hard Feathers.—Firm, close feathering, such as is found on game fowls.

Hen.—A mature female domestic fowl.

Hen Feathered.—Said of a male fowl with a tail like a hen, as in the males of Sebrights and some varieties of game fowls.

Hen Tailed.—Same as hen feathered.

Henny.—A term applied to a male fowl, usually a game, that has tail or other plumage resembling that of a hen.

High-in-Back.—A term used in England to describe hump or roach back.

Hock.—The joint between the thigh and the shank. See *17*, Fig. 1.

Hollowed Place in Comb.—A depression in the comb of a fowl; same as a thumb mark. Fig. 24.

Hood.—Neck feathers that curve forwards over the head.

Horn Comb.—Same as antler comb and **V**-shaped comb.

Horseshoe Lacing.—Lacing forming a orseshoe about the tip of a feather. Fig. 13.

Hump Back.—A fowl with a hump back is one that has a knob, lump, or prominence on the back.

Hybrid.—The offspring from two birds of different *species;* as from mating a goldfinch with a canary, or a turkey with a guinea.

Ideal.—Of a perfection that is seldom realized.

FIG. 13

Inbred Fowl.—An offspring from closely related fowls.

Inbreeding.—Breeding, or following a course of breeding, from nearly related fowls.

Incubate.—See hatch and sit.

Irregular Lacing.—Incomplete or imperfect lacing about the edge of a feather.

Jaw.—In a fowl, the jaw is that part of the head that supports the upper and lower mandibles.

Keel.—(1) The lower edge of the breastbone. (2) The loose flesh and feathers hanging below the breast in ducks and other poultry.

Knee Joint.—Same as hock joint. See *17*, Fig. 1.

Knob.—The protuberance on a goose at the juncture of the head and the bill.

FIG. 14

Knock Kneed.—A malformation of the legs of a fowl, in which the hock joints come close together instead of being well apart as they should be. Fig. 14.

Lacing.—The edging along the margin of a feather; it is usually darker **in color** than the body of the feather. Fig. 15.

Leader.—The spike, or heel, on a rose comb—the part that extends to the rear. See *a*, Fig. 22.

Leaf Comb.—A comb consisting of two small sections, each shaped like a leaf. Fig. 16.

Leggy.—A fowl is said to be leggy when it has too great length in legs.

Leg and Toe Feathering. The feathering on both the shanks and feet; booting. See *25*, Fig. 1.

Lesser Sickles. — T h e smaller tail feathers next to the full, flowing sickles. See *29*, Fig. 1.

FIG. 15

FIG. 16

Line Breeding.—Breeding, or following a course of breeding, from a limited number of original fowls. In line breeding the fowls mated are not so closely related as those mated in inbreeding. Line breeding is really a modified form of inbreeding.

Loop.—A double fold in the comb, as in a Minorca female.

Lopped Comb.—A comb that falls over on either side. Same as comb over. Figs. 8 and 24.

Low Built.—Said of a fowl that is very short in the legs and hence carries its body close to the ground.

Lump Comb.—Same as strawberry comb.

Made Form.—The form that may be produced in a fowl by training.

Main Tail Feathers.—The stiff feathers of the tail under and between the sickles and coverts. See *31*, Fig. 1.

Mandibles.—The horny upper and lower parts of the beak or bill.

Marbled.—A term used to describe ticked or laced feathers on the breast of Pyle Game cocks.

Markings.—Striping, lacing, barring, or marks of any kind on the plumage.

Mazarine.—Deep-blue or purplish markings across a black feather.

Mealy.—A term used to describe plumage that should be one solid color but is covered with irregular dots of mixed or faulty color.

Moon.—A rounded spot of color tipping the feathers of fowls of some varieties.

Mossiness.—An effect produced by irregular dark markings. Fig. 17. See frosting.

FIG. 17

FIG. 18

Molt.—(1) To cast off or shed the feathers of fowls. (2) The act or process of molting. (3) The season or period of molting.

Mottled. — Marked with spots or blotches of different colors.

Mulberry Color.—See gypsy color.

Muff, Muffle, Muffling.—A growth of feathers on either side of the head, usually seen on bearded fowls, and very marked in Faverolles. See 6, Fig. 1.

Natural Form.—The natural appearance of a fowl without training.

Non-Sitter.—A fowl that does not incubate eggs.

FIG. 19

Novice.—A beginner; an inexperienced person.

Open Barring.—Barring in which the bars are wide apart. Fig. 18.

Open Lacing.—Narrow lacing about the edge of a feather and forming a ring around a spot of another color, giving the feather the appearance of having a large open center. Fig. 19.

Overhang.—A term used by poultrymen to describe the overhanging skull as found in Aseel Game, Malay Game, and Brahma fowls. Some pigeons, also, have the same kind of a projection on the skull.

Overlap.—To lie partly over; said of the colors on plumage when they meet on a ragged edge, giving the appearance of one color overlapping another.

Parti-Colored.—Of several colors, like the Light Brahma or Houdan.

Pea Comb.—A small, low comb divided lengthwise into three parts, and having the appearance of three small single combs placed side by side, as on the Brahma and Aseel. Figs. 5 and 20.

Pearl Eyed.—See daw eyed.

Pen.—(1) An enclosure. (2) A female swan.

FIG. 20

Penciling.—Narrow lines or markings. The term penciling is applied to several kinds of markings on poultry: (1) The bars on the feathers of Penciled Hamburgs. (2) The concentric lines that follow the outline of the feather in Dark Brahmas and Partridge Cochins. Fig. 21. (3) The fine gray markings on Rouen drakes. (4) The stippling as found on Leghorns and Black-Breasted Red Game females.

Pen Manners.—The behavior of fowls in pens in the show room.

Pen of Fowls.—In the show room, a pen of one male and four females.

Peppered.—Plumage is said to be peppered when it is dotted with spots.

Pile.—The spelling used in England for Pyle.

FIG. 21

Pinion.—(1) The outermost section of the wing of a bird, bearing the pinion feathers. (2) To cut off the outer part of a bird's wing that bears a considerable proportion of the feathers used in flying, in order to prevent flying.

Pit.—An enclosed space in which fowls are pitted against each other; hence, a fighting place for fowls.

Plumage.—The feathers and down.

Point.—One of the tapering, sharp-ended serrations of the upper part of a single comb. See *a*, Fig. 25.

Poulard.—A female fowl, usually a pullet, in which the egg-producing organs have been destroyed.

Poult.—A young turkey.

Poultry.—All domestic fowls.

Prepotency.—The superiority of one parent over the other in transmitting characters to the offspring; that is, in stamping its individuality on the offspring.

Primaries.—The flight feathers. See *37*, Fig. 1.

Producer.—A fowl that produces offspring better than itself.

Pullet.—A female fowl less than a year old. Show-room practice allows a fowl to be exhibited as a pullet during the entire show season that follows the hatching.

Pullet Bred.—Bred in line from a mating made expressly for producing pullets for exhibition. Both males and females from such matings are called pullet bred. Compare with cockerel bred.

Pure Bred.—Fowls that have no alien blood in them are said to be pure bred.

Purply.—The effect produced by purple bars across a black feather.

Quill.—See feather, and *c*, Fig. 12.

Quill Bound.—A condition in which the feather is retained in its sheath, instead of the sheath cracking and falling off.

Racy.—A fowl that is slender, trim, active, alert, or tight feathered is said to be racy.

Reachy.—Said of fowls that have an upright carriage and are tall, such as game fowls.

Ribbon.—The bright-blue band across the wings of Rouen and other ducks.

Roach Back.—A back with a hump; same as hump back.

Rocker Comb.—A term formerly applied to the Wyandotte comb; same as cradle comb.

Rooster.—Common name for a cock or a cockerel.

Rose Comb.—A broad, level comb, wide in front, tapering to a spike, or point, in the rear, and covered on

the top with small projections, or points, as in Hamburgs and Rose-Comb Bantams. Fig. 22. At *a* is shown the spike.

Rosy Wings.—Wings of Pyle females, which are marked with salmon color; wings of the same color were formerly called foxy colored.

Ruff.—Same as muff.

Rusty Color. — The reddish-brown shadings on the outside of the wings of Black-Breasted Red Game and Brown Leghorn females. In England, the same shading is called foxy.

FIG. 22

Saddle.—That portion of the back of a male fowl between the middle of the back and the base of the tail.

Saddle Feathers.—The flowing feathers growing from the saddle of a fowl.

Saddle Hackles.—The long, flowing feathers that grow from the saddle of a male and hang down on both sides of the body; also called saddle hangers and saddle feathers. See *27*, Fig. 1.

Salmon.—A reddish or pinkish orange color, like that found on the breast of Red Pyle Game females and Brown Leghorn females.

Scales.—Thin, horny growths covering the shanks and feet.

Scaly Leg.—A diseased condition of the shanks and feet, caused by the scaly-leg mite.

Secondaries.—The long quill feathers of the wings that grow on the second joint or next to and above the primaries. See *36*, Fig. 1.

Section.—A distinctly defined part of a standard-bred fowl.

Self-Color.—A uniform color.

Serrated.—Notched along the edge like a saw.

Serration.—One of the points of a single comb. See *a*, Fig. 25.

Shaft.—See feather, and *d*, Fig. 12.

Shafty.—A term describing a dark-colored feather with a light shaft. Fig. 23.

Shank.—That part of the leg between the toes and the hock joint. See *18*, Fig. 1.

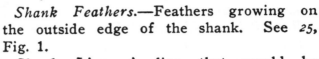

Shank Feathers.—Feathers growing on the outside edge of the shank. See *25*, Fig. 1.

Shank Line.—A line that would be formed by drawing a straight line along the rear edge of the shank upwards through the body of a fowl.

Sheath.—The covering over a new feather; it splits and falls off as the feather develops.

FIG. 23

Sheen.—The glistening brightness, or gloss, on plumage.

Shoulder.—The front or upper part of the wing; it is round or bow shaped and is hidden in fowls of some breeds by the breast plumage and hackle; in game fowls it stands out prominently. See *34*, ·Fig. 1.

Shoulder Butt.—Same as shoulder.

Show-Room Form.—The form that a fowl has in the show room.

Sickles.—The top pair of curved feathers in the tail of male fowls. One or two pairs similar to these, but below them, are called the lesser sickles. See *28* and *29*, Fig. 1.

Side Spike.—Same as side sprig.

Side Sprig.—An extra point, or growth, at the side or near the end of a single comb. Fig. 24.

· *Silvery.*—A term applied to the appearance of the shoulders of barred fowls that are deficient in barring and that have light, or silvery markings

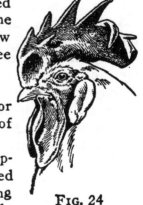

FIG. 24

on these parts instead of the customary barring.

Single Color.—Same as whole color.

Single Comb.—A ·thin, serrated, fleshy growth on the top of the head of a fowl, as in Plymouth Rocks and

Leghorns. Fig. 25. At *a* is one of the serrations, or points; at *b*, the blade.

Single Mating.—A mating from which both males and females fit for exhibition are produced from a single pair of breeding fowls. See double mating.

Sit.—To cover eggs for hatching; incubate.

Sitters.—Fowls that sit on and incubate eggs. The sitting proclivities are stronger in some breeds than in others. Fowls in which the sitting proclivities are weak are said to be non-sitters.

FIG. 25

Sitting.—The act of sitting to incubate eggs; also, the number of eggs for a sitting, usually from 11 to 15. See clutch.

Slipped Wing.—A wing in which the flight, or secondary, wing feathers hang loose or out of place. Fig. 26.

Smooth Legs.—Legs that have no feathers, stubs, or down on the shanks.

Smut.—A term applied to dark color. overlying any section of a fowl.

FIG. 26

Solid Color.—Of one uniform color throughout; self-color.

Spangle.—A dark marking at the point, or tip, of a feather. Fig. 27.

Spike.—The rear point on a rose comb; also sometimes called a leader. See *a*, Fig. 22.

Splashed Feathers.—Feathers in which there is an uneven mixture of color.

Split Crest.—A rounded crest that is split and falls over on both sides.

Sport.—A fowl that varies from the normal type; a white offspring from black parents.

FIG. 27

Spur.—A horny growth on the inside of the shank of a cock. See *23*, Fig. 1.

Squirrel Tail.—A tail in which the feathers are carried so far forward as almost to touch the head, like the tail of a squirrel. Fig. 28.

Stag.—A young game cock; also, a turkey cock.

Standard Mating.—A mating in which the fowls conform to Standard description; sometimes called single mating when the purpose is the production of both males and females.

Station.—Manner of standing; attitude, or pose of a fowl. A fowl is said to have good station when it has a form typical of the breed

FIG. 28

to which it belongs, has good symmetry, and the proper height and reach. Station is a term applied more especially to game fowls. Compare with carriage.

Steppings.—A term used in England to describe the effect produced by the ends of the secondary feathers, each one of which is shorter than the one immediately below it, giving the appearance of a flight of steps.

Stippling.—The effect produced on plumage by dots of dark and of light shades of color, as in Brown Leghorn females. Fig. 29.

Strain.—Fowls of one variety that have been bred in line for a number of generations from a few original fowls.

Strawberry Comb.—A lump comb, somewhat resembling a strawberry in shape, as in Malays and Silkies. Fig. 30.

Striping.—Markings of dark color that extend down the middle of a

FIG. 29

feather and taper to a

FIG. 30

point near the tip of the feather, as in Light Brahmas, Brown Leghorns, and some other fowls. Fig. 31.

Stub.—A short piece of the quill of a feather; especially, a short piece of the quill of a feather occasionally found on the shanks of smooth-legged fowls.

Style.—A fowl is said to have style when it presents a fine, spirited appearance, and has good symmetry, station, and carriage.

Supplementary Lacing.—An outside edging or lacing of a different shade or tint than the color next to it, that is found on both laced and solid feathers. When it occurs on laced feathers, as in edging of white around the outside of black lacing, it is the same as double lacing. Fig. 10.

Surface Color.—The color on the parts of the feathers exposed to view.

Sword Feather.—A main tail feather of a Japanese Bantam male.

Symmetry.—The blending of all sections or parts of a fowl into a harmonious whole.

Tail Coverts.—The curved, soft feathers about the sides of the lower part of the tail feathers. See *30*, Fig. 1.

Fig. 31

Tail Feathers.—The stiff, or main, feathers of the tail. See *31*, Fig. 1.

Team.—Three or more fowls shown by one exhibitor.

Thigh.—The upper segment of the leg; it is included between the body of the fowl and the upper extremity of what is known as the drumstick.

Thoroughbred.—(1) Of the best or the purest breeding; in this sense, now generally replaced by the term standard bred. (2) A term descriptive of game cocks of high courage and spirits.

Throat.—Same as gullet.

Thumb Mark.—(1) A hollow place in the side of a single comb. Fig. 24. (2) An opening or split in the front or center of a rose comb.

Ticked.—Plumage is ticked when it has spots of color different from the rest of the plumage.

Tight Feathered.—Fowls are said to be tight feathered when the feathers lie close to the body; close feathered.

Tom.—A male turkey; a gobbler.

Top Color.—The color of the plumage on the back.

Topknot.—A tufted growth of feathers on the top of the head of a fowl; a crest. Figs. 9 and 16.

Training.—The teaching or drilling of a fowl to pose in the show room.

Tricolored.—Of three colors.

Trimming.—A fraudulent way of preparing a fowl for the show room. See faking.

Trio.—Three; in poultry, a male and two females.

Trunk.—The body of a fowl, as distinguished from its appendages, the legs, neck, head, etc.

Tucked Up.—A fowl is said to be tucked up when the abdomen lacks fulness and makes a sharp upward turn to the tail, as in game fowls.

Twisted Comb.—A comb twisted into curves or some other faulty shape. Fig. 32.

Fig. 32

Type.—The form peculiar to any breed.

Under Plumage.—The fluff or under part of the plumage, seen only when the feathers are separated. See feather, and *b*, Fig. 12.

Utility Fowl.—A fowl for egg production and market purposes, as distinguished from an exhibition fowl.

Variety.—A subdivision of a breed; distinguished from other varieties of the same breed by the plumage colors. See breed.

V-Shaped Comb.—A comb having two points or prongs; also called antler comb, and horn comb. Fig. 2.

Vulture Hock.—A hock like that of a vulture, which has stiff feathers growing from the hock joint. See *16*, Fig. 1.

Washiness.—A state or quality of a feather that appears to have had the color washed out of it.

Waster.—A fowl unfit for breeding purposes, but fit for food.

Wattles.—Pendant growths of flesh that hang on each side of the beak; most prominently developed in male fowls.

Web.—(1) The upper part of a feather where the barbs are stuck together; the flat, thin feather structure beyond the fluff part of the feather. See feather and *a,* Fig. 12. (2) The skin growing between the toes. (3) The skin between the joints of the wing.

Web Foot.—A foot with webs between the toes. When a fowl other than a water fowl has a foot with webs between the toes, it is said to have a web foot.

Wheaten.—An uneven brown like that on ripe standing wheat; peculiar to some females of the Black-Breasted Red Games and the Faverolles.

Whip Tail.—The fine, slim tail of the modern game or game bantam fowl.

Whiskers.—Feathers growing from the side of the face; same as muff. Sometimes applied to the muffling below the beak. See *6,* Fig. 1.

Whole Color.—A fowl is said to be of a whole color when all of its plumage is of one color, as buff or black, but this does not mean that all the plumage must be of one shade of the color.

Willow Color.—A greenish yellow color peculiar to the shanks of some game fowls.

Wing Bar.—A bar of dark color across the middle of a wing. See *35,* Fig. 1.

Wing Bay.—A triangular surface showing on the wing where it is folded; located between the wing bar and the point of the wing. See *36,* Fig. 1.

Wing Bow.—The surface of the wing between the wing bar and the shoulder. See *33,*. Fig. 1.

Wing Butts.—The ends of the flight feathers; a misnomer for wing points.

FIG. 33

Wing Coverts.—The feathers that cover the roots of the secondary flight feathers.

Wing Fronts.—The fronts of the wings, properly called shoulders; improperly called wing butts.

Wing Points.—The extreme outer ends of the flight feathers.

Work, Full of Work.—A term used in England to describe a well-finished rose comb, the points of which are perfect or nearly perfect.

Wry Tail.—A tail carried to one side. Fig. 33.

PIGEONS

VARIETIES

There are almost innumerable breeds and varieties of pigeons. The names of the most common are given in the following list:

Archangels.

Barbs.—Black, White, Red, Yellow, Dun.

Berlin Tumblers.—Red, Yellow, Blue, Black.

Blondinettes.—Spangled or Laced, Brown or Laced, Black or Laced, Blue or Laced, Sulphur or Laced.

Breasters.—Black, Yellow, Red, Blue.

Brunettes.

Brunswicks.

Burmese, or *Leghorn Runts.*

Capuchins.

Carneau.—Red, Yellow, Rose-Wing Red, miscellaneous colors.

Carriers.—Black, Dun, Blue, White.

Cumulets.

Damascenes.

Dragoons.—Blue, Silver (brown bars), Silver (black bars), Red, Yellow, White.

Egyptian Swifts.—Blue, Black, White, Red, Yellow, Speckled, Mottled.

Exhibition Homers.—Black, Blue, Checkered, White, Yellow, Red, Red or Red Checkered, Silver or Silver Dun.

Fairies.—Red, Black, Yellow, Blue.

Fantails.—Blue, Silver, Black, White, Yellow, Red, Saddle Backs, Silkies, Frizzled.

Fire Pigeons.

Flying Antwerps.—Dun, Blue, Blue Checker, Red Checker.

Flying Tumblers, or Rollers.—Black, Red, Blue, Silver, Yellow, Black Rosewing, Red Rosewing, Yellow Rosewing, Black Mottle, Red Mottle, Yellow Mottle, Red Breasted (white sides), Black·Breasted (white sides), Blue Breasted (white sides), Yellow Breasted (white sides), Black Saddle, Red Saddle, Yellow Saddle, Blue Saddle, Silver Saddle, Black Badge, Red Badge, Yellow Badge, Blue Badge, Silver Badge, Checkered Badge, Bronze, White.

Frillbacks.

Helmets.—Red, Yellow, Black.

Highflyer.—Plain Head or Crested, Dun, Red, Yellow, miscellaneous colors.

Hollander.—Plain Head, Red, Yellow, Crested Head, Yellow.

Hungarian.—Many colors.

Hyacinths.

Isabels.

Jacobins.—Red, Yellow, Black, Blue, White, Mottled.

Lahores.

Latz.

Magpies.—Blue, Black, Red, Yellow.

Maltese.—Black, Blue, Silver, White, Red, Yellow, mixed colors.

Moreheads.

Nuns.—Black, Red, Yellow.

Oriental Frills.—Same colors as Satinettes.

Owls.—African, Blue, Black-White, Silver, Checkered, White (blue tail), White (black tail), English, Blue, Blue Powdered, Silver, Black, White, Red, Yellow, Checkered.

Pigmy Pouters.—Red, Yellow, Black, Blue, Lavender, Silver, Mealy, Creamy, Checkered, White, Red (white bars), Yellow (white bars), Black (pied), Black (white bars), Blue (pied), Blue (black bars).

Plain Ice.—Blue, Silver, Powdered Silver.

Porcelains.

Pouters.—Black Pied, Blue Pied, Red Pied, Yellow Pied, White.

Priests.—Red, Yellow, Black, Blue.

Quakers.

Ruffled Neck Moreheads.

Runts.—Blue, Silver, Black, White, Pied.

Satinettes.—Peaked, Plain Head.

Scandaroons.—Red, Yellow, Black, Blue, White, Red Saddled, Yellow Saddled, Black Saddled, Blue Saddled.

Shields.

Short-Faced Tumblers.—Almonds; Agates, Red Yellow; Mottles, Black; Rosewings, Black, Red; Splashes; Wholefeathers, Red, Yellow; Kites; Blues, Balds, Blue, Silver, Red, Black, Yellow; Beards, Blue, Silver, Red, Black, Yellow.

Show Antwerps.—Silver Dun, Blue, Blue Checker, Red Checker.

Snells.

Spot Fairies.

Spots.—Black, Blue, Red, Yellow.

Starlings.

Suabians.

Swallows.—Red, Yellow, Blue, Black, Checkered.

Swiss, or *Crescents.*—Clear Legged, Booted, Long Muffled.

Swiss Mandaine.—Many colors.

Tippler.—Solid and mixed colors.

Trumpeters.—Black, Black Rosewing, Black Mottle, Red Mottle, White.

Turbiteens.—Plain Head, Point Crest or Shell Crown; Red, Yellow, Black, Blue, Silver.

Turbits.—Yellow, Red, Blue, Silver, Black, Checkered, Creamy, White Bars.

Ural Ice.—Light, Dark.

Victorias.

Whiskered Owls.

White King.

TERMS USED BY PIGEON FANCIERS

The following is a glossary of the terms in common use by pigeon fanciers:

Arrow Pointed.—In the form of an arrow. Example, the penciling or lacing of a Blondinette.

Bald or *Baldhead.*—The white head of a colored pigeon. Example, the Bald Tumbler.

Barrel-Headed.—An elongated skull, free from angles. Example, the Show Homer.

Bar (tail).—The colored band at extremity o. tail.

Bars (wing).—The bands of black or other colors across the lower part of the wing. Example, the Blue Dragoon.

Beard.—A clearly defined V-shaped patch of white feathers on the throat, directly under the lower mandible. Example, the Long-Faced Beard Tumbler.

Beetle Brow.—Overhanging eye wattles, as seen in soft-eyed Carriers.

Bib.—The colored feathering running in clearly defined outline below the head, along the throat and upper part of the breast. Example, the Nun.

Bishopped.—Having a patch of white feathers at the butt end of the wing.

Blaze.—A white mark on a colored pigeon (generally on the forehead). Example, the Blaze-Face.

Bolting Eye.—An eye that is prominent, wild looking, and staring. Example, a young carrier.

Box Beak.—A beak both mandibles of which are uniform in strength and shape and close fitting. Example, the Carrier.

Broken (in feather).—An indiscriminate mixture of variously colored feathers. Example, the Almond Tumbler.

Broken (in eye).—An erratic coloring of the iris.

Bull Eye.—An eye, the iris of which, as well as the pupil, is very dark in color. Example, the White Dragoon.

Cap.—A colored covering at the top of the head above the eye. Example, the Swallow.

Carriage.—The natural position of a pigeon.

Cere.—The skin-like substance around the eye. Example, the Dragoon.

Chain.—An inverted growth of feathering on each side of the neck. Example, the Jacobin.

Checker.—Two distinct shades of one color. Example, the Checkered Dragoon.

Chuck.—The V-shaped patch of white under the lower mandible. Example, the Beard Tumbler.

Clean-Leg.—Free from feathering below the hock.

Clean-Cut.—Evenly defined.

Condition.—Robust health and perfection of plumage.

Crescent.—A half-moon shaped mark on the breast. Example, the Suabian.

Crest.—An inverted growth of feathers at the back of the head. Example, the Turbit.

Crop.—The craw, or first stomach.

Down-Faced.—Downward contortion of the beak.

Dewlap.—(See Gullet.)

Eye Wattles.—The fleshy excrescence around the eye (chiefly applied to Carriers and Barbs).

Feather-Legged.—Feathered below the hocks. Example, the Blondinette.

Flights (outer or primary).—The first ten feathers of each wing.

Flights (inner or secondary).—The remaining long feathers of the wing.

Foul-Thighed.—Colored feathers on white thighs.

Frill.—A fringe of feathers on the breast, growing in inverted position from the throat downwards. Example, the Turbit.

Frog-Shaped.—Depressed in crown, but free from angles and not flat.

Gay.—Showing too much white (as applied to the crop markings of a Pouter and the shoulder markings of a Mottled Tumbler).

Girth.—The waist of the Pouter.

Gullet.—An abnormal development of loose skin extending from the lower mandible to the top of the neck. Example, the Owl.

Hackle.—The lower feathers at the back of the neck.

Handkerchief Markings.—A triangular shaped patch of white feathers on the back of a colored pigeon. Example, the Mottled Tumbler.

Hood.—The upper covering of the head. Example, the Jacobin.

Jew Wattle.—The wattle on the lower mandible.

Keel.—The lower part of the breast.

Lacing or *Penciling.*—Clearly defined markings, around the outer edge of a feather. Example, the Blondinette.

Limb.—The leg and thigh (as applied to the Pouter).

Mandible.—A portion of the beak.

Mane.—The ridge of feathers at the back of the neck. Example, the Jacobin.

Mealy.—Undecided color, generally applied to Silver-Dun Antwerps and Homers.

Muffed.—Having a covering of feathers on the hocks, legs, and feet. Example, the Trumpeter.

Peak.—Pointed feathers at the back of the head. Example, the Turbit.

Pinch-Eyed.—Irregularity of outline as applied to the eye cere or eye wattle. Example, the Dragoon.

Profile.—The side face.

Rose (breast).—The rose-like feathering on the breast of the Owl.

Rose (feather).—The shoulder markings of the Pouter, Mottled Trumpeter, and Tumbler; the same term is also applied to the radiating point of the hood, mane, and chain of the Jacobin.

Rose (head).—The feathering on the frontal of the Trumpeter.

Rosette.—Feathering on the breast, in the form of a rose. Example, the Owl.

Saddle.—The upper portion of the back.

Self-Colored.—One color only.

Shell.—The shell-shaped growth of feathers at the back of the head. Example, the Swallow.

Shod (as applied to the Fantail).—Deflecture of the lower feathers of the tail.

Skull.—The upper portion of the head.

Slobbered (as applied to the cut of a Baldhead Tumbler). Indistinct and uneven.

Snakey.—Serpentine in shape. Example, the head and neck of the Magpie.

Snip.—A clearly defined elongated spot of white, generally on the forehead. Example, the Snip (German Toy).

Solid Color.—(See Self-Colored).

Spangled.—A "broken" arrangement of feathering.

Spindle-Beaked.—Having a beak that is long and thin.

Splash.—An indiscriminate mixture of several colors. Example, the Splash Short-Faced Tumbler.

Spot.—A colored mark on a white pigeon, generally on the frontal or forehead.

Squab.—A very young pigeon, pinfeathered.

Squeaker.—A (feathered) young pigeon, just learning to feed.

Stockings.—The feathering on the thighs and legs. Example, the Pouter.

Stop.—An abrupt termination of the skull at the base of the beak. Example, the Short-Faced Tumbler.

Tuft.—An inverted growth of feathers behind the wattle. Example, the Priest.

.: *Toys.*—Varieties of which color and markings are the chief properties.

Vent.—The passage from the body.

Veil.—Applied to the head markings of the Nun.

Wattle (beak).—The fleshy excrescence on the beak.

Whiskers.—The feathers between the root of the beak and the base of the eye.

Whole Feather.—A self-colored pigeon.

ARITHMETIC

MEASURES OF EXTENSION

Measures of extension are used in measuring lengths (distances), surfaces (areas), and solids (volumes), and are divided, accordingly, into linear measure, square measure, and cubic measure.

Linear measure has one dimension (length), square measure has two dimensions (length and breadth), and cubic measure has three dimensions (length, breadth, and thickness).

LINEAR MEASURE

12 inches (in.)	= 1 foot	ft.
3 feet	= 1 yard	yd.
5½ yards	= 1 rod	rd.
320 rods	= 1 mile	mi.

in.	*ft.*	*yd.*	*rd.*	*mi.*
12 =	1			
36 =	3 =	1		
198 =	16½ =	5½ =	1	
63,360 =	5,280 =	1,760 =	320 =	1

SQUARE MEASURE

144 square inches (sq. in.)	= 1 square foot	sq. ft.
9 square feet	= 1 square yard	sq. yd.
30¼ square yards	= 1 square rod	sq. rd.
160 square rods	= 1 acre	A.
640 acres	= 1 square mile	sq. mi.

sq. in.	*sq. ft.*	*sq. yd.*	*sq. rd.*	*A.*	*sq. mi.*
144 =	1				
1,296 =	9 =	1			
39,204 =	272¼ =	30¼ =	1		
6,272,640 =	43,560 =	4,840 =	160 =	1	
4,014,489,600 =	27,878,400 =	3,097,600 =	102,400 =	640 =	1

SURVEYORS' SQUARE MEASURE

625 square links (sq. li.)............ = 1 square rod .. sq. rd.

16 square rods................... = 1 square chain . sq. ch.

10 square chains................. = 1 acre......... A.

640 acres...................... = 1 square mile .. sq. mi.

36 square miles (6 miles square) ... = 1 township..... Tp.

A square measuring 208.71 ft. on each side contains 1 A.

The following are the comparative sizes, in square yards, of acres in different places:

	sq. yd.		*sq. yd.*
England and America	4,840	Amsterdam	9,722
Scotland	6,150	Dantzic.............	6,650
Ireland	7,840	France..............	11,960
Hamburg	11,545	Prussia	3,053

CUBIC MEASURE

1,728 cubic inches (cu. in) ...... = 1 cubic foot....... cu. ft.

27 cubic feet............... = 1 cubic yard ...... cu. yd.

128 cubic feet............... = 1 cord of wood.

cu. in.	*cu. ft.*	*cu. yd.*
1,728 =	1	
46,656 =	27 =	1

MEASURES OF WEIGHT

AVOIRDUPOIS WEIGHT

16 ounces (oz.).............. = 1 pound........... lb.

100 pounds................. = 1 hundredweight .... cwt.

20 hundredweight ⎫
2,000 pounds....... ⎭ .... = 1 ton.............. T.

oz.	*lb.*	*cwt.*	*T.*
16 =	1		
1,600 =	100 =	1	
32,000 =	2,000 =	20 =	1

LONG-TON TABLE

16 ounces (oz.).............. = 1 pound............ lb.
28 pounds................. = 1 quarter........... qr.
 4 quarters................ = 1 hundredweight .... cwt.
20 hundredweight ⎫
2,240 pounds....... ⎭ .... = 1 ton.............. T.

oz.	lb.	qr.	cwt.	T.
16 =	1			
448 =	28 =	1		
1,792 =	112 =	4 =	1	
35,840 =	2,240 =	80 =	20 =	1

TROY WEIGHT

24 grains (gr.)............... = 1 pennyweight....... pwt.
20 pennyweights.......... = 1 ounce............ oz.
12 ounces................. = 1 pound............ lb.

gr.	pwt.	oz.	lb.
24 =	1		
480 =	20 =	1	
5,760 =	240 =	12 =	1

APOTHECARIES' WEIGHT

20 grains (gr.)............... = 1 scruple .... sc. or ℈
 3 scruples................. = 1 dram......... dr. or ℨ
 8 drams.................. = 1 ounce......... oz. or ℥
12 ounces................. = 1 pound........ lb. or ℔

gr.	℈	ℨ	℥	lb
20 =	1			
60 =	3 =	1		
480 =	24 =	8 =	1	
5,760 =	288 =	96 =	12 =	1

MEASURES OF CAPACITY

LIQUID MEASURE

 4 gills (gi.).............. = 1 pint................. pt.
 2 pints................. = 1 quart............... qt.
 4 quarts............... = 1 gallon.............. gal.
31½ gallons................ = 1 barrel.............. bbl.
 2 barrels ⎫
63 gallons ⎭ .... = 1 hogshead........... hhd.

$$gi. \quad pt. \quad qt. \quad gal. \; bbl. \; hhd.$$

$$4 = 1$$
$$8 = 2 = 1$$
$$32 = 8 = 4 = 1$$
$$1{,}008 = 252 = 126 = 31\tfrac{1}{2} = 1$$
$$2{,}016 = 504 = 252 = 63 \; = 2 = 1$$

APOTHECARIES' FLUID MEASURE

60 minims, or drops ($\mathfrak{m}$) .... = 1 fluid dram........... f3
8 fluid drams............. = 1 fluid ounce......... f3
16 fluid ounces............ = 1 pint................ O.
8 pints.................. = 1 gallon.............. Cong.

DRY MEASURE

2 pints (pt.)............... = 1 quart................ qt.
8 quarts................. = 1 peck................ pk.
4 pecks.................. = 1 bushel.............. bu.

$$pt. \quad qt. \; pk. \; bu.$$

$$2 = 1$$
$$16 = 8 = 1$$
$$64 = 32 = 4 = 1$$

AVOIRDUPOIS POUNDS IN A BUSHEL

Commodities	Lb.	Commodities	Lb.
Barley................	48	Malt.................	34
Beans................	60	Oats.................	32
Buckwheat.............	48	Potatoes..............	60
Clover seed............	60	Rye.................	56
Corn (shelled)..........	56	Timothy seed.........	45
Corn (in the ear)........	70	Wheat...............	60

The following units are also in commercial use:

1 quintal of fish.................... = 100 lb.
1 barrel of flour.................... = 196 lb.
1 barrel of pork or beef............. = 200 lb.
1 gallon of petroleum .... =   6½ lb.
1 keg of nails...................... = 100 lb.

MEASURES OF TIME

60 seconds (sec.).........	= 1 minute.................	min.
60 minutes..............	= 1 hour..................	hr.
24 hours...............	= 1 day..................	da.
7 days................	= 1 week.................	wk.
4 weeks..............	= 1 month................	mo.
12 months.............	= 1 year.................	yr.
100 years.............	= 1 century..............	C.

sec.	min.	hr.	da	wk.	yr.
60 =	1				
3,600 =	60 =	1			
86,400 =	1,440 =	24 =	1		
604,800 =	10,080 =	168 =	7 =	1	
31,556,936 =	525,948 =	8,765 =	365 =	52 =	1

The following is a list of the months, in regular order, with the number of days each contains:

	Days			*Days*
1. January (Jan.).......	31		7. July	31
2. February (Feb)	28		8. August (Aug.)	31
3. March (Mar.)	31		9. September (Sept.)..	30
4. April (Apr.)	30		10. October (Oct.)	31
5. May	31		11. November (Nov.) ..	30
6. June	30		12. December (Dec.) ...	31

In leap years, 1 da. is added to Feb., giving it 29 da. The following lines will assist in remembering the number of days in each month:

"Thirty days have September,
April, June, and November;
All the rest have thirty-one,
Except the second month alone,
To which we twenty-eight assign,
'Till leap year gives it twenty-nine."

In many business transactions, the year is regarded as 360 da., or 12 mo. of 30 da. each.

MEASURES OF ANGLES OR ARCS

CIRCULAR MEASURE

60 seconds (″) .... = 1 minute.................
60 minutes................. = 1 degree................. °
360 degrees................ = 1 circle................. ⊙

$$60'' = \qquad 1'$$
$$3,600'' = \qquad 60' = \quad 1°$$
$$1,296,000'' = 21,600' = 360° = 1⊙$$

A *quadrant* is one-fourth of a circle, or 90°; a *sextant* is one-sixth of a circle, or 60°. A right angle (∟) contains 90°. The unit of measurement is the degree, or $\frac{1}{360}$ of the circumference of a circle.

Circular, or *angular*, *measure* is used principally by surveyors, navigators, astronomers, and by technical men generally, for measuring angles and arcs of circles.

METRIC SYSTEM OF MEASURES

The metric system is based on the meter, which, according to the U, S. Coast and Goedetic Survey Report of 1884, is equal to 39.370432 in. The value commonly used is 39.37 in. and is authorized by the U. S. government.

There are three principal units—the *meter*, the *liter* (pronounced 'lee-ter'), and the *gram*, the units of length, capacity, and weight, respectively. Multiples of these units are obtained by prefixing to the names of the principal units the Greek words *deca* (10), *hecto* (100), and *kilo* (1,000); the submultiples, or divisions, are obtained by prefixing the Latin words *deci* ($\frac{1}{10}$), *centi* ($\frac{1}{100}$), and *mili* ($\frac{1}{1000}$). These prefixes form the key to the entire system. The abbreviations of the principal units of these submultiples begin with a small letter, while those of the multiples begin with a capital letter.

MEASURES OF LENGTH

10 millimeters (mm.)........ = 1 centimeter.............cm.
10 centimeters............. = 1 decimeter.............dm.
10 decimeters............. = 1 meter.................m.
10 meters................. = 1 decameter............Dm.
10 decameters............. = 1 hectometer...........Hm.
10 hectometers............ = 1 kilometer.............Km.

MEASURES OF SURFACE (NOT LAND)

100 square millimeters
 (sq. mm.)............... = 1 square centimeter ...sq. cm.
100 square centimeters...... = 1 square decimeter....sq. dm.
100 square decimeters....... = 1 square meter........sq. m.

MEASURES OF VOLUME

1,000 cubic millimeters
 (cu. mm.)............... = 1 cubic centimeter ....cu. cm.
1,000 cubic centimeters...... = 1 cubic decimeter .....cu. dm.
1,000 cubic decimeters....... = 1 cubic meter........cu. m.

MEASURES OF CAPACITY

10 millimeters (ml.)......... = 1 centileter..............cl.
10 centileters............. = 1 decileter..............dl.
10 decileters............. = 1 liter...................l.
10 liters................. = 1 decaliter..............Dl.
10 decaliters............. = 1 hectoliter ....Hl.
10 hectoliters............. = 1 kiloliter...............Kl.
The liter is equal to the volume occupied by 1 cu. dm.

MEASURES OF WEIGHT

10 milligrams (mg.)......... = 1 centigram.............cg.
10 centigrams............. = 1 decigram.............dg.
10 decigrams............. = 1 gram.................g.
10 grams................. = 1 decagram.............Dg.
10 decagrams............. = 1 hectogram............Hg.
10 hectograms............. = 1 kilogram.............Kg.
1,000 kilograms............ = 1 ton...................T.

The gram is the weight of 1 cu. cm. of pure distilled water at a temperature of 39.2° F.; the kilogram is the weight of 1 liter of water; the ton is the weight of 1 cu. m. of water.

MEASURES OF MONEY
UNITED STATES MONEY

10 mills (m.).................. = 1 cent .... **c.**
10 cents.................... = 1 dime................. **d.**
10 dimes.................... = 1 dollar................. **$**
10 dollars.................. = 1 eagle................. **E.**

m.	*ct.*	*d.*	$	*E.*
10 =	1			
100 =	10 =	1		
1,000 =	100 =	10 =	1	
10,000 =	1,000 =	100 =	10 =	1

The term *legal tender* is applied to money that may be legally offered in payment of debts. All gold coins are legal tender for their face value to any amount, provided their weight has not diminished more than $\frac{1}{200}$. Silver dollars are also legal tender to any amount; but silver coins of lower denominations than $1 are legal tender only for sums not exceeding $10. Nickel and copper coins are legal tender for sums not exceeding 25c.

The legal coins of the United States are:

GOLD COINS	*Weight in Grains*
1-dollar piece.......................	= 25.8
2½-dollar piece, or quarter eagle.......	= 64.5
3-dollar piece.......................	= 77.4
5-dollar piece, or half eagle........	= 129.0
10-dollar piece, or eagle.............	= 258.0
20-dollar piece, or double eagle......	= 516.0

SILVER COINS	,*Weight*
Standard dollar................. =412.5	grains
Half dollar, or 50-cent piece..... = 192.9	grains, or 12½ grams
Quarter dollar, or 25-cent piece.. = 96.45	grains, or 6¼ grams
Dime, or 10-cent piece.......... = 38.58	grains, or 2½ grams

COPPER AND NICKEL COINS	*Weight*
5-cent piece..................... =77.16	grains, or 5 grams
3-cent piece..................... = 30.00	grains
1-cent piece..................... = 48.00	grains

ENGLISH MONEY

4 farthings (far.)......... = 1 penny.................. d.
12 pence................ = 1 shilling.................. s.
20 shillings.............. = 1 pound, or sovereign........ £

$$
\begin{array}{rcccc}
far. & d. & s. & £ \\
4= & 1 \\
48= & 12= & 1 \\
960= & 240= & 20= & 1
\end{array}
$$

The unit of English money is the *pound sterling*, the value of which in United States money is $4.8665. The fineness of English silver is .925; of the gold coins, .916⅔. What is called sterling silver when applied to solid-silver articles has the same fineness. Hence the name *sterling silver*.

The other coins of Great Britain are the *florin* (= 2 shillings), the *crown* (= 5 shillings), the *half crown* (= 2½ shillings), and the *guinea* (= 21 shillings). The largest silver coin is the crown, and the smallest the threepence (¼ shilling). The shilling is worth 25c. (24.3+c.) in United States money. The guinea is no longer coined. The abbreviation £ is written before the number, while s. and d. follow. Thus, £25 4s. 6d. = 25 pounds 4 shillings 6 pence.

Rule.—To reduce pounds, shillings, and pence to dollars and cents, reduce the pounds to shillings, add the shillings, if any, and multiply the sum by 24½; if any pence are given, increase this product by twice as many cents as there are pence.

Example.—Reduce £4 7s. 11d. to dollars and cents.
Solution.— $(4 \times 20 + 7) \times .24\frac{1}{2} + 2 \times 11 = \$21.39.$

Rule.—To reduce pounds to dollars, and vice versa, exchange being at $4.8665: Multiply the number of pounds by 73, and divide the quotient by 15; the result will be the equivalent in dollars and cents. Or, multiplying the dollars by 15 and dividing the product by 73 will give its equivalent in pounds and decimals of a pound.

Example 1.—Reduce £6 to dollars and cents.
Solution.— $6 \times 73 \div 15 = \$29.20.$
Example 2.—Reduce $17 to pounds.
Solution.— $17 \times 15 \div 73 = £3.493.$

The monetary units of leading foreign nations and their equivalents in United States money are as follows. These rates are proclaimed each year by the Secretary of the Treasury.

Country	Monetary Unit		Value in U. S. Gold
Canada..........	Dollar	= 100 cents........	$1.00
Great Britain....	Pound	= 20 shillings.......	4.86⅔
France..... ⎫ Belgium.... ⎬ ... Switzerland ⎭	Franc	= 100 centimes.....	.193
Italy............	Lira	= 100 centesimi	.193
Spain............	Peseta	= 100 centimos.....	.193
German Empire..	Mark	= 100 pfennigs	.238
Denmark ⎫ Norway ⎬...... Sweden ⎭	Crown	= 100 öre.........	.268
Russia...........	Ruble	= 100 copecks......	.515
Japan...........	Yen	= 100 sen.........	.498

HEAT

SPECIFIC HEATS OF METALS

The specific heat of a substance is the number of heat units required to raise a unit mass of the substance one degree in temperature. The specific heat of water is very nearly constant for all temperatures, but that at its temperature of maximum density (4° C. or 39.1° F.) is considered unity. The specific heats of most substances increase with increasing temperatures.

HEAT UNITS

One *British thermal unit* (B. T. U.) is the quantity of heat required to raise the temperature of 1 lb. of pure water 1° F. at or near its maximum density, 39.1° F.

One *calorie* is the quantity of heat required to raise the temperature of 1 Kg. of water 1° C. at or near 4° C.

· 1 B. T. U. = .252 calorie and 1 calorie = 3. 968 B. T. U.

One *small*, or *gram, calorie* (a heat unit also in some use) is the quantity of heat required to raise the temperature of 1.gram of water 1° C. at or near 4° C.

CENTIGRADE AND FAHRENHEIT DEGREES

Deg. C.	Deg. F.	Deg. C.	Deg. F.	Deg. C.	Deg. F.	Deg. C.	Deg. F.
0	32.0	26	78.8	51	123.8	76	168.8
1	33.8	27	80.6	52	125.6	77	170.6
2	35.6	28	82.4	53	127.4	78	172.4
3	37.4	29	84.2	54	129.2	79	174.2
4	39.2	30	86.0	55	131.0	80	176.0
5	41.0	31	87.8	56	132.8	81	177.8
6	42.8	32	89.6	57	134.6	82	179.6
7	44.6	33	91.4	58	136.4	83	181.4
8	46.4	34	93.2	59	138.2	84	183.2
9	48.2	35	95.0	60	140.0	85	185.0
10	50.0	36	96.8	61	141.8	86	186.8
11	51.8	37	98.6	62	143.6	87	188.6
12	53.6	38	100.4	63	145.4	88	190.4
13	55.4	39	102.2	64	147.2	89	192.2
14	57.2	40	104.0	65	149.0	90	194.0
15	59.0	41	105.8	66	150.8	91	195.8
16	60.8	42	107.6	67	152.6	92	197.6
17	62.6	43	109.4	68	154.4	93	199.4
18	64.4	44	111.2	69	156.2	94	201.2
19	66.2	45	113.0	70	158.0	95	203.0
20	68.0	46	114.8	71	159.8	96	204.8
21	69.8	47	116.6	72	161.6	97	206.6
22	71.6	48	118.4	73	163.4	98	208.4
23	73.4	49	120.2	74	165.2	99	210.2
24	75.2	50	122.0	75	167.0	100	212.0
25	77.0						

TEMPERATURE

The temperature of a body is its degree of sensible heat. For the measurement of temperatures there are three kinds of thermometers: the Fahrenheit, abbreviated F. or Fahr., commonly used in America; the Centigrade, abbreviated C. or Cent., used in France and by scientists everywhere; and the Réaumur, abbreviated R or Réau., used in Germany.

Standard Points	Degrees F.	Degrees C.	Degrees R.
Boiling point of water at sea level; i. e., pressure = 1 atmosphere.......	212	100	80
Melting point of ice.......	32	0	0
Absolute zero. i. e., the total absence of heat; theoretical only......	−460	−273	−219

Between boiling point and freezing point = 180° F. = 100° C. = 80° R.

$$\text{Temp. F.} = \frac{9}{5}\text{ Temp. C.} + 32° = \frac{9}{4}\text{Temp. R.} + 32°.$$

$$\text{Temp. C.} = \frac{5}{9}(\text{Temp. F.} - 32°) = \frac{5}{4}\text{Temp. R.}$$

$$\text{Temp. R.} = \frac{4}{9}(\text{Temp. F.} - 32°) = \frac{4}{5}\text{Temp. C.}$$

MISCELLANEOUS TABLES

The following table is used in counting certain articles:

12 of anything............	= 1 dozen...................	doz.
12 dozen.................	= 1 gross...................	gr.
12 gross.................	= 1 great gross.............	g. gr.
20 of anything............	= 1 score	

units	doz.	gr.	g. gr.
12 =	1		
144 =	12 =	1	
1,728 =	144 =	12 =	1

The following table is used in the paper trade:

24 sheets..................... = 1 quire.................... qr.
20 quires.................... = 1 ream.................... rm.
2 reams..................... = 1 bundle.................. bdl.
5 bundles................... = 1 bale.................... B.

$$
\begin{array}{lll}
sheets & qr. & rm.\ bdl.\ B. \\
24 = & 1 \\
480 = & 20 = & 1 \\
960 = & 40 = & 2 = 1 \\
4{,}800 = & 200 = & 10 = 5 = 1
\end{array}
$$

It is now becoming customary to consider 500 sheets as a ream, and to discard the higher denominations.

BOOKS

The terms folio, quarto, octavo, etc., show the number of leaves into which a sheet of paper is folded.

Folio .... = 2 leaves, or 4 pages
Quarto .... = 4 leaves, or 8 pages
Octavo .... = 8 leaves, or 16 pages
Duodecimo .... = 12 leaves, or 24 pages
16mo .... = 16 leaves, or 32 pages
18mo .... = 18 leaves, or 36 pages
24mo .... = 24 leaves, or 48 pages
32mo .... = 32 leaves, or 64 pages

METRIC EQUIVALENTS OF POUNDS, FEET, ETC.

The government publishes the equivalents in pounds, etc., of the metric system, but the American shipper wants to know what the pounds, inches, feet, and gallons, to which he is accustomed, are in the metric system. The following is a convenient table showing the metric values of our measures. Some countries demand that the metric system should be used in the consular papers, and in most countries, especially in Latin-America, the consignees ask for the weights, etc., in the metric system. This table will be found valuable for reference by invoice clerks and shipping clerks in the export departments of manufacturing establishments.

Pounds	Kilos	Pounds	Kilos
1	= .4536	60	=27.216
2	= .9072	70	=31.751
3	= 1.3608	80	=36.287
4	= 1.8144	90	=40.823
5	=2.2680	100	= 45.36
6	=2.7216	200	= 90.72
7	=3.1751	300	= 136.08
8	=3.6287	400	= 181.44
9	=4.0823	500	=226.80
10	= 4.536	600	=272.16
20	= 9.072	700	=317.51
30	=13.608	800	=362.87
40	=18.144	900	=408.23
50	=22.680	1,000	=453.60

1,000 kilos = 1 metric ton (Tonelada metrico).

	Centimeters		Centimeters
1 inch	= 2.54	7 feet	=213.36
1 foot	= 30.48	8 feet	=243.84
1 yard	= 91.44	9 feet	=274.32
2 feet	= 60.96	10 feet	=304.80
3 feet	= 91.44	11 feet	=335.28
4 feet	=121.92	12 feet	=365.76
5 feet	=152.40	13 feet	=396.24
6 feet	=182.88	14 feet	=426.72

DIFFERENCE OF SUN TIME BETWEEN NEW YORK CITY AND OTHER PARTS OF THE WORLD

When it is noon at New York, it is, at

Buffalo	11:40 A. M.	Boston	12:12 P. M.
Cincinnati	11:18 A. M.	Quebec	12:12 P. M.
Chicago	11:07 A. M.	London	4:55 P. M.
St. Louis	10:55 A. M.	Paris	5:05 P. M.
San Francisco	8:45 A. M.	Rome	5:45 P. M.
New Orleans	10:56 A. M.	Constantinople	6:41 P. M.
Washington	11:48 A. M.	Vienna	6:00 P. M.
Charleston	11:36 A. M.	St. Petersburg	6:57 P. M.
Havana	11:25 A. M.	Peking	12:40 A. M.

TABLE OF DISTANCES

1 mile.............................. = 5,280 ft.; 1,760 yd.;
320 rd.; 8 fur.

1 furlong............................. = 40 rd.

1 league............................. = 3 mi.

1 knot,* or nautical mile.............. = 6,080 ft., or 1⅛ mi.

1 nautical league..................... = 3 naut. mi.

1 fathom............................. = 6 ft.

1 meter.............................. = 3 ft. 3⅜ in., nearly

1 hand............................... = 4 in.

1 palm............................... = 3 in.

1 span............................... = 9 in.

1 cable's length...................... = 240 yd.

MEASURES OF VOLUME

1 cubic foot.......................... = 1,728 cu. in.

1 ale gallon.......................... = 282 cu. in.

1 standard, or wine, gallon............ = 231 cu. in.

1 dry gallon.......................... = 268.8 cu. in.

1 bushel............................. = 2,150.4 cu. in.

1 British bushel...................... = 2,218.19 cu. in.

1 cord of wood....................... = 128 cu. ft.

1 perch.............................. = 24.75 cu. ft.

1 ton of round timber................. = 40 cu. ft.

1 ton of hewn timber................. = 50 cu. ft.

A box 12⅟₈ in. long, wide, and deep contains 1 bu.
A box 19⅜ in. long, wide, and deep contains 1 bbl.
A box 8¼ in. long, wide, and deep contains 1 pk.
A box 6⁷⁄₁₆ in. long, wide, and deep contains ½ pk.
A box 4⁵⁄₁₆ in. long, wide, and deep contains 1 qt.

Cylinders having the following dimensions, in inches, contain the measures stated, very closely; the diameters are given first:

Gill	= 1¾ in. × 3 in.	Gallon.......	= 7 in. × 6 in.
Pint	= 3½ in. × 3 in.	8 gallons.....	= 14 in. × 12 in.
Quart........	= 3½ in. × 6 in.	10 gallons....	= 14 in. × 15 in.

---

*A knot is really a measure of speed and not of distance; when used in this sense, it is equivalent to 1 naut. mi. in 1 hr. Thus, a vessel traveling 20 naut. mi. per hr. has a speed of 20 knots.

PLASTERING, PAINTING, AND CALCIMINING

Plastering, painting, and *calcimining* are usually estimated by the square yard. Allowances for doors, windows, etc. are not regulated by any established usage.

Rule.—*Multiply the perimeter* of the room by the height of the ceiling for the area of the walls. To this add the area of the ceiling, and from the sum make such deductions as are specified. Reduce the results to square yards, and multiply the price per square yard by the number denoting the area in square yards.*

Example.—At 22c. per sq. yd., what will it cost to plaster a room 65 ft. long, 22 ft. wide, and 15 ft. high, deducting in full for 8 doors 4 ft. 6 in. wide and 11 ft. 6 in. high, 10 windows 3 ft. 6 in. wide and 8 ft. high, and a baseboard 6½ in. high extending around the room?

Solution.—

Perimeter of the room............ $= 65 \times 2 + 22 \times 2 = 174$ ft.

Area of walls.................... $= 174 \times 15 = 2610$ sq. ft.

Area of ceiling.................. $= 65 \times 22 = 1430$ sq. ft.

Total............................. $= 4040$ sq. ft.

Area of doors................. $= 4\frac{1}{2} \times 11\frac{1}{2} \times 8 = 414$ sq. ft.

Area of windows.............. $= 3\frac{1}{2} \times 8 \times 10 = 280$ sq. ft.

Area of baseboard......... $=$ (perimeter less width of 8 doors) $\times \frac{6\frac{1}{2}}{12} = (174 - 4\frac{1}{2} \times 8) \times \frac{6\frac{1}{2}}{12} = 74\frac{3}{4}$ sq. ft.

Total, after deduction................. $= 3271\frac{1}{4}$ sq. ft.

Area in square yards .... $= 3271\frac{1}{4} \div 9 = 363\frac{17}{36}$ sq. yd.

Cost.............................. $= \$.22 \times 363\frac{17}{36} = \$79.96$

PAPERING

Wallpaper as made in the United States, is 18 in. (½ yd.) wide, and is sold in single rolls and double rolls; a single roll is 8 yd. long, and a double roll is 16 yd. long. When cutting the paper, paper hangers divide the rolls into strips of sufficient length to reach

---

*The perimeter is the sum of the lengths of the sides of the room.

from the baseboard to a short distance (say 6 in.) above the lower edge of the border. There is always considerable waste in cutting, owing to the matching of the figures forming the design, and the fact that there is a part of a strip left over after cutting up the roll. The parts of strips thus left over are used for the surface above doors and below windows, and other irregular places. Although double rolls are usually counted as 2 single rolls, there is a choice between them in certain cases. Thus, suppose the strips were required to be 9 ft. (3 yd.) long, only 2 strips could be cut from a single roll, or 4 strips from 2 single rolls, while 5 strips could be cut from a double roll. The length of a roll of border is the same as the length of a roll of paper.

On account of the waste in cutting, the various sizes and shapes of rooms, the number of windows, doors, etc., it is difficult to estimate exactly the number of rolls required. Two rules are given, both of which are used in practice:

Rule.—I. *From the perimeter of the room, subtract the widths of openings (windows and doors), and reduce the result to half yards; the number of half yards so obtained will be the total number of strips required. Find the number of strips that can be cut from a roll, and divide the first result by the second; the quotient will be the number of rolls required.*

II. *Divide the number of half yards of the perimeter of the room by the number of strips that can be cut from a roll; the quotient will be the number of rolls required.*

If computed by the first rule, the number of rolls obtained may be too small, and if computed by the second rule, too large. But, since paper dealers will usually take back all rolls that are intact, the second rule will generally give the best results, as it will prevent the loss of time required to send to the dealer for extra rolls, in case they are needed.

· **EXAMPLE.**—Find how much paper will be needed to cover the walls and ceiling of a room 15 ft. × 20 ft., the border for both walls and ceiling to be 18 in. wide. The

baseboard is 8 in. high, and the height of walls from floor to ceiling is 9 ft.

SOLUTION.—Since the widths of the openings are not specified, it will be necessary to use rule II.

Perimeter of room $= 2 \times 15 + 2 \times 20 = 70$ ft. $= 23\frac{1}{3}$ yd. $= 46\frac{2}{3}$ half yards, or 47 strips. Assuming that the strips extend the height of the baseboard above the bottom edge of the border, the length of a strip is (since 18 in. $= 1\frac{1}{2}$ ft.) $9 - 1\frac{1}{2} = 7\frac{1}{2}$ ft. $= 2\frac{1}{2}$ yd. Hence, the number of strips in a single roll is $8 \div 2\frac{1}{2} = 3$ strips, and the number of rolls required is. $47 \div 3 = 15\frac{2}{3}$, or 16 rolls.

In papering the ceiling, the direction in which the strips are to run must be considered. If the strips run lengthwise of the room, the distance between the edges of the border is $20 - 2 \times 1\frac{1}{2} = 17$ ft., and the length of the strips must be at least 18 ft., or 6 yd., long; hence, but 1 strip can be cut from a single roll, and but 2 strips from a double roll. The width of the room in half yards is $(15 \div 3) \times 2 = 10$; hence, allowing for the border, 9 strips, or 9 single rolls, will be required.

If the strips run crosswise of the room, the length of a strip between the edges of the border will be $15 - 2 \times 1\frac{1}{2} = 12$ ft., and the length of a strip must be at least 13 ft., or $4\frac{1}{3}$ yd.; hence, 1 strip may be obtained from a single roll, or $16 \div 4\frac{1}{3} = 3$ strips from a double roll. The length of the room in half yards is $(20 \div 3) \times 2 = 13\frac{1}{3}$; hence, allowing the paper to extend 6 in. beyond the inner edge of the border, at both ends of the room, 12 strips will be required. The number of double rolls required will be $12 \div 3 = 4$ double rolls. Consequently, in this case, there is less waste when the paper runs crosswise than when it runs lengthwise.

Since the perimeter of the room is 70 ft., or $23\frac{1}{3}$ yd., $23\frac{1}{3} \div 8 = 3$ single rolls of border for the walls, and the same amount for the ceiling will be required. Therefore, 16 single rolls of paper are required for the walls, 4 double rolls for the ceiling, 3 single rolls of border for the walls, and 3 single rolls for the ceiling.

CARPETING

Carpet is made in various widths. Ingrain carpet is usually 36 in., or 1 yd., wide; Brussels carpet is 27 in., or ¾ yd., wide. Carpet borders are 22½ in., or ⅝ yd., wide. A linear yard of ingrain carpet contains 1 sq. yd., and a linear yard of Brussels carpet contains ¾ sq. yd.

Rule.—*To find the number of linear yards of carpet required for a room, if no allowance is made for cutting and matching the strips, divide the area of the room in square yards by the area of a linear yard of the carpet.*

EXAMPLE.—How many yards of Brussels carpet will be required to cover a floor 36 ft. long and 21 ft. wide, making no allowance for cutting and matching?

SOLUTION.—Area   of   floor $=36\times21=756$ sq.   ft. $=\dfrac{756}{9}$ $=84$ sq. yd. A linear yard of Brussels carpet has an area of ¾ sq. yd. Hence, the number of linear yards required is $84\div\frac{3}{4}=112$ yd.

In practice, there is usually considerable loss due to cutting and matching. To find the number of yards required for a room, when allowance is made for loss, the width of the room is divided by the width of a single strip. The quotient is the number of strips required, supposing them to run lengthwise of the room. The number of strips multiplied by the length in yards of a single strip, making allowance for the loss required for matching, is the number of linear yards required.

EXAMPLE.—How many yards of Brussels carpet will be required to cover a room 23 ft. long and 15 ft. wide, making an allowance of 1 ft. on each strip for matching? The carpet is supposed to run lengthwise.

SOLUTION.—Width of room $=15$ ft. $=180$ in. Width of carpet $=27$ in. Number of strips $=180\div27=6\frac{2}{3}$. Hence, 7 strips must be used, the excess, 9 in., being cut off or turned under. Allowing 1 ft. for matching, length of strip $=23+1$ $=24$ ft. $=8$ yd. Number of linear yards required $=7\times8$ $=56$ yd.

The number of linear yards of carpet border required for a room is equal to the perimeter of the room in yards.

EXAMPLE.—How many yards of border will be required. in carpeting a room 42 ft. long and 26½ ft. wide?

SOLUTION.—Perimeter of room $= 42 \times 2 + 26\frac{1}{2} \times 2 = 137$ ft.

$$= \frac{137}{3} = 45\frac{2}{3} \text{ yd.}$$

BOARD MEASURE

In measuring lumber, the unit is the *board foot,* which is a board 1 ft. long, 1 ft. wide, and 1 in. (or less) thick. One board foot is equal to $\frac{1}{12}$ cu. ft.

Rule.—*To find the number of board feet in any piece of lumber, multiply the length in feet by the breadth in feet, and this product by the thickness in inches, if it be more than 1 inch; or, otherwise, multiply the length in feet by the breadth in inches, and this product by the thickness in inches, and then divide by 12.*

EXAMPLE.—How many board feet are contained in a joist 18 ft. long, 14 in. wide, and 12 in. thick?

SOLUTION.— $\dfrac{18 \times 14 \times 12}{12} = 252$ board feet.

Lumber is sold by the thousand (M) feet, the term foot being always used instead of the longer term, board foot.

Rule.—*To find the cost of lumber, divide the number of feet by 1,000 and multiply by the cost per M.*

EXAMPLE.—What will be the cost of 19 boards 14 ft. long, 15 in. wide, and 1½ in. thick, at $23.50 per M?

SOLUTION.—Number of thousand feet $= \dfrac{19 \times 14 \times 15 \times 1\frac{1}{2}}{12 \times 1,000}$

$= .498\frac{3}{4}$. Hence, $.498\frac{3}{4} \times 23.50 = 11.72$.

Shingles are sold in bundles of 250 (¼ M). The lengths of all shingles in bundle are the same (usually 12 in., 14 in., or 16 in.), but their widths vary. The average width, however, is generally 4 in., the width of all bundles being alike. When laying shingles, 4 in. is usually exposed to the weather, the remaining portions being concealed by the other shingles.

Rule.—*To find the number of shingles required to cover a roof, compute the total area of the roof in square inches, and divide this area by the product of the average width of the shingles and the length that is exposed to the weather.*

EXAMPLE.—What will it cost to shingle a roof, each side measuring 40 ft. × 16 ft., if the shingles cost $4.50 per **M**?

SOLUTION.—Since the size of the exposed portion is not stated, it will be assumed as 4 in.×4 in. Then, for one side, $\frac{40\times16\times144}{4\times4}=5{,}760$ shingles will be required, and for both sides, $5{,}760\times2=11{,}520$ shingles. Therefore, the cost will be $11.52\times\$4.50=\$51.84$.

Multiply by 144 in order to reduce the square feet (40×16) to square inches. Allowance should also be made for waste.

MASONRY

In estimating the cubical contents of stone walls, the *perch* of $24\frac{3}{4}$ cu. ft. is used.

Rule.—*To find the number of perches of masonry in a wall, divide the volume of the wall in cubic feet by $24\frac{3}{4}$.*

In estimating the contents of stone foundations for buildings, the length of the wall is measured on the outside, thus counting each corner twice. If a wall 2 ft. thick measures 12 ft.×20 ft. on the outside, and the corners are assumed to be parts of the longer sides, there will be 2 walls each 20 ft. long, and 2 walls each 8 ft. long. The actual length is therefore $2\times20+2\times8=56$ ft. The length estimated on the outside is $2\times20+2\times12=64$ ft. To find the actual length of such a wall, subtract 4 times the thickness of the wall from the length measured on the outside. Thus, in the above case, actual length $=64-4\times2=56$ ft.

Usually, masons make no allowance for windows or doors in estimating their work. In estimating the quantity of stone required for the wall, such allowances should be made.

EXAMPLE.—(a) How many perches of stone will be required to build the walls of a church 60 ft. long by

32. ft. wide, the walls being 24 ft. high and 2¼ ft. thick? There are 8 windows, each 5 ft. wide and 11 ft. high, and 2 doors, each 6 ft. wide and 9 ft. high. (*b*) What will be the cost of laying the walls at $3.50 per perch?

SOLUTION.—

Length of wall (outside) $= 2 \times 60 + 2 \times 32 = 184$ ft.

Actual length $= 184 - 4 \times 2\frac{1}{4} = 175$ ft.

Actual cubical contents $= 175 \times 24 \times 2\frac{1}{4} = 9,450$ cu. ft.

Allowance for windows $= 5 \times 11 \times 2\frac{1}{4} \times 8 = 990$ cu. ft.

Allowance for doors $= 6 \times 9 \times 2\frac{1}{4} \times 2 = 243$ cu. ft.

Net contents $= 9,450 - (990 + 243) = 8,217$ cu. ft.

(*a*)   Perches required for wall $= 8,217 \div 24\frac{3}{4} = 332$.

(*b*)   Since, in estimating the cost of the work, no allowance is made for corners, doors, and windows,·

Cubical contents $= 184 \times 24 \times 2\frac{1}{4} = 9,936$ cu. ft.

Perches of stonework $= 9,936 \div 24\frac{3}{4} = 401\frac{5}{11}$.

Cost of laying walls $= 401\frac{5}{11} \times \$3.50 = \$1,405.09$.

BRICKWORK

Brickwork is generally estimated by the thousand bricks laid in the wall, but measurements by the cubic yard and by the perch are also used. To allow for mortar, ¼ in. is added to the length and to the thickness in making calculations. The following data will be found useful in calculating the number of bricks in a wall. For each superficial foot of wall 4 in. in thickness (the width of 1 brick), allow 7½ bricks; for a 9-in. wall (the width of 2 bricks), allow 15 bricks; and so on, estimating 7½ bricks for each additional 4 in. in thickness of wall. If brickwork is to be estimated by the cubic yard, allow 500 bricks to 1 cu. yd. This figure is based on the use of 8¼ in. × 4 in. × 2¼ in. bricks, with mortar joints not over ⅜ in. thick. If the joints are ⅛ in. thick, as in face brickwork, 1 cu. yd. will require about 575 bricks. In making calculations of the number of bricks required, an allowance of, say, 5% should be made for waste in breakage, etc.

BINS, CISTERNS, ETC.

It is frequently necessary to estimate the capacity of a bin, box, or vessel in bushels, barrels, or gallons. The volume of the bin or vessel in cubic feet or cubic inches is divided by the number of cubic feet or cubic inches in a bushel, barrel, or gallon, as the case may be. For convenience of reference, the following table of capacities is given:

DRY MEASURE

1 heaped bushel = 2,747.71 cu. in. = 1.59 cu. ft., nearly
1 stricken bushel = 2,150.42 cu. in. = 1.25 cu. ft., nearly
1 peck   =   537.6   cu. in.
1 quart   =   67.2   cu. in.
1 pint   =   33.6   cu. in.

LIQUID MEASURE

1 hogshead = 8.422   cu. ft.
1 barrel   = 4.211   cu. ft.
1 gallon   = 231   cu. in.
1 quart   = 57.75   cu. in.
1 pint   = 28.875 cu. in.

Rule.—To find the capacity of a bin or other vessel in dry measure or in liquid measure, divide the volume of the bin or vessel in cubic inches by the number of cubic inches in the unit of measure.

The following table of approximate capacities is very convenient in rough calculations:

1 cubic foot = .63 heaped bushel
1 cubic foot = .80 stricken bushel
1 cubic foot = 7.50 liquid gallons
1 cubic foot = $\frac{13}{60}$ barrel

The following short rules are approximate, but the results are sufficiently accurate for all practical purposes.

Rule.—To find the capacity of a bin in heaped bushels, multiply the volume in cubic feet by .63.

Rule.—To find the capacity of a bin in stricken bushels, multiply the volume in cubic feet by .8.

Rule.—To find the number of gallons in a cistern or other vessel, multiply the volume in cubic feet by 7.5.

Rule.—*To find the number of barrels in a cistern, multiply the volume in cubic feet by* $\frac{18}{80}$.

Rule.—*To find the number of gallons in a cylindrical vessel, multiply the square of the diameter in inches by the height in inches, and that product by .0034.*

GAUGING OF CASKS

A *cask* resembles two frustums of cones with their larger bases placed together.

The *bung diameter* of a cask is the diameter measured half way between the two ends; it is usually the greatest diameter.

The *mean diameter* of a cask is the mean between the bung diameter and the head diameter. The mean diameter is found by adding together the head diameter and bung diameter and dividing the sum by 2.

Rule.—*To find the number of gallons in a cask, multiply the square of the mean diameter in inches by the length in inches, and that product by .0034.*

EXAMPLE.—The diameter of a cask is 27 in. at the head, 33 in. at the bung, and the cask is 3 ft. long; how many gallons will it hold?

SOLUTION.—Mean diameter $= \dfrac{27+33}{2} = 30$ in. Length $= 3$ ft. $= 36$ in. Capacity $= 30^2 \times 36 \times .0034 = 110.16$ gal.

To find the number of liters in the cask, multiply by .0129 instead of .0034. If the cask is partly filled, stand it on end, find the mean diameter of the part filled, multiply its square by the height, and that product by .0034.

COAL AND HAY

A ton (2,000 lb.) of Lehigh coal, egg size, measures 34½ cu. ft. in the bin; Schuylkill coal, 35 cu. ft.; pink-gray and red-ash coal, 36 cu. ft.; Wyoming coal, 31 cu. ft.

The bulk of a ton of hay is dependent on the pressure to which it is subjected. Roughly speaking, a ton of

hay lying unpressed measures 500 cu. ft.; when in a small stack, 400 cu. ft.; and in mows compressed with grain, or in well-settled stacks, 300 cu. ft.

Shipping Ton.—Freight on very light articles is usually estimated by the space occupied.

$$40 \text{ cu. ft.} = \begin{cases} 1 \text{ United States shipping ton} \\ 31.16 \text{ imperial bushels} \\ 32.143 \text{ United States bushels} \end{cases}$$

$$42 \text{ cu. ft.} = \begin{cases} 1 \text{ British shipping ton} \\ 32.719 \text{ imperial bushels} \\ 33.75 \text{ United States bushels} \end{cases}$$

POSTAL DISTANCES AND TIME

In the following list are given the approximate distances by postal routes and the time by rail between New York City and the points indicated. The times mentioned are subject to changes due to varying conditions.

Cities in the United States	Miles	Hours
Albany, N. Y.	142	3½
Atlanta, Ga.	882	24¼
Baltimore, Md.	188	6
Binghamton, N. Y.	207	5½
Bismarck, N. Dak.	1,738	60½
Boise, Idaho	2,736	92½
Boston, Mass.	217	7
Buffalo, N. Y.	410	9½
Cape May, N. J.	172	5
Carson City, Nev.	3,036	109¾
Charleston, S. C.	804	21¼
Chattanooga, Tenn.	853	32
Cheyenne, Wyo.	1,899	54
Chicago, Ill.	900	23
Cincinnati, Ohio	744	23

Cities in the United States	Miles	Hours
Cleveland, Ohio	568	19½
Columbus, Ohio	624	20.
Concord, N. H.	292	9½
Deadwood, S. Dak.	1,975	65½
Denver, Colo.	1,930	61½
Des Moines, Iowa	1,257	37½
Detroit, Mich.	743	21
Galveston, Tex.	1,789	56½
Harrisburg, Pa.	182	6
Hartford, Conn.	112	4
Helena, Mont.	2,423	89
Hot Springs, Ark.	1,367	55
Indianapolis, Ind.	808	23
Jacksonville, Fla.	1,077	32
Kansas City, Mo.	1,302	38¼
Louisville, Ky.	854	30
Memphis, Tenn.	1,163	40
Milwaukee, Wis.	985	29¼
Montgomery, Ala.	1,057	30½
Montpelier, Vt.	327	10¼
New Orleans, La.	1,344	40
Omaha, Neb.	1,383	43
Philadelphia, Pa.	90	3
Pittsburg, Pa.	431	13
Portland, Me.	325	12
Portland, Ore.	3,181	114½
Prescott, Ariz.	2,724	94
Providence, R. I.	189	6
Richmond, Va.	344	11¼
St. Louis, Mo.	1,048	29
St. Paul, Minn.	1,300	37
Salt Lake City, Utah	2,452	71½
San Francisco, Cal.	3,250	106
Santa Fé, N. Mex.	2,173	82
Savannah, Ga.	905	26
Scranton, Pa.	146	4½
Tacoma, Wash.	3,209	102
Topeka, Kans.	1,370	48

Cities in the United States	Miles	Hours
Trenton, N. J.	57	2
Vicksburg, Miss.	1,288	50
Vinita, Okla.	1,412	42
Washington, D. C.	228	6½
Wheeling, W. Va.	496	14¼
Wilmington, Del.	117	5
Wilmington, N. C.	593	20

The postal distances and time between New York and foreign cities are as follows:

By Postal Route to	Miles	Days
Adelaide, via Vancouver	12,845	31
Alexandria, via London	6,150	12
Amsterdam, via London	3,985	8
Antwerp, via London	4,000	8
Athens, via London	5,655	11
Bahia, Brazil	5,870	14
Bangkok, Siam, via San Francisco	12,900	43
Batavia, Java, via London	12,800	34
Berlin, via London	4,385	9
Bombay, via London	9,765	22
Bremen, via London	4,235	8
Buenos Ayres	8,045	24
Calcutta via London	11,120	24
Cape Town, via London	11,245	25.
Constantinople, via London	5,810	11
Florence, via London	4,800	9
Glasgow	3,370	8
Greytown, via New Orleans	2,815	7
Halifax, N. S.	645	2
Hamburg, via London	4,340	9
Hamburg, direct	4,820	9
Havana	1,366	3
Hong Kong, via San Francisco	10,590	27
Honolulu, via San Francisco	5,645	12
Liverpool	3,540	7
London, via Queenstown	3,740	7
London, via Southampton	3,760	8
Madrid, via London	4,925	9

By Postal Route to	Miles	Days
Melbourne, via Vancouver	12,265	30
Mexico City (railroad)	3,750	5
Panama	2,355	6
Paris	4,020	8
Rio de Janeiro	6,204	17
Rome, via London	5,030	9
Rotterdam, via London	3,935	8
St. Petersburg, via London	5,730	9
San Juan, Porto Rico	1,730	6
Shanghai, via San Francisco	9,920	25
Stockholm, via London	4,975	10
Sydney, via Vancouver	11,570	29
Valparaiso, via Panama	5,910	22
Vienna, via London	4,740	9
Yokohama, via San Francisco	7,345	20

INFORMATION OF INTEREST

Birthday Stone for Each Month of the Year.—Stones of different kinds are often considered proper for birthdays coming in different months of the year. They are: Garnet for January, amethyst for February, bloodstone for March, diamond for April, emerald for May, pearl for June, ruby for July, sardonyx for August, sapphire for September, opal for October, topaz for November, and turquoise for December.

Names of Wedding Anniversaries.—Wedding anniversaries are named according to the name of the article considered appropriate for anniversary presents at different times. The names are:

1st year—Cotton
2d year—Paper
3d year—Leather
5th year—Wooden
7th year—Woolen
10th year—Tin
12th year—Silk and fine linen

15th year—Crystal
20th year—China
25th year—Silver
30th year—Pearl
40th year—Ruby
50th year—Golden
75th year—Diamond

Care of Birds and Fish.—Caged birds, especially the canary, should always be kept in good cages that are perfectly clean and free from vermin. The greater part of all the cages now used have a hanger at the top of the cage, which can be removed. This should be separated from the cage at least once every month. Here is where the red mites hide. The best kind of roosts or perches can be made from the smaller branches of the elder. The outer covering should be scraped and the pith removed from the center of the pieces of elder. The red mites crawl into these perches, which can be scalded once a week with hot water, thus destroying the mites.

The best seed for canaries is Sicilian canary seed and a little German rape seed. A small portion of hemp seed may be added. Never mix the hemp seed with the other seed; if you do, the birds will throw the other seed out in their diligent search for the hemp seed. Hemp seed is too fattening for them to have much of it. Feed the hemp seed separate. Canaries must have some kind of green feed, and nothing is better for them than a few leaves of dandelion or lettuce. They should never be fed cabbage or heavy greens.

· It is a pleasure to have an aquarium in the house with fish and growing plants. The plants contained in the aquarium should be sufficiently numerous to throw off enough oxygen to supply the fish. The function of plant life in the water is to decompose the carbonic-acid gas under the action of sunlight, using the carbon to build up the structures and to liberate the oxygen which is necessary to the fish. Fish in breathing absorb the free oxygen in the water, and they also absorb it from the air. The proportion of oxygen or of air that water will contain varies with the temperature. Thus, for about every 16° drop in temperature water will take up and retain about double the volume of oxygen or of atmospheric air. Boiling the water expels the oxygen. When all of the oxygen is exhausted the water will no longer support the life of the fish. The cooler the water, the

greater amount of oxygen will there be and the greater number of fish can be kept in it. The fewer fish, and the more space there is in the aquarium, the better will the fish prosper. An aquarium should be kept clean and free from slimy deposits. The water should be changed frequently enough to keep it pure.

RULES OF BUSINESS

There are a few rules or guides for good business that can be safely followed at all times. It is always best, however, to ask advice of your banker or a lawyer of experience relative to financial matters that may cause a loss.

If a note is lost or stolen, it does not release the maker; he must pay it if the consideration for which it was given and the amount can be proved.

Notes bear interest only when so stated.

Principals are responsible for the acts of their agents.

Each individual in a partnership is responsible for the whole amount of the debts of the firm, except in cases of a special partnership. The word "limited" in connection with a firm name indicates that a limitation of responsibility for each member is fixed.

Ignorance of the law excuses no one.

An agreement without consideration of value is void.

A note made on a Sunday is void, also one dated ahead of its issue. It may be dated back at pleasure.

Contracts made on Sunday cannot be enforced.

A note by a minor is void in some states, and in others it is voidable on judicial decision.

A contract made with a minor or a lunatic is void.

A note obtained by fraud or from a person in a state of intoxication cannot be collected.

It is a fraud to conceal a fraud.

Signatures made with a lead pencil are good in law.

The acts of one partner binds the rest.

"Value received" is usually written in a note, and should be, but it is not necessary. If not written it is presumed by the law or may be supplied by proof.

The maker of an "accommodation" bill or note (one for which he has received no consideration) having lent his name or credit for the benefit of the holder, is not bound to the person accommodated, but is bound to all other parties, precisely as if there were a good consideration.

No consideration is sufficient in law if it be illegal in its nature.

Checks or drafts must be presented for payment without unreasonable delay.

An indorsee has a right of action against all whose names were on the bill when he received it.

. If the letter containing a protest of non-payment be put into the post office, any miscarriage does not affect the party giving notice.

` Notice of protest may be sent either to the place of business or residence of the party notified.

CHECKS

How to Draw Checks.—A check is merely an order for a bank to pay a stipulated sum of money to the person whose name appears on the check, from the funds of the drawer of the check.

Checks may be made payable either to order or bearer. In the former case, the payee should be known to the proper bank officials, and must indorse the check before the money is paid. In case the check reads "pay to bearer," any one holding the check should indorse it, and if he is known to the bank, he is entitled to present it and receive the money stipulated.

Every person who writes a check should be very careful to protect himself against dishonest intentions of the person to whom the check is issued. A check should always be written with pen and ink. Never use a lead

pencil when drawing a check. The amount which is stipulated on the check should be started as far to the left as possible so that no writing or figures could be inserted to increase the amount of the check. The space remaining should be filled in by a very heavy line so that nothing could be added after the amount inserted. The figures of a check should be plainly written and care should be taken that the figures correspond. Although a bank cannot be held responsible for the payment of a check made payable to bearer, or wrong person, if the circumstances warrant such action, a bank may refuse to cash it until they are satisfied that it is the right party.

Checks Should Be Presented for Payment as Soon as Possible.—The receiver of a check may avoid considerable trouble or loss of money by presenting checks for payment as soon as possible after they are received. The drawer of a check usually prefers to have his checks paid as soon as possible, to avoid keeping track of outstanding checks. Should the holder of a check neglect to present it for payment at once and the bank should become insolvent, he cannot compel the bank to make good the loss he has sustained if more than the ordinary time has elapsed before he presents the check that is given him.

Certified Checks.—A certified check is a common check that has been certified by the cashier of the bank on which it is drawn; that is, he has written or stamped across the face, usually with red ink, the word "certified," the date, and his signature.

The certifying of a check is the same as accepting a draft, and makes the bank responsible for its payment, and not the drawer. Remember, that when you have a check certified it is at once deducted from your account; therefore, if you do not use it, you must deposit it to your credit before it can again be added to your account.

Certificate of Deposit.—A certificate of deposit is a written acknowledgment of a bank that it has received from the person named a sum of money as a deposit, subject to withdrawal on demand and on surrender of

the certificate. Generally, persons holding certificates of deposit are not allowed to draw a check for all or part of it.

Receipt.—A receipt is a written acknowledgment of having received a specified value, with the date, source of receipt, signature of the party that received the value, and such other particulars as may be necessary to make it plain and unquestionable.

NOTES

Note.—A note is an absolute promise, in writing, to pay on a certain date, or on demand, a specified sum of money to a person named therein, or to his order, or to the bearer, and is signed by the maker.

Joint Note.—A joint note is one signed by two or more parties and reading, "We promise to pay." It is supposed that each party to the note has been equally benefited; therefore, only his proportionate share can be collected from each.

A joint-and-several note reads, "We jointly and severally promise to pay." In this form of note, the makers are united in the obligation, and the payee can collect from all the makers together, or the entire face of the note from any one of them, if he is worth that amount.

Protests.—Have all the notes in your favor made payable at a bank; then, a few days before they become due, if not previously discounted, deposit them for collection. The bank will then see that they are properly presented when due, and will protest if not paid.

Protesting is a formal statement made by a notary public that the paper was presented for payment and payment refused. A notice of protest is sent to the maker and to each indorser. If there are indorsers and no protest is made, the indorsers in some states, are released. When there are no indorsers, it is quite common to waive protest by writing on the back of such paper "Protest Waived."

Unless inscribed with the words "with interest," notes do not draw interest until after maturity; but if not paid at maturity, they draw interest at the legal rate until paid.

Due Bill.—A due bill is a written acknowledgment of something due from one party to another. They are not usually made payable to order, are frequently without date, and seldom mention the name of the place or state.

DRAFTS

Sight Draft.—A sight draft is a draft drawn by one person on another, and payable on presentation, or at sight. They are treated as cash by those receiving them.

Time Draft.—Time drafts are drawn payable a certain number of days after sight and to be of value must be accepted by the party on whom they are drawn. Acceptance is shown by writing across the face, usually in red ink because of its prominence, the word "accepted," the date, and the signature of the acceptor. The due date is figured so many days after the date of acceptance, and not after the date on which it was drawn.

Often there is seen attached to the end of a draft a slip reading, "No Protest." "Take this off before presenting." This informs the banker that the drawer does not wish the paper protested, and is done so that if the paper is not accepted, the drawer will not have to pay the protest fees.

Bank Draft.—For convenience and safety in making remittance from one part of the country to another, in funds that are at par, and yet without actually transferring the cash, bank drafts are bought from local banks and forwarded, instead of using checks, etc.

SIMPLE-INTEREST RULES

4%.—Multiply the principal by the number of days to run, separate the right-hand figure from the product and divide by 9.

5%.—Multiply by the number of days and divide by 72.

6%.—Multiply by the number of days, separate the right-hand figure and divide by 6.

8%.—Multiply by the number of days and divide by 45.

9%.—Multiply by the number of days, separate the right-hand figure and divide by 4.

10%.—Multiply by the number of days and divide by 36.

12%.—Multiply by the number of days, separate the right-hand figure and divide by 3.

The following method of computing interest for short terms is an accurate and speedy one: The interest on any sum for 60 days at 6 per cent. can be found by drawing a perpendicular line 2 places to the left of the decimal point of the principal. The result will be the interest in dollars and cents. Thus, the interest on $2,035.45 for 60 days at 6% will be $20.35.

DISCOUNT RATES

The following table of equivalent discounts will be found useful by those in whose business several different rates of discount are allowed from list prices:

10 and 5 off=14½% off
15 and 5 off=19½% off
20 and 5 off=24% off
20 and 10 off=28% off
25 and 10 off=32½% off
30, 10, and 5 off=40⅐% off
40, 10, and 5 off=48²⁄₁₀% off
50 and 10 off=55% off
60, 10, and 5 off=65⅘% off
70, 10, and 5 off=74²⁄₂₀% off

YEARS AT WHICH A GIVEN AMOUNT WILL DOUBLE, AT SEVERAL RATES OF INTEREST

Rate %	At Single Interest	At Compound Interest		
		Compounded Yearly	Compounded Semi-Annually	Compounded Quarterly
1	100	69.666	69.487	69.400
1½	66.66	46.556	46.382	46.298
2	50.00	35.004	34.830	34.743
2½	40.00	28.071	27.899	27.812
3	33.33	23.450	23.278	23.191
3½	28.57	20.150	19.977	19.890
4	25.00	17.673	17.502	17.415
4½	22.22	15.748	15.576	15.490
5	20.00	14.207	14.036	13.946
5½	18.18	12.946	12.775	12.686
6	16.67	11.896	11.725	11.639
6½	15.38	11.007	10.836	10.750
7	14.29	10.245	10.075	9.989
7½	13.33	9.585	9.914	9.328
8	12.50	9.006	8.837	8.751
8½	11.76	8.497	8.346	8.241
9	11.11	8.043	7.874	7.788
9½	10.52	7.638	7.468	7.383
10	10.00	7.273	7.121	7.026
12	8.34	6.110		

LEGAL HOLIDAYS

Legal holidays are days set apart by statute or by executive authority for fasting and prayer, or those given over to religious observance and amusements, or for political, moral, or social duties or anniversaries, or merely for popular recreation and amusement under such penalties and provisions alone as are expressed in positive legislative enactments.

In the United States there are no established holidays of a religious character having a legal status without legislation. The days established by statutory or by executive authority, which are observed as legal holidays, are given in the list that follows:

January 1. *New Year's Day:* In all the states and territories except Massachusetts and New Hampshire.

January 8. *Anniversary of the Battle of New Orleans:* In Louisiana.

January 19. *Lee's Birthday:* In Alabama, Florida, Georgia, North Carolina, South Carolina, and Virginia.

February 12. *Lincoln's Birthday:* In Arizona, Connecticut, Colorado, Illinois, Minnesota, New Jersey, New York, North Dakota, Pennsylvania, Washington, and Wyoming.

February 22. *Washington's Birthday:* In all the states and territories except Mississippi and New Mexico.

March 2. *Texas Independence Day:* In Texas.

April 6. *Confederate Memorial Day:* In Louisiana.

April 19. *Patriot's Day:* In Massachusetts.

April 21. *Anniversary of the Battle of San Jacinto:* In Texas.

April 26. *Confederate Memorial Day:* In Alabama, Florida, and Georgia.

May 10. *Confederate Memorial Day:* In North Carolina and South Carolina.

May, Second Friday. *Confederate Memorial Day:* In Tennessee.

May 20. *Anniversary of the Signing of the Mecklenburg Declaration of Independence:* In North Carolina.

May 30. *Decoration Day:* In all the states and territories except Alabama, Arkansas, Florida, Georgia, Idaho, Louisiana, Mississippi, New Mexico, North Carolina, South Carolina, Texas, and Virginia.

June 3. *Jefferson Davis's Birthday:* In Alabama, Florida, Georgia, and South Carolina.

July 4. *Independence Day:* In all states and territories.

July 24. *Pioneer's Day:* In Utah.

August 16. *Bennington Battle Day:* In Vermont.

September, First Monday. *Labor Day:* In all the states and territories except Arkansas, Louisiana, Mississippi, Nevada, New Mexico, North Dakota, Oklahoma, and Vermont.

September 9. *Admission Day:* In California.

October 12. *Columbus Day:* In California, Colorado, Connecticut, Maryland, Missouri, Montana, New Jersey, New York, and Pennsylvania.

October 31. *Admission Day:* In Nevada.

November 1. *All Saints' Day:* In Louisiana.

November 25. *Labor Day:* In the parish of Orleans, Louisiana.

November, Fourth Thursday. *Thanksgiving Day:* In all the states and territories. The exact day is fixed by the proclamation of the President of the United States and the governors of the states.

December 25. *Christmas Day:* In all the states and territories.

Shrove Tuesday. *Mardi Gras:* In Alabama and in the parish of Orleans, Louisiana.

Good Friday: In Alabama, Louisiana, Maryland, Minnesota, Pennsylvania, and Tennessee.

Arbor Day: In Colorado, third Friday in April; Idaho, last Monday in April; in Nebraska, April 22; Utah, April 15. This day is observed in other states on dates appointed by the governors.

General Election Day, being the Tuesday after the first Monday of November in every year when such elections are held is a holiday in Arizona, California, Florida, Idaho, Illinois, Indiana, Iowa, Louisiana, Maryland, Minnesota, Missouri, Montana, Nevada, New Hampshire, New Jersey, New York, North Dakota, Oklahoma, Oregon, Pennsylvania, Rhode Island, South Carolina, South Dakota, Tennessee, Texas, Washington, West Virginia, Wisconsin, and Wyoming.

Sundays are holidays, and also any day appointed by the governor in any of the several states as a *fast day*, or a day for prayer. There are no statutory holidays in Mississippi, but by common consent the Fourth of July, Thanksgiving Day, and Christmas are observed as such. In Kansas the only legal holidays by legislative enactment are February 22, May 30, first Monday of September, and Thanksgiving Day, but by common consent New Year's Day, Fourth of July, and Christmas are also observed.

Saturday, after 12 o'clock noon, is a legal holiday throughout the year in Connecticut, District of Columbia, Florida, Maine, Maryland, Massachusetts, Michigan, Missouri, New Jersey, New York, Pennsylvania, Rhode Island, and Washington; in Louisiana and Missouri, in cities of 100,000 inhabitants and over; in Ohio and Virginia, in cities of 50,000 inhabitants and over; in Delaware, in the city of Wilmington and in Newcastle county, except St. George's Hundred, where Saturdays from June to September only are holidays; in South Carolina, in Charleston county; and in Colorado, in Denver during June, July, and August.

Holidays falling on Sunday are observed the day before in Kansas, Mississippi, Nevada, Vermont, and West Virginia, and on the same day in Louisiana; but elsewhere in the United States, on the following Monday.

In Canada the following are legal holidays in all the provinces: New Year's Day, Good Friday, Easter Monday, Christmas Day, the birthday of the reigning sovereign, any day appointed by proclamation for a public

holiday or a general fast or thanksgiving, and the day next following New Year's, Christmas, and the sovereign's birthday, when these days fall on Sunday. In Quebec, in addition to the above, the following are observed: The Epiphany, the Annunciation, the Ascension, Corpus Christi, St. Peter and St. Paul's Day, All Saints' Day, and Conception Day.

In England and Ireland the bank holidays are: Good Friday, Easter Monday, the Monday in Whitsun week, the first Monday in August, sovereign's birthday, Christmas, and the 26th of December if a week day; in Scotland, New Year's Day, Christmas (if either day fall on Sunday, then the following Monday), Good Friday, first Monday in May, first Monday in August, and the sovereign's birthday. In addition to the above, any day so proclaimed by the reigning sovereign is to be observed as a bank holiday throughout the United Kingdom, or in any part thereof.

CORRESPONDENCE

LETTER WRITING

The importance of letter writing, both in business and as an educational accomplishment, cannot be overestimated. Business must, to a large extent, be transacted by means of correspondence; and one of the leading requisites of business success is the ability to discharge the important duties pertaining to correspondence in a manner satisfactory to all concerned.

The essential parts of a letter are:

1. Heading, including date.
2. Address.
3. Salutation.
4. Body.
5. Complimentary close.
6. Subscription, or signature.
7. Superscription, or outside address.

The incidental parts are:

1. The postscript, with its continuations or iterations, paulo-postscript, post-paulo-postscript, and so on.

2. Nota bene.

3. Enclosure.

4. Stamp.

5. Return directions.

The writing of the place and date at the lower left-hand corner of the paper, at the end of a letter, though quite admissible and somewhat customary in the matter of social letters, is, in the case of business letters, annoying to those that desire to note at once the date of the letter. It is better not to indulge in any cecentricities in such matters. For people that do not have anything else to do it may be allowable; but busy people do not have time to look in unusual places for headings, addresses, signatures, etc.

The salutation is the greeting, as "Dear Sir," "Sir," "My dear George," and the like, with which it is usual to begin a letter. What the salutation shall be must be determined, of course, by the relation between the writer and the party addressed. The most formal, private, or unofficial salutations are "Sir" and "Madame." These are almost impersonal and belong to such persons as we may wish to accost with civility. "Sir" is the correct salutation in addressing officers of the government who have no special title inherent in the office they hold. When it is used the complimentary close should be "Yours respectfully," or something correspondingly distant.

General Form.—The following letter shows the usual arrangement of the various parts of an ordinary business letter. If the street address is given in the heading, the heading and date should be written in two lines; if the street address is not given, the heading and date should be written in one line. The address, if of more than two lines, should be neatly balanced. A colon should follow the salutation; a dash is often used after the colon, but this is unnecessary.

(Heading and Date)

540 Sewell St., PORTLAND, ME.,

February 22, 1912.

(Address)

MR. JOHN W. PLAYFAIR,

President First National Bank,

558 Jackson Boulevard,

Chicago, Ill.

(Salutation)

DEAR SIR:

(Body)

Mr. George Williams of your city has called to interest me in the purchase of a large tract of timber and mining lands in Northern Wisconsin. Mr. Williams impresses me favorably, and his propositions appear quite reasonable on their face.

I have, however, deferred giving him a final answer until I hear from you regarding his standing in business circles in Chicago. He speaks of you as an acquaintance, and since I claim you as a friend, your advice will be as welcome as it must be valuable.

(Complimentary Close)

I am, dear sir,

Very sincerely yours,

(Signature)

WILLIAM HUTCHESON.

The superscription is the outside address—the one written on the envelope, and the one for the postmaster and

Return in 5 days to
540 Sewell St.,
Portland, Me.

Stamp

MR. JOHN W. PLAYFAIR,

President First National Bank,

558 Jackson Boulevard,

Chicago, Ill.

the letter carrier to note. Like the address, the superscription consists of three parts: the name, the title, and the business address or residence.

The accompanying illustration shows a specimen superscription.

SUGGESTIONS

The first and most important rule to be observed by a writer of a letter is to *be courteous*.

Neatness.—Always be careful, in the writing of a letter, to avoid blots, corrections, or erasures. Make the letter perfect as to neatness, even if it has to be rewritten. An essential as important as neatness is correct spelling.

Brevity.—One of the essential qualities of business correspondence that cannot be too strongly dwelt upon is *brevity*, for business men have no time to waste, and appreciate conciseness of expression. Brevity of expression, if combined with neatness, clearness, and courtesy always makes a good impression upon the true business man. One of the greatest helps to success in any walk of life is the ability to express ideas accurately and concisely.

Deliberation.—No one should write a letter when angry, nor, as a rule, when inclined to say severe things. If one receives a letter provoking him to anger, it is better to wait a little before answering; then probably the style of his reply will be entirely changed. Words hastily spoken, and letters written in haste or anger, one usually would like to recall. Hasty or vindictive words make enemies and endanger business, while kind words make and hold friends. Make it a rule never to write a letter when strongly excited.

Many writers experience difficulty in the opening and closing sentences of a letter. The opening should be perfectly natural and should introduce the subject uppermost in the mind. Avoid in the opening such set phrases as "I now take my pen in hand to tell you that I am well, etc.," "I thought I would drop you a line to let you know, etc." A familiar letter usually ends

with an expression of compliment or affection in addition to the complimentary close.

Promptness of Answers.—From the standpoint of the recipient of the letter, correspondence demands close and courteous attention. Letters, especially business letters, should be answered with reasonable promptness.

Date of Letter Answered.—The answer to a business letter should contain a reference to the date of the letter answered; thus, "In answer to your letter of the 10th inst."

Enclosing Stamp.—A letter asking a favor or treating of business in which only the writer and not the recipient is interested, should have a stamp enclosed for an answer.

Legibility.—Do not write so that your correspondent will be unable to read your letter, or meet with great difficulty in so doing. Sign your name to the letter, so that there can be no possible doubt as to the spelling. Some business men cultivate a characteristic signature, which they use for checks and business papers. Such a signature is often purposely almost illegible, and obviously should not be used for a letter except to a well-known correspondent.

FIRST AID TO THE INJURED

PREPARATION

In every place where a large number of persons are employed and where accidents are liable to occur, a supply of articles needed to render first aid should be available. These should include one or more stretchers, bandages, absorbent cotton, carron oil (equal parts of raw linseed oil and lime water), splints, soap, towels, blankets, aromatic spirits of ammonia, etc. The necessary quantity of any of these or other articles depends on the nature and size of the works.

Sterilizing.—Many disease germs may be killed by heat; others by chemicals called disinfectants, such as bichloride of mercury, carbolic acid, etc. The solutions used in washing wounds should be made up of about the following strengths: Bichloride of mercury, 15 gr. to 1 qt. of water; or, liquid carbolic acid, 2 teaspoonfuls to 1 qt. of water. The substances should be thoroughly dissolved before the solution is used.

ACCIDENTS AND INJURIES

FAINTING

Fainting, or *swooning,* with loss of sensation, motion, and consciousness, may result from a severe blow or wound, from loss of blood, from great emotion (extreme fear or joy), from electric shocks, etc. The patient becomes pale, inanimate, and is in a condition of apparent death; if not soon relieved, death may result.

The patient should be laid with the head lower than the feet, and ligatures or bands of some sort should be

FIG. 1

tied around the arms and legs close to the body, so as to confine the circulation to the trunk and head. The tongue should be kept out of the throat, in order to allow free access of air, and the respiration may be

helped by pressing in and down on the ribs and chest and allowing the chest to expand by its own elasticity.

Artificial Respiration.—The process just described is one form of *artificial respiration,* and may in some cases be effective. If the desired results are not soon obtained, place the patient on his back with a pad (a roll of clothing will do) under the back just below the shoulders, so as to raise the pit of the stomach. The patient's tongue should be drawn out and held by an assistant, or, it should be fastened against the lower teeth by a rubber band passing under the chin or clasped between the patient's teeth, the lower jaw being held up by a bandage tied over the head. Grasp the forearms half way between the elbows and wrists, and draw the arms back rather quickly but steadily in vertical planes until they meet above the patient's head, as in Fig. 1, and hold them thus for 2 sec. This motion draws the ribs up, expands the chest, and air enters. Now bring the arms back to the sides of the body, and press firmly

Fig. 2

on the sides and front of the chest over the lower ribs, as in Fig. 2; the object of this movement is to contract the chest and force the air out ot the lungs. If enough assistants are present, one can stand astride the patient and press firmly against the sides and top of the chest

while the arms are held down along the sides. This series of movements, constituting one inspiration and one expiration, should be repeated about once every 4 sec., or fifteen times per min., for 1½ or 2 hr. if necessary, unless in the meantime a physician pronounces life extinct. While working over the patient prevent unnecessary crowding of persons, avoid rough usage, and do not allow the patient to remain on his back unless his tongue is secured. Under no circumstances should the patient be held up by his feet, nor should he be placed in a warm bath unless under medical direction.

TRAUMATIC SHOCK

Severe injuries may sometimes result in *traumatic shock* (*trauma* meaning wound), in which the victim appears confused and listless and perhaps stupefied, but not unconscious. The pulses and respiration are perceptible, though feeble and irregular. Sometimes the bowels move involuntarily. Intelligence is not usually wholly lost, and the patient can be made to respond to questions if repeatedly urged. This condition may last a few moments or several hours, and may terminate in death.

Place the patient in a horizontal position with head lowered, and warm him by rubbing and by using warm linen or blankets. Let him inhale the odor from dilute ammonia water. If he can swallow, give a little hot brandy and water with a few drops of ammonia water added; 1 teaspoonful of aromatic spirits of ammonia in a wineglassful of water is also good. From 2 to 4 teaspoonfuls of turpentine in a quart of water, as hot as may be used without discomfort, may be injected into the bowels, often with good results.

Wounds consisting of severe bruises are sometimes characterized by numbness, coldness, and absence of bleeding until reaction begins. In such cases, use stimulants and antiseptics and keep the injured part as quiet as possible and protected by warm dressing.

HEMORRHAGE, OR BLEEDING

Hemorrhage, or *bleeding,* may come from the arteries, the veins, or the capillaries. The arteries are the channels through which blood flows from the heart to the various parts of the body, and the veins are the channels through which the blood returns to the heart. The capillaries form the network of very minute tubes through which the blood passes from the arteries to the veins and by which all the tissues of the body are nourished.

Arterial hemorrhage is usually distinguished by the bright red color of the blood and the regular pulsations with which it issues from the blood vessels; *venous hemorrhage* can be known by the dark-blue tint of the blood and the steadiness of its flow; in *capillary hemorrhage,* the blood has a reddish tint and exudes from the tissues or wells up from the surface of the wound. *Internal hemorrhage* may exist without any external flow of blood.

After excessive loss of blood, the patient's face and lips turn pale; he experiences chills, cold sweats, nausea, frequent vomiting, irregular respiration, feeble pulse, dizziness, buzzing in the ears, and finally unconsciousness, terminating either in death or in cessation of the bleeding. In the latter case, consciousness may soon return, but very often the tendency to fainting fits persists for a time.

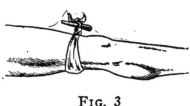

FIG. 3

Capillary hemorrhage is arrested by bathing the wounded part in cold sterilized water and bandaging it with a pad, or compress of sterilized gauze or lint.

Venous hemorrhage is more serious and cannot always be stopped by binding a pad over the wound; in this case, the limb must be bandaged on the side of the wound away from the heart. The limb should be raised and held above the

rest of the body and the patient should be made to lie perfectly quiet.

Arterial hemorrhage is more serious than either of the others. If a large artery or a number of small ones are ruptured, the blood may escape so rapidly that death occurs almost at once. Pressure enough to stop the flow should be applied to the artery where it passes over a bone between the wound and the heart. The location of the artery is revealed by the distinct pulsations. Pres-

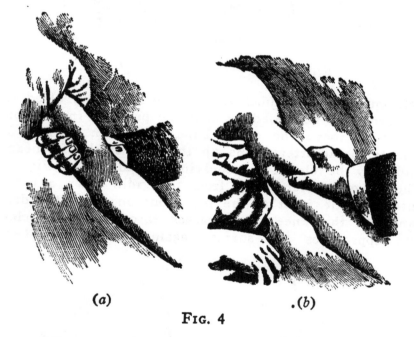

(a)   .(b)

Fig. 4

sure applied with the fingers will answer temporarily, and this method affords a way of finding the proper spot on which to press. A knot or any hard substance, in a handkerchief or a bandage may then be placed on the spot, tied loosely around the limb, and twisted with a stick, as in Fig. 3, until bleeding ceases. The stick may be then be fastened with another bandage.

The course of the main (brachial) artery in the arm is well indicated by the inner sleeve seam of a man's coat; this artery can be compressed by grasping the arm by

either method (*a*) or (*b*), Fig. 4. The pressure should always be downwards against the bone and not against

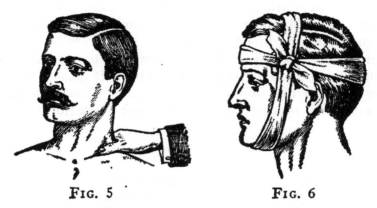

FIG. 5   FIG. 6

soft muscle. The subclavian artery supplying blood to the arm may be closed by applying pressure in the hollow just above the collar bone, as shown in Fig. 5. The temporal artery runs up the side of the forehead, and may be closed by applying a pad, as in Fig. 6. The femoral artery runs from the groin down a little inside of the front of the leg about one-third the distance to the knee, then passes through the muscles and approaches the surface again behind the knee.

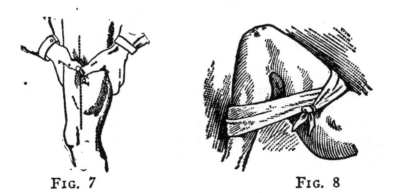

FIG. 7   FIG. 8

Pressure applied as at *P*, Fig. 7, may stop bleeding from a wound above the knee, and a pad applied as in Fig. 8 is applicable for a wound below the knee.

ELECTRIC SHOCK

Electric shock may produce severe burns, unconsciousness, or death, depending on the strength of the current through the body as well as on its duration and flow. If the skin is thin and moist and the contacts with the conductors good, comparatively low voltage, 220 or possibly less, may be sufficient to send considerable current through the body. On the other hand, a person with thick, dry skin, as on the palms of the hands, may sometimes make slight accidental contact with a circuit of several thousand volts without serious results. A very small current through the region of the heart may paralyze its action and cause death; currents of greater density stimulate the heart to increased action, but paralyze the nerve centers controlling respiration and may cause death by suffocation, the same as in drowning.

Accidental contact with an electric conductor should be broken as quickly as possible; if maintained until heart action ceases, as a result of suffocation, death invariably results. In breaking the contact (provided, of course, the power cannot be immediately turned off the circuit), use the feet to push the victim and the conductor apart—never the hands. Current passing from one foot through the legs and the other foot to ground does comparatively little injury, since the important nerve centers and the heart are not in its path. As soon as the contact is broken, the victim, if he has not lost consciousness; soon recovers. If the victim is unconscious but has not ceased breathing, an effort should be made to revive him, the same as in an ordinary fainting fit. If respiration has ceased, artificial respiration should be tried and continued for some time, even though the heart action is so feeble as to be almost imperceptible. The first and most important requirement in producing respiration by artificial means is to hold the tongue so that it cannot obstruct the throat.

Burns caused by contact with electric conductors should be protected with sterilized gauze. Such burns

are generally deep, sometimes even carbonizing the bones, especially those of the fingers. They heal quickly, however—ordinarily in from 3 to 6 weeks.

WOUNDS

Before being used on a wound, all instruments, bandages, etc., should be sterilized by heating in steam or boiling water or by baking or by treating with a germ-destroying solution. The water used in washing a wound should first be boiled, in fact nothing unsterilized should be permitted to come in contact with the wounded surface. The germs entering a wound from the skin of the patient or from the object that produced the wound may be removed by thoroughly washing with sterilized water, and the sterilized dressings will prevent further infection.

The first treatment of a wound includes checking the bleeding; the removal of all foreign matter and a thorough washing; drawing the lips of the wound together or gently straightening bruised or torn flesh; applying several layers of sterilized gauze, with absorbent cotton next the wound if it is likely to bleed or discharge, and holding all in place with a suitable bandage. Sterilized adhesive strips are, sometimes necessary to hold the wound together.

FRACTURES

The signs of *fracture* are: (1) Loss of power in the limb, or part, injured. (2) Pain and swelling at the seat of the injury. (3) Distortion of the injured limb —it will be longer or shorter than the other or will lie in some unnatural position. By gentle pulling, the limb may be brought back to its natural shape, but on being released will immediately return to the distorted position. (4) On gently moving the limb, a grating sensation (crepitation) may be felt where the ends of the broken bone rub against each other. (5) If near the surface, the break may be felt from the outside. A fracture should be handled with extreme gentleness; rough usage may do much harm.

Before attempting to move a patient suffering from fracture, the injured part should be supported in a rigid

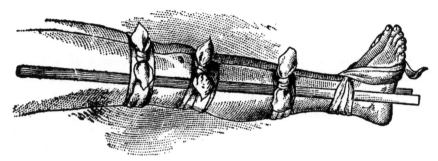

Fig. 9

position by tying on splints. Almost any substance stiff enough to support the injured part will answer for a temporary splint; for example, a stocking leg or a coat sleeve filled with earth, sand, moss, hay, chaff, or paper and securely tied at each end, a barrel stave, a piece of board, a roll of paper, etc. If hard substances are used for splints, the leg should be padded. If feasible, the splints should extend past the nearest joints, and should be securely bandaged so that both the fracture and the joints are held rigid, as in Fig. 9.

Fig. 10

Until the physician comes, a fractured jaw should be held in place by a bandage passed under the chin and over the head. If the collar bone is broken, the arm should be raised gently, and a pad made by tightly rolling a handkerchief or a piece of cloth should be placed in the armpit; the forearm should be supported horizontally across the chest by a large arm sling, and the arm and sling should be held firmly in position by a broad bandage placed around the

body and just above the elbow. Fractured ribs may be temporarily treated by fastening broad bandages around the body, tying the knot on the side opposite the fracture, as in Fig. 10.

DISLOCATIONS AND SPRAINS

A *dislocation* is the displacement of the bones of a joint. Ordinarily, a physician is needed, and little can be done before his arrival except to make the patient as comfortable as possible.

A *sprain* should be kept very quiet. If possible, keep the injured member in water as hot as can be borne for 1½ hr. or more; then bandage with moderate firmness in such a manner as to prevent any movement of the joint, using splints for this purpose if necessary.

EFFECTS OF HEAT

Burns.—The general treatment of a burn consists in relieving the pain, in combating the depression, and increasing the warmth of the patient. The pain may usually be relieved by excluding the air from the burned portion; stimulants should be given, if necessary, to relieve the depression. A covering of flour may be spread over the burned surface; or bicarbonate of soda, either in the form of paste or powder, can be used; any oil, such as sweet oil, raw linseed oil, or carron oil, or a dressing, such as vaseline, cold cream, etc., is effective.

In removing the clothing from over a burn or in dressing it, the blisters should not be broken. If any clothing adheres, it should be saturated with oil and allowed to remain. The patient should not be exposed to cold.

Heat exhaustion is generally accompanied by weakness, cool skin, pale face, weak voice, rapid and feeble pulse, increased respiration, dim vision, and possibly by unconsciousness. The patient should be placed in a horizontal position with the head low, and stimulants and hot applications should be administered. Occasional doses of brandy should be given, also a teaspoonful of

aromatic spirits of ammonia in a little hot milk or water every half hour. If the patient cannot swallow, these remedies may be injected into the rectum.

Sunstroke, which may occur in any hot, moist temperature, is accompanied by high fever. In a few cases. unconsciousness and death come very quickly; but usually the progressive symptoms are intense headache, dizziness, oppression, nausea, vomiting, occasionally diarrhea, and unconsciousness with delirium and restlessness. The face is flushed, the eyes bloodshot, the skin very hot and dry (temperature from 107° to 112° F.), the breathing labored and sometimes noisy, and the pulse frequent and full.

Both the symptoms and the treatment are directly opposite those for heat exhaustion. In cases of sunstroke, every effort should be made to reduce the excessive bodily temperature. Rubbing with ice, a cold bath, a cold pack, and cold rectal injections are all good.

RESTORING OF APPARENTLY DROWNED PERSONS

TREATMENT WHEN SEVERAL ASSISTANTS ARE AT HAND

As soon as the patient is taken from the water, expose the face to the air, toward the wind if there is any, and wipe dry the mouth and nostrils; rip the clothing so as to expose the chest and waist, and give two or three quick, smarting slaps on the chest with the open hand. If the patient does not revive, proceed immediately *to expel water from the stomach and chest,* as follows: Separate the jaws and keep them apart by placing between the teeth a cork or small bit of wood; turn the patient on his face, a large bundle of tightly rolled clothing being placed beneath the stomach (see Fig. 1);

press heavily on the back over the stomach for ½ min., or as long as fluids flow freely from the mouth.

To Produce Breathing.—Clear the mouth and throat of mucus by introducing into the throat the corner of a handkerchief wrapped closely around the forefinger; turn the patient on the back, the roll of clothing being so placed as to raise the pit of the stomach above the level of the rest of the body (see Fig. 2). Let an assistant, with a handkerchief or piece of dry cloth, draw the tip of the tongue out of one corner of the mouth (which prevents the tongue from falling back and

FIG. 1

choking the entrance to the windpipe), and keep it projecting a little beyond the lips. Let another assistant grasp the arms just below the elbows and draw them steadily upwards by the side of the patient's head, and to the ground, the hands nearly meeting (which enlarges the capacity of the chest and induces inspiration). While this is being done, let a third assistant take a position astride the patient's hips, with his elbows resting on his own knees, his hands extended ready for action. Next, let the assistant standing at the head turn down the patient's arms to the side of the body

(see Fig. 3), the assistant holding the tongue changing hands, if necessary, to let the arm pass. Just before the patient's hands reach the ground, the man astride the body will grasp the body with his hands, the balls of the thumbs resting on either side of the pit of the stomach, the fingers falling into grooves between the short ribs. Now, using his knees as a pivot, he will at the moment the patient's hands touch the ground throw (not too suddenly) all his weight forwards on his hands, and at the same time squeeze the waist between them, as if he wished to force something in the chest upwards out of the mouth; he will increase

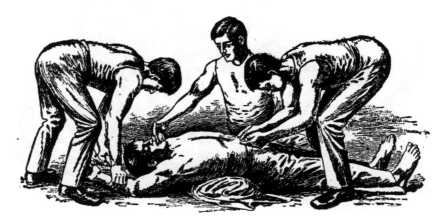

Fig. 2

the pressure while he slowly counts one, two, three, four (about 5 sec.), then suddenly let go with a final push, which will spring him back to his first position. This completes expiration.

At the instant the pressure is taken from the waist the man at the patient's head will again steadily draw the arms upwards to the sides of the patient's head, as before (the assistant holding the tongue again changing hands to let the arm pass, if necessary), holding them there while he slowly counts one, two, three, four (about 5 sec.).

Repeat these movements, deliberately and persever-
ingly, 12 to 15 times in every minute—thus imitating the
natural motions of breathing.

If natural breathing is not restored after a trial of
the bellows movement for the space of about 4 min.,
then turn the patient a second time on the stomach,
rolling the body in the opposite direction from that in
which it was first turned, for the purpose of freeing
the air passage from any remaining water. Continue
the artificial respiration from 1 to 4 hr., or until the
patient breathes, according to the preceding instructions;

FIG. 3

and for a time, after the appearance of returning life,
carefully aid the short gasps until deepened into full
breaths. Continue the drying and rubbing, which should
have been unceasingly practiced from the beginning by
assistants, taking care not to interfere with the means
used to produce breathing. Thus, the limbs of the
patient should be rubbed, always in an upward direction
toward the body with firm, grasping pressure and energy,
using the bare hands, dry flannels, or handkerchiefs, and
continuing the friction under the blankets or over the
dry clothing. The warmth of the body can also be
promoted by the application of hot flannels to the

stomach and armpits and bottles or bladders of hot water, heated bricks, etc. to the limbs and soles of the feet.

After Treatment.—When breathing has been established, let the patient be stripped of all wet clothing, wrapped in blankets only, put to bed comfortably warm, but with free circulation of fresh air, and left to perfect rest. Give whisky, or brandy, and hot water in doses of a teaspoonful, or a tablespoonful, according to the weight of the patient, or any other stimulant at hand, every 10 or 15 min. for the first hour, and as often thereafter as may seem expedient. After reaction is fully established, there is great danger of congestion of the lungs, and if perfect rest is not maintained for at least 48 hr. it sometimes occurs that the patient is seized with great difficulty of breathing, and death is liable to follow unless immediate relief is afforded. In such cases, apply a large mustard plaster over the breast. If the patient gasps for breath before the mustard takes effect, assist the breathing by carefully repeating the artificial respiration.

The foregoing treatment should be persevered in for some hours, as it is an erroneous opinion that persons are irrecoverable because life does not soon make its appearance.

MODIFICATION OF TREATMENT

To Produce Respiration.—If no assistant is at hand and one person must work alone, place the patient on his back with the shoulders slightly raised on a folded article of clothing; draw forward the tongue and keep it projecting just beyond the lips; if the lower jaw be lifted, the teeth may be made to hold the tongue in place; it may be necessary to retain the tongue by passing a handkerchief under the chin and tying it over the head. Grasp the arms just below the elbows and steadily draw them upwards by the sides of the patient's head **to the** ground, the hands nearly meeting, as shown

in Fig. 1. Next, lower the arms to the sides and press firmly downwards and inwards on the sides and

FIG. 1

front of the chest over the lower ribs, drawing toward the patient's head, as shown in Fig. 2. Repeat these movements 12 to 15 times every minute, etc.

FIG. 2

Remarks.—Prevent unnecessary crowding of persons round the body, especially if in an apartment.

Under no circumstances hold the body up by the feet.

On no account place the body in a warm bath, unless under medical direction, and even then it should be employed only as a momentary excitant.

MEMORANDA

MEMORANDA

MEMORANDA

MEMORANDA

MEMORANDA

MEMORANDA

MEMORANDA

MEMORANDA

$279.13 from 100 Pullets in Six Months

I am still in the same position as when I enrolled, but on one hundred pullets have made the price of the Course a couple of times over, besides my regular wages. I intend to stay right at this until I can start in business for myself. I enjoy the Course ever so much and have the chicks here and can try on them things that I learn from the Course, even to caponizing.

I raise 90 per cent. of all chicks from one day old. Here is my egg record for the last 6 months and I never owned a chicken before enrolling in your Course.

Cost of Feed		Eggs	Sold for
Jan.	$19.00	1803	$59.61
Feb.	22.20	1745	42.00
Mar.	14.88	1792	33.40
Apr.	19.75	2225	43.78
May	11.54	2411	35.35
June	18.00	1930	45.00

I had about one hundred and fifteen pullets in January and now have about one hundred. I am pretty proud of that record, so you can guess what I think of your Course.

R. C. MAXWELL, Pittsfield, Mass.

AN I.C.S. COURSE TURNS FAILURE INTO SUCCESS

S. R. EMERICK, 733 W. 2d St., Shelbyville, Ind.: "The day that the I.C.S. knocked at my door, I was not in any position to make money, in fact I was not fit for anything. The day I enrolled for my Poultry Farming Course was the best day of my life, for it has made a man of me. I am now my own employer, being the owner of "The Natural Poultry Yard," having taken up the breeding of utility birds and breeding for egg production. The Lesson Papers of my Course are my business guides. Any one who will follow the instructions as set forth in the Course cannot help but succeed, for the Lesson Papers are easy to understand and to remember. Any one who thinks of going into the poultry business should first let the I.C.S. prepare him for success."

AN I.C.S. COURSE IS BEST

A. E. EASTMAN, 47-51 Birch St., Manchester, N. H.: "Your Course in Poultry Farming treats the subject thoroughly in all its branches. Although I have read many poultry books and am a subscriber to several poultry papers, I received many valuable suggestions from the Course that I have been unable to obtain from any other source. I can cheerfully recommend your Course of instruction to any one desiring a full knowledge of poultry raising."

GAINED $1.50 PER BIRD

JOHN CLARK, Box 8, Norman Place, Tenafly, N. J.: "I have found your Poultry Farming Course very beneficial to me. Before I took up the Course I was losing money on my birds, but this past year I have gained an average of $1.50 per bird. This I would not have been able to do if I had not taken your Course."

A GRADUATE'S SUCCESS

W. A. SLATER, Box 115, Jamestown, N. Y.: "Your I.C.S. Poultry Course I found very practical and a benefit to me in many ways. When I started into the chicken business, the second year I lost 50 per cent. of my stock. After graduating from your Course, I have this year raised 95 per cent. of the chicks hatched and have succeeded in getting more eggs from my flocks than ever before. I am now manager of Slater's Poultry Farm."

3

Failed Repeatedly—Now Successful

I cannot recommend your Course in Poultry Husbandry too highly, as it has made me a success after repeated failures. It is the most complete Course in Poultry Husbandry that has ever come to my notice. It covers every branch and detail of poultry farming. I have bought about every book advertised, the writers of which gave an outline of how they ran their farms but stopped at the gate, but your Course taught me how to raise my own poultry and run my little farm. Your Course taught me what to do and why to do it. I am no longer in the dark concerning poultry. My hens laid 70 per cent. more eggs in the first half of this year than they ever laid in a whole year before. Your lessons on diseases of poultry have saved many a growing chick for me this season. My loss of young chicks this season through natural causes has been less than 7 per cent. of all chicks hatched. Last season my loss from natural causes was about 60 per cent.

Every person that contemplates going into the poultry business, or those who have failed, should enroll in your Schools, for it will make one a success from the start, and it will make a success out of a failure.

WM. T. SCHEIDE,
R. F. D. 1, Lima, Ohio.

AN I.C.S. COURSE WOULD HAVE SAVED HIM $5,000

WALTER B. DAVIS, Davis Poultry Farm, Kings Highway and E. 23d St., Brooklyn, N. Y.: "I have about completed your Course on Poultry Farming and I beg to state that I consider it the greatest asset a poultry farmer can have to begin with. It covers the details in every way. From my own personal experience I can safely say that had I been familiar with this Course a year ago I would have saved $5,000 on my poultry farm. (This figure is a conservative estimate.)"

DOUBLES HIS SALARY

PAUL GELUK, c/o Patterson Ranch, Oxnard, Calif.: "I was a foreman in the Dundee Chemical Works when I decided to enroll for the Complete Poultry Course. At the present time I have charge of the Poultry Department for the Patterson Ranch Company at Oxnard, Calif. My salary since the time of enrolment has been doubled. While I did not have much education before enrolling, I experienced no difficulty, as your Lesson Papers are easy to learn. All the advancement I have made is entirely through my I.C.S. Course, as I never handled any poultry before I took charge here."

A CITY MAN'S SUCCESS

J. K. SHAUGHNESSY, Federal St., Agawam, Mass.: "I had always hankered for country life and chickens. If any man will invest in the I.C.S. Poultry Farming Course he will have no trouble to make a success of the business. My present position, secured through your Students' Aid Department, is that of manager and half owner of the Sanitary Poultry Yards. We have a capacity of 1,600 layers and expect to increase each year. I am dry picking all my market stock and am getting ten cents more per pound than any man around this section and also top prices for my eggs."

GAINED A POSITION AS MANAGER

C. W. LARSON, R. F. D. No. 3, Box 40-A, St. Paul, Minn.: "I was working as a clerk when I enrolled with the I.C.S. for the Poultry Farming Course. I would strongly advise any one who contemplates going into the poultry industry to take up this Course which will assure him all success. It was because I was known to be a student of your Course that I was able to secure a position as manager of the Victoria Poultry Farm, an up-to-date plant, at a good salary. You are at liberty to refer prospective students to me."

The I. C. S. a Public Benefactor

I have just received my Diploma in your Agricultural Course, and am much pleased with the painstaking manner in which my Instruction Papers were handled by your people. The proposition, in a nutshell, is that, if the student does his (or her) part, the I. C. S. will do theirs.

The benefits to be derived from a Course in Agriculture in the I. C. S. are manifold; the most important, perhaps, is that it teaches the tiller of the soil to grow not only a better crop, but realize a greater production, as well as to do it with a great deal less of labor and expense, thereby making the tilling of the soil more of a pleasure than a drudge. Farmers, as well as others, are waking up to the truth that scientific farming is the only proper method to pursue, especially in these days of worn-out land, problems of drainage, and other things too numerous to mention. In this connection, your instruction on manures is worth the price of the whole Course. I might say the same of your instruction on drainage, etc.

I have endeavored to make my letter brief, but, on account of the great scope or magnitude of your Agricultural Course, it would be difficult to say it all upon a hundred sheets of paper of this size.

Any one who can show how two plants can be grown where but one could be made to grow before, and with less labor, expense, etc., is no less than a public benefactor, and this you do in your Agricultural Course.

WAYNE CANFIELD
City Hall, Wilkes-Barre, Pa.

PAID FOR HIS COURSE WITH 15 HENS

Wilbur H. Dresher, Jeddo, Pa., writes that he has been able, through the knowledge gained from our Poultry Farming Course, to make 15 hens pay the price of his Course in less than 1 year. He praises the Schools for teaching him how to reduce his feed bills through scientific feeding, and for showing him how to take care of the health of his flock.

LABORER BECOMES SUPERINTENDENT

F. B. Oliver, Smithville Flats, N. Y: "I have been employed in the poultry business nearly the entire time since I enrolled in the I.C.S. for the Poultry Farming Course and my monthly salary has been substantially increased. I have likewise advanced from a farm laborer to superintendent of a poultry plant. My Course has been so very beneficial to me that I intend to enroll for the Agricultural Course."

PRAISES COURSE

H. S. Ferguson, Manager, Deep Fork Dairy, Okmulgee, Okla.: "I have taken a Course in Soil Improvement, Farm Crops, Livestock and Dairying with the International Correspondence Schools and can truly recommend same to any one who wishes to take up such a Course. I owe what I am to the Course and am sure any one may be benefited the same as myself. It does not require a college education to take a Course with this School, as they are willing to help you with anything you do not fully understand. Give them a trial and be convinced."

NOW PROPRIETOR

Ray L. Chamberlin, South Road, Orange, Mass., was earning a small salary when he enrolled for the Complete Poultry Course. Since receiving his Diploma he has become manager and half owner of the Wyolette Poultry Yards. He declares that the lessons on diseases and enemies of poultry are worth the price of the whole Course; also, that the lesson on poultry feeding has made a big increase in his egg yields.

NOW MANAGER

Wm. M. Freshley, Madison, Ohio, declares that he has gained considerable help from his I.C.S. Poultry Farming Course. He is now proprietor of the Silver Campine Farm. He recommends the Course to poultrymen as well as to beginners.

7

Salary More Than Doubled

E. A. BAKER, Proprietor   F.W. EASTMAN, Manager
P. O. Box, 2898   Greensboro
Boston, Mass.   Vermont

BAKER FARM, GREENSBORO, VERMONT
Pure Bred Holstein Cattle

At the time I enrolled with the I.C.S. I was working as a farm hand. In two years' time my present position came to me at a salary more than twice what I was earning when I enrolled and a share in the profits besides. I cannot recommend the I.C.S. too highly. I have two students of the School in my employ and both, I feel sure, will succeed.   F. W. EASTMAN

HIS COURSE BROUGHT SUCCESS

OBLETON R. REID, Lothair, Ky.: "I have been engaged in the poultry business for some   , without much success at first. Every year I would lose from 200 to 300 young chickens. I was just stumbling along in the dark. Then I enrolled for your Complete Poultry Course. I consider this the best investment I ever made and advise any person who enters the poultry business to take a Course from the I.C.S. first. The knowledge that I have gained from your instruction has put me on the road to success. Instead of heavy losses I have this year, up to this time, lost only eight or ten chicks, and I have now (June 9th) about four hundred broilers ready for market."

FOUND COURSE A MONEY SAVER

ERNEST STARTUP, 840 Whitney Ave., New Haven, Conn., began his I.C.S. studies while employed as a butler. He writes: "Having kept a small flock of fowls as a side line with some degree of success, I became determined to start a poultry farm of my own. In order to obtain more knowledge on the subject I enrolled for the Special Poultry Course. Now, although only half through the Course, I am more than delighted that I had sense enough to enroll. I find the Instruction Papers full of the very things one wants to know and they clearly show that the secret of success is nothing more than common sense and right methods. I honestly believe that had I started a poultry farm without taking this Course, I would have lost more money in the first week than I have paid for the Course."

ADDED $500 PROFIT

T. E. CASTLE, Virginia City, Mont.: "At the time I enrolled with the International Correspondence Schools for the Poultry Farming Course, I was conducting a small poultry plant as a side issue to my business of editing and managing a country newspaper. I had been handling poultry for a number of years and thought I was pretty well versed in the intricacies of the profession, until I took up the study of my Course. I have learned more than I ever thought I knew before and have added $500 to my profits as proprietor of the Castle Hennery. It makes no difference how much one may know of the poultry business, if he will study your Course and apply its teachings he must necessarily make his business a success."

9

Found His Course Profitable

HARRY L. GOODWIN, Farmington, Me., was a printer 43 years old when he enrolled with the I. C. S. for the Poultry Farming Course. At that time he was interested in poultry and had been for years a writer for the press. He says that his Course has enabled him to secure much better results with Barred Rocks, Rhode Island Reds, and Indian Runner Ducks than he had formerly been able to attain. During the past year he has written 61 articles for publication in farming and poultry journals, for which he is receiving payment, thereby considerably increasing his income. He feels that his Course has already paid for itself in more ways than one, and that it has been a very profitable investment.

HIS MOST SATISFACTORY INVESTMENT

Martin J. Rooney, 408 S. Ohio St., Butte, Mont.: "The I.C.S. Course in Poultry Farming is thorough in every particular. I can honestly say that I consider the price I paid for the Course one of the most satisfactory investments I ever made."

WORTH FIVE TIMES ITS COST

George A. Van Vleck, Hollis, L. I., N. Y.: "If I had paid five times the price of your Poultry Farming Course, I would consider it one of my best investments, since it has enabled me to get such results from my flock. I am now part owner of the Hillside Poultry Yards. No one needs to make mistakes for lack of knowledge who has mastered your Course."

NOW MANAGER

Albert E. Edwards, c/o The Davidson Farm, R. F. D. No. 1, Jermyn, Pa.: "Although I left school at the age of eleven to work in a grocery store, I had no difficulty in mastering your Poultry Farming Course. Without the knowledge I have obtained from it, I could not have taken the responsibility of handling 6,000 chicks at one time, ranging from two days to three months, in a colony system.

Any one who is in the business, or intends to go into it, should take the Course, since he could save enough from his feed bill in a year to pay for it, besides producing better stock for better prices. I was employed as a carpet weaver on piece work. I am now the baby-chick manager on the C. P. Davidson farm."

THE BEST MONEY HE EVER SPENT

Chas. H. Carroll, 71 Clark St., Auburn, N. Y.: "Although I was raised on a large farm where we kept fowls, I felt the need of your Poultry Farming Course. Since receiving my Diploma I can truly say that it was the best money I ever spent, as I can now manage any poultry farm with assurance of success."

WORTH MORE THAN SEVEN YEARS' EXPERIENCE

Fred. Busse, Carlstadt, N. J.: "I have had seven years' experience in the raising of poultry and I find that I have learned more in three months from your Poultry Farming Course than I found out in the whole seven years previous. I recommend the Course as a great help to any one raising poultry whether on a large or small scale."

11

The Man Who Raised the $100,000 Hen

Greensboro, Caroline County, Maryland

EGLANTINE FARM PRODUCTS
(Trade Mark)

I am glad to say that it was my good fortune to have enrolled three years ago as a student in your Poultry Farming Course. The education gained from this study fitted me for the position of head poultryman at Eglantine Farm. Since coming here I have had charge at all times of the poultry department. I have looked after the mating of the fowls, the incubating of the eggs, and the rearing of the chicks. It was my good fortune to select the pullets of our own breeding that have done so remarkably well in the North American Egg-Laying Contest.

FRANK VADAKIN,
Head Poultryman, Eglantine Farms,
Greensboro, Md.

The Best Source

BROOKVALE FARM
The Home of Burr's
WHITE ORPINGTONS

G. M. BURR, Proprietor   MESHOPPEN, PA.

It gives me pleasure to acknowledge the great assistance your thorough Course of Instruction in Poultry Farming has been to me. I had made several attempts to establish a poultry business, but met with many discouragements, and it was not until I had mastered the underlying principles of poultry raising that I met with any gratifying degree of success. I have now a well-established and successful poultry business, and was the winner of a sixth prize in the Cyphers Company's first annual contest of successful poultry growers. I am using on my plant the International Sanitary Hover. I have had excellent success with it, and, in my opinion, it is superior to any other brooder made. As a breeder of single-comb White Orpingtons, I find my I.C.S. Course full of valuable information and practical instruction for all phases of the work. I know that any one going into the poultry business needs such instruction to make a success of it, as in my own case.

G. M. BURR

Considers Course a Valuable Investment

I wish to express my appreciation not only for the value of your Poultry Course but also of the interest and personal attention given the student. For several years I have considered myself a competent poultryman, well grounded in the business from incubation to the showroom, the market, or the laying house. After a year's study I find my knowledge on every subject broader and more practical. From each lesson I have learned something of value and consider that any lesson, taken alone, would be well worth the money price of the entire Course. As a result of my year's application of the Poultry Course to my business, I find increased egg production, marked improvement in my laying stock and breeders from feeding correctly. I am breeding higher-quality stock and on the whole my plant is much improved. I know the Course to be practical and workable. It's scientific, yet easily understood by a plain man like myself. By my own experience I know it can be applied to any kind of plant with benefit. I believe it to be equally valuable to the beginner and the experienced. It has made and saved me many times its cost. I wish the I.C.S. all prosperity.   JACK GORDON,
571 Natoma St., San Francisco, Calif.

CANNOT FAIL TO SUCCEED

BERT WHITE, Box 477, Burlingame, Kans.: "Any one interested in poultry should invest in the Poultry Farming Course with the I.C.S. From personal experience I can say that any one that will study the Course cannot fail to succeed. Each subject is well explained and easily understood. Since I began to study my Course the profits of my flock are rapidly increasing."

WORTH MANY TIMES ITS COST

WILLIAM F. HALLOWAY, River Side Farm, Newark, Md.: "I wish to express my gratitude to the faculty of the International Correspondence Schools for the assistance they have rendered me and the interest they have taken in my progress and success since I enlisted for a Course in Soil Improvement and Farm Crops. The Instruction Papers are very lucid and cover every point of importance with the utmost care, thereby making it easy for the person to grasp the meaning of what is taught. I think any one who contemplates making farming his life vocation will find an International Correspondence Schools' Course in Agriculture worth many times the cost."

HIS COURSE PROFITABLE

J. C. THRENHAUSER, Fair Haven, Pa.: "I cannot express my appreciation of the value of your Poultry Farming Course, since the benefits derived are far beyond my anticipation. Since taking your Course I have spent some time at the government experiment station. Their course in some respects is quite like yours, but it is not so extensive or so complete. I have been offered two positions to take charge of poultry farms, both of which I declined, because I can do much better by caring for my own poultry."

PUTS PRICELESS VALUE ON COURSE

RALPH W. WESTON, Box 26, Honolulu, Hawaii: "I can say in all faith that the methods and instruction set forth in the I.C.S. Poultry Farming Course are of priceless value. I have applied these methods in a small way and find the results as stated. The Course is worth many times the expenditure of time and money."

EARNINGS INCREASED—HEALTH IMPROVED

ERNEST BROWETT, R. F. D. 4, Pitt Poultry Farm, McDonald, Pa.: "When enrolling I was a coal miner. Now I am managing the poultry farm of F. A. Thomassy. The Course has brought me better health and earnings. No one should try to raise a small or large flock of poultry without an I.C.S. Course."

Dollars and Cents Knowledge

Having been a subscriber to your Mechanical Course in former years, I was pleased to learn that you were issuing a Course in Poultry Farming. Knowing the need of information on this subject, I subscribed for the Course.

In reading and studying the first Instruction Papers, I began to realize the greatness and perfection of the Course. Step by step the student is led to proficiency and also I find that each step has been carefully examined beforehand from one standpoint—the question of dollars and cents. In this lies the crux of the matter, the secret of success.

THOMAS H. POLLARD
916 Eighth Ave., Brooklyn, N. Y.

I.C.S. Course a Necessity Not a Luxury

Secretary, Twin Valley Poultry Association
and American Partridge Rock Club

Breeder of
IMPERIAL PARTRIDGE PLYMOUTH ROCKS

In speaking of your Poultry Course, will say that it has no equal. It is not "Can you afford it?" but "Can you afford to do without it?" No one will make a mistake in taking an I.C.S. Poultry Course. I owe my success to your Poultry Course.

ROBERT H. RAMSEY,
Lewisburg, Ohio

17

Praise From Farm Owner

Permit me to express my gratefulness to you for the I.C.S. chemical analysis of my soil. In keeping with the knowledge that I gained from the studies of the I.C.S. Agricultural Courses, the analysis of my soil has made it more clear to me that my soil is lacking in the plant foods nitrogen, phosphorus, potassium, calcium, magnesium, and organic matter, and also gave me the quantity of these foods that should be added to the acre for profitable results. In addition to these, it proved that my soil is not acid, and saved me of the expenditure for 30 tons of lime, which I thought my soil needed. I left the farm in 1900 after working 5 years as a farm hand, but returned again 3 years ago, taking up farming for myself. It was then, seeing my deficiency, I immediately enrolled for the Agricultural Course of the I.C.S. I greatly appreciate the time spent in and the understanding received by studying these Courses. I am sure half of my success would have been lost had I done other than studying.

JAS. H. DOUGLAS,
1511 Laurel St., N. S., Pittsburgh, Pa.